Performing the *Pied-Noir* Family

After the Empire:
The Francophone World and Postcolonial France

Series Editor: Valérie K. Orlando, University of Maryland

Advisory Board: Robert Bernasconi, Memphis University; Claire H. Griffiths, University of Chester, UK; Alec Hargreaves, Florida State University; Chima Korieh, Rowan University; Mildred Mortimer, University of Colorado, Boulder; Obioma Nnaemeka, Indiana University; Alison Rice, University of Notre Dame; Kamal Salhi, University of Leeds; Tracy D. Sharpley-Whiting, Vanderbilt University; Nwachukwu Frank Ukadike, Tulane University

Recent Titles

Performing the Pied-Noir Family: Constructing Narratives of Settler Memory and Identity in Literature and On-Screen by Aoife Connolly

The Algerian War in Film Fifty Years Later, 2004–2012 by Anne Donadey

Remnants of the Franco-Algerian Rupture: Archiving Postcolonial Minorities by Mona El Khoury

Theory, Aesthetics, and Politics in the Francophone World: Filiations Past and Future edited by Rajeshwari S. Vallury

Paris and the Marginalized Author: Treachery, Alienation, Queerness and Exile edited by Valérie K. Orlando and Pamela A. Pears

French Orientalist Literature in Algeria, 1845–1884: Colonial Hauntings by Sage Goellner

Corporeal Archipelagos: Writing the Body in Francophone Oceanian Women's Literature by Julia L. Frengs

Spaces of Creation: Transculturality and Feminine Expression in Francophone Literature by Allison Connolly

Women Writers of Gabon: Literature and Herstory by Cheryl Toman

Backwoodsmen as Ecocritical Motif in French Canadian Literature: Connecting Worlds in the Wilds by Anne Rehill

Front Cover Iconography and Algerian Women's Writing: Heuristic Implications of the Recto-Verso Effect by Pamela A. Pears

The Algerian War in French-Language Comics: Postcolonial Memory, History, and Subjectivity by Jennifer Howell

Writing through the Visual and Virtual: Inscribing Language, Literature, and Culture in Francophone Africa and the Caribbean edited by Ousseina D. Alidou and Renée Larrier

State Power, Stigmatization, and Youth Resistance Culture in the French Banlieues: Uncanny Citizenship by Hervé Tchumkam

Violence in Caribbean Literature: Stories of Stones and Blood by Véronique Maisier

Performing the *Pied-Noir* Family

Constructing Narratives of Settler Memory and Identity in Literature and On-Screen

Aoife Connolly

LEXINGTON BOOKS
Lanham • Boulder • New York • London

Published by Lexington Books
An imprint of The Rowman & Littlefield Publishing Group, Inc.
4501 Forbes Boulevard, Suite 200, Lanham, Maryland 20706
www.rowman.com

6 Tinworth Street, London SE11 5AL, United Kingdom

Copyright © 2020 The Rowman & Littlefield Publishing Group, Inc.

Excerpts from THE LAST LIFE: A Novel by Claire Messud. Copyright © 1999 by Claire Messud. Reprinted by permission of Houghton Mifflin Company. All rights reserved.

Excerpts from *Le Premier Homme* by Albert Camus. Copyright © Gallimard: 1994.

All rights reserved. No part of this book may be reproduced in any form or by any electronic or mechanical means, including information storage and retrieval systems, without written permission from the publisher, except by a reviewer who may quote passages in a review.

British Library Cataloguing in Publication Information Available

ISBN 978-1-4985-3735-3 (cloth)
ISBN 978-1-4985-3737-7 (pbk)
Library of Congress Control Number: 2020944042

For Patricia and Gene

Contents

Acknowledgments	ix
Introduction	1
1 Camus, Meursault, Daru, Cormery: The First *Pied-Noir* Men	19
2 Performing French Algerian Femininity	57
3 Performing *Pied-Noir* Masculinity	105
4 Performing Childhood and Adolescence through French Algerian Narrators	147
Conclusion	191
Bibliography	199
Index	215
About the Author	223

Acknowledgments

I am indebted to the Irish Research Council for awarding me a Government of Ireland Postgraduate Scholarship and to the College of Arts, Social Sciences, and Celtic studies at National University of Ireland (NUI), Galway, for awarding me a Galway Doctoral Research Scholarship. Their generous financial support facilitated research related to the PhD thesis upon which this book is based. Further thanks goes to the College of Arts, Social Sciences, and Celtic studies at NUI, Galway, for providing bursaries for research-related travel. I would also like to thank the School of Languages, Law and Social Sciences at Technological University Dublin for their financial support in the final phases of this project.

I would especially like to thank Professor Philip Dine (who supervised the original research) for sharing his invaluable expertise and for his continued encouragement and advice, as well as for introducing me to the history and literature of Algeria.

I would like to thank all staff and colleagues from NUI, Galway, particularly Dr. Marion Krauthaker, Dr. Sylvie Lannegrand, and Dr. Maria Scott for their insightful input as members of my Graduate Research Committee. Dr. Catherine Emerson and Professor Jane Hiddleston provided valuable feedback as examiners and I am particularly grateful to Professor Hiddleston for her continued support. I am equally grateful to Lexington's anonymous reviewers for their comments and suggestions.

My gratitude also extends to those who kindly offered theses, articles, or books: Dr. Claire Eldridge, Dr. Amy Hubbell, Dr. Mairéad Ni Bhriain, Dr. Máire Áine Ní Mhainnín, Dr. John Strachan, and M. Bernard Zimmermann. Many thanks also to Dr. Aliaa Shalaby for her help with Arabic and to the staff at Lexington Books for their patience and enthusiasm.

Special thanks to Kevin for his support and encouragement and to my family—especially to my parents, to whom I owe my greatest debt of gratitude.

Introduction

I. FRANCE'S CONTESTED LEGACY OF COLONIALISM

Contemporary efforts to portray France as a thriving, modern, and united postcolonial nation have been partially successful. Widespread rejoicing following the country's World Cup win by its ethnically diverse soccer teams in both 1998 and 2018 perhaps served most obviously to highlight the notion of a flourishing France in which issues associated with colonial history were no longer pertinent. However, periodic public manifestations of anger reveal fractures within the French Republic. Intermittent rioting in the Parisian *banlieues* [high-density housing projects located on the fringes of cities], populated primarily by inhabitants of North African origin, provides an explicit example of postcolonial division. Riots in 2005 revived particularly bitter memories when authorities used a law enacted during the Algerian War in 1955 to enforce a curfew in the *banlieues*.[1] Moreover, Andrew Hussey considers disturbances in 2005, along with rioting in Gare du Nord in March 2007, as "only the latest and most dramatic form of engagement with the enemy," in a battle that dates from colonial times.[2] The nation has equally faced social unrest in its former colonies, most notably in the French Caribbean in 2009 and subsequently in French Guiana. In fact, as Manu Saadia notes, France's anti-government *gilet jaune* [yellow vest] movement, which began in November 2018, evoked "an uncanny parallel between the quasi-colonial situation in French Guiana," where poor living standards prompted protests and strikes in 2017, and "the [neglected] rural regions of metropolitan France, where protestors [...] wearing their iconic yellow utility vests" blocked roads.[3] In this way, the *gilet jaune* movement suggested a split between what one commentator referred to as "des métropoles mondialisées" [globalized cities], the *banlieues*, and "la ruralité enterrée" [forgotten rurality].⁴ Moreover, the slogans of some protestors, such as "À bas le capitalisme, le colonialisme et le sexisme" [Down with capitalism, colonialism and sexism],⁵ coupled with the subsequent development of the "gilet noir" [black vest] movement, comprised largely of immigrants from the former colonies seeking rights for the undocumented, point to ever-present tensions between France's Republican values and a present that is still informed by practices from the colonial past.

While the *gilet jaune* movement included protestors from diverse backgrounds with a multitude of preoccupations as well as activists from both the far right and far left, explicit reminders of France's colonial legacy continue to surface. Issues associated with immigration from the former colonies still prove controversial, as was evident in 2009 when President Nicolas Sarkozy launched a debate on French identity.⁶ The success of the far-right, anti-immigrant *Front national* [National Front], renamed the *Rassemblement national* [National Rally] in 2018, further hints at an enduring malaise that should be considered, not just in terms of the general rise of right-wing populism in Europe and the United States, but also in light of the nation's historic involvement in overseas territories. Indeed, the party's president from 1972 to 2011, Jean-Marie Le Pen, was a *parachutiste* [paratrooper] during the Algerian War who subsequently denied repeated allegations that he practiced torture while serving there. Continued controversies surrounding the Islamic veil equally hark back to France's relations with its overseas empire, as do debates on the banning of ostentatious religious symbols in schools (2004) and the ban on covering one's face in public places (2011). These episodes, in addition to a former French minister's alleged assertion that "It's a French woman's duty to wear a bikini,"⁷ and attempts to ban the burkini swimsuit in 2016, reveal a sustained political and legal focus on Islamic practices that relate to the country's colonial legacy. The perpetuation of this theme in Michel Houllebecq's best-selling *Soumission* (2015), which imagines France under Islamic rule, equally underscores a preoccupation with the subject in art and the popular imagination.⁸ The contemporaneous radicalization of French-born Muslim youth, exemplified at its most extreme by acts of terrorism such as the 2015 *Charlie Hebdo* and Bataclan attacks in Paris, exposes old wounds from the colonial past.⁹ Such attacks are certainly part of a global jihadist movement but are also symptoms of a violent history that merits further attention.

A less visible, but nevertheless pivotal, aspect of this history are the former settlers of Algeria known as the *pieds-noirs*, a million of whom migrated to France as the Algerian War drew to its bloody close. Against the backdrop of heated debates about immigration in Europe and the United States, an examination of this particular community is timely. Until recently, studies of the settlers were dated or of doubtful objectivity. This book takes its place alongside contemporary efforts to address the lack of critical attention given to a group that, as symbols of a failed colonial system, few wished to remember. These include works by French-language researchers such as Éric Savarèse and Emmanuel Comtat, as well as English-language academics such as Claire Eldridge, Sung-Eun Choi and Fiona Barclay.[10] While scholarly publications on the subject tend to draw most of their research from interviews, *pied-noir* associations, or the print media, this book focuses on fictional and autobiographical narratives in literature and on-screen. The current study, which considers works by the *pieds-noirs* up to the present day, provides an update to Lucienne Martini's 1997 survey, *Racines de papier: Essai sur l'expression littéraire de l'identité pieds-noirs* [Paper Roots: Essay on the Literary Expression of the *Pieds-Noirs*], itself the work of a *pied-noir*. However, whereas Martini and others tend to regard works by the settlers as transmitters of memory and therefore reflective of identity, this study argues that those analyzed here actively construct an identity and collective memory.[11] In its critical analysis of literature and film, it complements Amy Hubbell's 2015 monograph on the themes of repetition and return, which, she argues, are primary constituents of *pied-noir* identity. The current study, however, focuses on affective and ideological attachment to the *pied-noir* family—an extremely significant theme in works by the settlers, including those of Albert Camus, the community's foremost public intellectual—which scholars have thus far largely neglected. This study uncovers a renewed investment in the family as a partial response to exile. Moreover, through the family prism, this book provides a comprehensive examination of discourses on settler masculinity, femininity, childhood, and adolescence. In so doing, it reveals the construction of distinctive performances of gender and youth and brings to light neglected representations including homosexual, Jewish, and young narrative voices, which have significant implications with regard to nontraditional and emergent identities that are themselves contested. It is useful to note here that some commentators do not consider the Jewish population to be part of the *pied-noir* community but they are included in this study as French citizens at the time of Algerian independence.[12] Moreover, the research presented here reveals significant overlaps in all the works studied, which itself suggests that even unconventional narratives are not as straightforwardly divergent as would appear. More broadly, this study confirms Michel Foucault's concept of the "rebound effect" ("l'effet de retour") of colonialism on the Western world,[13] by bringing to light unexpected ways in which discourses related to the processes of French colonization and decolonization influence identities in modern-day France despite the fact that Algeria, the jewel in the colonial crown, gained its independence in 1962.

II. TACKLING TABOO SUBJECTS: THE ALGERIAN WAR AND THE *PIEDS-NOIRS*

The Algerian War (1954–1962) remains the most traumatic aspect of France's colonial past and arguably the most traumatic war of decolonization fought by Western colonial powers. The French had occupied Algeria since 1830 and it had formed three administrative *départements* [departments] of France since 1848. Following the conquest of Algeria in 1830, immigration began from all over Europe, particularly from Spain, Italy, and Malta as well as from France, although administrative statistics from 1843 show that there were also settlers from Germany, Switzerland, and Ireland.[14] Many of these settlers hoped to escape the poverty of their birth countries, while some were political exiles from France's Second Empire or from the annexation of Alsace-Lorraine following the Franco-Prussian War. When efforts to colonize Algeria with a majority of settlers from metropolitan France proved to be largely unsuccessful, officials decided to naturalize Jews in Algeria as French citizens in 1870, and subsequently naturalized European settlers by passing laws in 1889 and 1893. These populations together formed the *Français d'Algérie* [French of Algeria].

At the beginning of the war in 1954, approximately one million European settlers lived alongside some nine million indigenous Algerians. Since Algeria was officially part of "la plus grande France" [greater France], the French administration could not conceive of a situation in which the nation was at war with itself. The state referred to this *guerre sans nom* [war without a name] as *les événements* [the events] or *opérations de maintien de l'ordre* [operations to maintain order]. In fact, France only officially recognized the war in 1999.

The conflict was particularly violent, involving guerrilla warfare by the pro-independence FLN (Front de libération nationale) [National Liberation Front] and counterterrorism strategies by the French army that included the use of torture. Violence worsened from 1961, when some of the *Français d'Algérie* became involved in the *Organisation de l'Armée Secrète* (OAS) [Secret Army Organization], a terrorist group opposing Algerian independence. As bloodshed increased on both sides, it became apparent that the *Français d'Algérie*, now known as the *pieds-noirs* [black feet], would not be able to continue living in the territory and the vast majority fled to France in 1962. The slogan at the time was "la valise ou le cercueil" [the suitcase or the coffin], subsequently immortalized in the eponymous novel by OAS activist Anne Loesch.[15] Since many of the former settlers had never been to France before, their repatriation was particularly traumatic. Government leaders initially denied the exodus, referring to the settlers in 1962 as "vacanciers" [holiday-makers]. Indeed, Charles de Gaulle did not acknowledge the scale of the repatriation until October of 1962.[16] Despite the booming economy, due to the particular circumstances of the *Trente Glorieuses* [Thirty Glorious Years] of sustained economic growth following World War II, the government was reluctant to accept the influx of almost a million citizens and hoped that the majority of the *pieds-noirs* would return to Algeria. It is worth noting here that historian Jean-Jacques Jordi, himself a *pied-noir*, links this influx to the "quinze glorieuses" or fifteen years of economic expansion that took place between 1955 and 1970.[17] In the initial aftermath of their arrival, however, many settlers felt unwelcome. Press articles from 1962 suggest a growing resentment toward the former settlers and a feeling that they did not deserve to benefit from privileges or jobs in metropolitan France as they had profited from colonial life.[18]

In the years that followed, the French were encouraged to forgive and forget a particularly brutal period, with amnesties accorded in the 1960s, 1970s, and 1980s to those guilty of war crimes. This collective amnesia continued into the 1990s. Thus, historian Pierre Nora neglected to include Algeria in his influential work *Les Lieux de mémoire* (1984–1992) [Sites of Memory]. Algeria's absence is all the more remarkable since Nora had published a critical text about the *Français d'Algérie* in 1961, based on his experience as a teacher in Oran. Commenting on this apparent oversight, Richard Derderian rightly wonders whether some events are "simply too contentious and too divisive to be enshrined and perpetuated in the kinds of symbolic sites of memory that inspire Nora's collection."[19] In fact, a riposte to Nora's original volume, this time highlighting the significance of colonial memory and written by UK and American-based academics, did not appear until 2020.[20]

In France, the conflict and its commemoration remain highly contested. In 2012, an official from France's National Archives explained its website's short essay on "the end of the Algerian war," which contained no mention of the *harkis* (Algerian auxiliaries who sided with the French), nor any specific reference to the *pieds-noirs* or to the OAS, by stating that the subject was still too raw to permit further detail.[21] Associations representing both the *pieds-noirs* and the *harkis* condemned the adoption of a controversial law that same year, which stated that March 19, 1962—the date of the cease-fire in Algeria—would be a national day of remembrance for civilian and military victims of the conflict. The large number of casualties after this date for those within the *harki* and *pied-noir* communities meant that some viewed this choice as inflammatory.[22] For many of the *pieds-noirs*, two events that took place after the cease-fire have been a significant source of trauma: the French army opened fire on a crowd of *Français d'Algérie* during a demonstration on the Rue d'Isly in Algiers on March 26, 1962, leaving over forty dead; and indigenous Algerians killed many more during independence celebrations in Oran on July 5, 1962—an incident in which the army was slow to intervene.[23]

The teaching of colonial history has sparked further tension, most notably in 2005, when the second paragraph of article 4 of the "loi du 23 février" [February 23 law] stated that the positive role of colonization would be taught in schools—a clause that President Jacques Chirac (who himself served in the Algerian War) eventually repealed. President Emmanuel Macron's statement, as a presidential candidate in 2017, that colonization was "un crime contre l'humanité" [a crime against humanity] sparked another outcry.[24] Indeed, Macron was greeted by cries of "Macron trahison" [Macron treason] by 150 *pied-noir* protestors in Toulon shortly after this statement.[25] Macron's public response, "je vous ai compris et je vous aime. Parce que la République, elle doit aimer chacun" [I have understood you and I love you, because the Republic must love everyone], revived further painful memories of the Algerian War.[26] His statement echoed Charles de Gaulle's "Je vous ai compris" [I have understood you] speech in Algiers in 1958, which served to allay many settlers' fears that the end of colonial Algeria was in sight, although de Gaulle subsequently went on to negotiate for independence and is consequently viewed as a traitor by many of the former settlers. Some of the *pieds-noirs* therefore saw Macron's choice of words as a deliberate provocation.[27] The president's decision in September 2018 to recognize the state's role in torture and in the death of pro-independence mathematician Maurice Audin, following his arrest in Algiers by the authorities in 1957, equally caused controversy. In an open letter to Macron, *pied-noir* Joseph Perez, president of the *Centre de documentation historique sur l'Algérie* [Center for historic documents on Algeria], accused Macron of demonstrating "compassion sélective" [selective compassion].[28]

Such enduring controversies are an indication of France's failure to engage with its colonial history. As Philip Dine notes, despite the publication of a vast number of works by private, often-unknown individuals on the subject of the war, academics frequently considered France to have a nonexistent literary corpus on the subject until very recently.[29] The opening up of archives in the 1990s, particularly those of the French army, undoubtedly facilitated a progressive advancement of knowledge in this regard. Scholars have now discussed the initial official silence surrounding the war and subsequent enduring gaps in the transmission of memory.[30] Nevertheless, the state's reluctance to confront the conflict resulted in "guerres de mémoires" [memory wars], which are still entrenched in the political landscape, as different communities continue to put their stories forward in a bid to carve out a place in the country's national narrative. Among vying groups that include French army officers, victims of torture, OAS commandos, and *harkis*, the *pieds-noirs* occupy a central position. It is in this context and amidst enduring stereotypical images of the former settlers as *gros colons* (rich settlers) or *petits blancs* (poor whites) that the current book seeks to shed new light on a population that is frequently essentialized.

III. THE FRENCH ALGERIAN FAMILY: A FUNDAMENTAL TROPE

Symbolic familial belonging is an enduring aspect of continuing memory wars, as revealed by a 2012 quotation from the celebrated historian of the war, and himself a French Algerian, Benjamin Stora: "Le risque existe d'une apparition de mémoire communautarisée, où chacun regarde l'histoire d'Algérie à travers son vécu, son appartenance familiale" [There is a risk that memories will be split between communities, where everyone considers the history of Algeria through their experience, their familial affiliation].[31] It is also worth noting that Frederick Cooper and Ann Laura Stoler point to the "dynamics of exclusion and inclusion" inherent in the process of colonization.[32] They suggest that tensions between these inclusionary and exclusionary practices from the age of empire "are still present today."[33] This study takes a preoccupation with the *pied-noir* family as, in some significant respects, a symptom of the simultaneously inclusionary and exclusionary model. Stoler also notes that private familial attachments connected to issues such as parenting, sex, and race were crucial to the power structures of empire.[34] This book argues that family loyalties remain crucial for those seeking to construct a community in a world influenced by the politics of empire.

Julia Clancy-Smith points to the significance of the family theme in colonial rhetoric by noting that the "*mère-patrie* [mother-fatherland] was a universally utilized concept employed to translate the relationship between rulers and ruled into a language expressing maternal bonds between mother and child."[35] Moreover, John Strachan reveals the reiteration in textbooks of the colonial-metropole relationship as a bond between mother or *la mère-patrie* [mother-fatherland] and infant, and thus of the European settlers as new members of a French family who were nonetheless *étrangers* or foreigners compared with ethnic French settlers.[36] However, as Strachan notes, settler children did not accept Republican values uncritically.[37] Indeed, the current book reveals new slants on representations of mother-child and family bonds in works by the *pieds-noirs*. Clancy-Smith's and Gouda's assertion that settlers "rarely used a language of family or kinship to describe their day-to-day encounters with the Arab and Berber populations," who were instead viewed as "the enemy," is also of particular interest.[38] This book argues that a developing concept of *pied-noir* identity represents the Arab and Berber populations as members, although often distant ones, of a French Algerian family, particularly in nostalgic evocations of the colonial past from a position of exile. The present monograph thus complements and builds on Patricia Lorcin's observation that "the concept of Algeria as an extended 'happy family' is a recurring theme" for the former settlers.[39]

For many scholars, a real or metaphorical family constitutes an essential aspect of *pied-noir* identity. Jordi, for example, comments on the "esprit de famille qui perdure" [enduring spirit of family] among the *pieds-noirs*.[40] Sociologist Clarisse Buono, the daughter of *pied-noir* parents, equally states, "Aujourd'hui en France, la collectivité des rapatriés d'Algérie se donne *a priori* à voir comme une grande famille" [Today in France, the community of repatriates from Algeria in principle show themselves to be a big family]—a family that is "éclatée, voire décomposée" [divided, even broken] and in which France appears as the "mère abusive" [abusive mother]—themes that resurface frequently.[41] The current study reveals how fictionalized narratives contribute to this impression. It acknowledges, however, that increasing affective attachment to the family is unquestionably a reaction to the sense of nonbelonging that accompanies exile. Thus, twenty years after his departure from Algeria, Maurice Benassayag describes how family and community became increasingly significant:

> La famille devait donc subsister comme le seul terrain où l'on n'avançât pas à découvert. La famille constitua le point d'ancrage et les nécessités de l'entraide donnèrent un peu plus de corps à ce lien. On peut avancer [. . .] que cette communauté conserve le sens de la famille.[42]

> [The family therefore had to survive as the only site where we were not forging ahead without cover. The family was the anchor and the requirements for mutual assistance gave a bit more weight to this link. One can suggest [. . .] that this community retains a sense of family.]

Settlers' narratives of family, encompassing identifiable performances of masculinity, femininity, and childhood, cannot be divorced from conflicting, pejorative depictions of "the native" under colonization or from subsequent anti-colonial discourses. During the war, for example, critics such as Frantz Fanon theorized the concept of evolving roles for a united indigenous population. This, in Fanon's view, saw a move away from traditional values and the birth of a new "famille algérienne" [Algerian family]: "une communauté spirituelle qui constitue le bastion le plus solide de la Révolution algérienne" [a spiritual community which forms the most solid bastion of the Algerian revolution].[43] An emphasis on a united *pied-noir* family equally undermines negative stereotyping of the settlers as in some way abnormal. Tellingly, the family trope can depoliticize colonial history, as is evident from historian Joëlle Hureau's claim: "Le gros œuvre de l'histoire des pieds-noirs apparaît essentiellement comme un conglomérat d'histoires familiales, similaires dans les grandes lignes. Plus qu'une histoire militaire ou politique, c'est une chronique domestique et prosaïque" [The ensemble of works on the history of the *pieds-noirs* essentially appears as a conglomeration of family stories which are broadly similar. Rather than a military or political story, it is a domestic, prosaic chronicle].[44]

The values of inclusion and exclusion that marked the colonial system continue as markers of a *pied-noir* identity in some texts. A 1979 publication is particularly striking in this regard: *Pieds-Noirs belle pointure: Onze portraits de famille* [The *Pieds-Noirs*, A Great Fit: Eleven Family Portraits]. In the preface to his eleven interviews with well-known personalities whom he proudly proclaims as *pied-noir*, author Richard Koubi notes that despite their diversity, those interviewed "restent conscients d'appartenir à une même famille dont ils portent et honorent le nom" [remain conscious of belonging to a family whose name they use and honor].[45] This text is notable for its appendix of other well-known *pieds-noirs*, including "cousins" from Morocco, Tunisia, and some of France's overseas departments and territories, who have excelled in the realms of politics, economics, science, arts, entertainment, the media, and sport.[46] The publication therefore appears as a means of identifying a *pied-noir* family, which is set apart from the metropolitan French but which, as seen by the success in France of the interviewees, has also earned admittance to a broader French community.

Another striking example of the family trope is Geneviève Baïlac's 1957 play *La Famille Hernandez* [The Fernandez Family], released as a film in 1964. Hureau, describing the play, cites a revealing quotation from Baïlac:

Le propos initial était de donner à l'«homme nouveau» qui naissait [. . .] en dépit des politiques, des différences fondamentales, des heurts de nature, un homme que l'on pouvait rencontrer dans la rue avec son langage pittoresque émaillé d'expressions empruntées à toutes les langues parlées en Algérie [. . .] son verbe haut et son humour méditerranéen [. . .], le moyen d'expression le plus adapté à sa nature»: le théâtre.[47]

[The initial aim was to give the "new man" that was emerging [. . .] in spite of politics, fundamental differences, personality clashes—a man that you could meet on the street with his quaint speech peppered with expressions borrowed from all the languages spoken in Algeria, his loud way of talking and Mediterranean humor [. . .]—the means of expression most adapted for his nature: theatre.]

The playwright underlines the theatrical performance of a "new" settler masculinity here but sidelines politics, as she does in the film version, which she wrote and directed. In this story, set in Bab-el-Oued in Algiers just before the outbreak of the Algerian War, the extended Hernandez family is part of a broader community who wash their children in the local fountain and willingly share their possessions. This family gives all their furniture away when they think they have won money, only for the neighbors to bring everything back when it turns out they were mistaken.[48] Their difference from the metropolitan French is underlined, not just by their strong accents and theatrical gestures but also by a comment from a new metropolitan teacher, who notes their similarities to but difference from "les méridionaux" [those from the South of France]: "Ici, [. . .] il y a du piment dans leurs veines" [Here, [. . .] they have the spice of life in their veins].[49] This early post-conflict representation of the *pieds-noirs* therefore stresses a unique identity that appears under threat at the end of the film, when, during an outdoor wedding party, a background radio announces that *parachutistes* [paratroopers] are en route to Algeria due to serious events. However, in a recording of a live theater sequel to the story twenty-five years later, many of the same actors perform their roles as larger-than-life *pieds-noirs* who still live in a happy community with indigenous Algerians, although this time they are based in an HLM (habitation à loyer modéré) [social housing development] on the outskirts of Paris.[50] In light of this exaggerated performance on-screen and onstage, the next section considers constructions of a community in exile.

IV. PERFORMING IDENTITY AND CONSTRUCTING A COMMUNITY

This book differs from other studies by drawing on theories of performativity and "invented tradition" to reveal how concepts of settler identity changed over time. Judith Butler's concept of gender as performative, involving both "theatrical and linguistic dimensions," is especially useful.[51] According to Butler, "acts, gestures, enactments, generally construed, are *performative* in the sense that the essence or identity that they otherwise purport to express are *fabrications* manufactured and sustained through corporeal signs and other discursive means."[52] Such acts and gestures relating to gender create "an illusion discursively maintained for the purposes of the regulation of sexuality."[53] Identity, therefore, is the result of discourses, which are understood in light of Foucault's definition of "le discours" [discourse] as "tantôt domaine général de tous les énoncés, tantôt groupe individualisable d'énoncés, tantôt pratique réglée rendant compte d'un certain nombre d'énoncés" [sometimes the general domain of all statements, sometimes a group of statements that can be individualized, sometimes a regulated practice that justifies a certain number of statements].[54] Sara Mills usefully sums up Foucault's concept of discursive practices that are laden with meaning as follows: "Discourse does not simply translate reality into language; rather discourse should be seen as a system which structures the way that we perceive reality."[55] In Butler's analysis, there is no "preexisting [gender] identity," and thus it is possible to disrupt discourse in this regard.[56] Her arguments are particularly relevant to this book's consideration of representations of gender and youth. Butler's concept of drag as a practice that can potentially subvert discourse and reveal "the imitative structure of gender itself—as well as its contingency" is equally pertinent,[57] as is her assertion that some drag performances are "denaturalizing parodies that reidealize heterosexual norms *without* calling them into question."[58]

The current study further applies the paradigm of performativity to a settler identity informed by the regulatory context of the colonial setting, as well as the particular circumstances of exile. With regard to an identity born of colonial processes, discourses are particularly significant. As Nicholas Thomas notes: "Colonialism has always been [. . .] a cultural process; its discoveries and trespasses are imagined and energized through signs, metaphors and narratives."[59] Furthermore, if as Butler suggests, "true gender is a fantasy instituted and inscribed on the surface of bodies,"[60] the current study argues that the *pied-noir* identity apparently assumed by a diverse group of settlers, who were known as *Français d'Algérie* until the Algerian War, is also a fantasy. Benedict Anderson's assertion that "all communities larger than primordial villages of face-to-face contact (and perhaps even these) are imagined,"[61] suggests that theories of performativity can apply to communities as well as individuals. Scholarship on "invented tradition" as "a set of practices, normally governed by overtly or tacitly accepted rules and of a ritual or symbolic nature, which seek to inculcate certain values and norms of behavior by repetition, which automatically implies continuity with the past,"[62] also underlines the performative and regulatory nature of a community's traditions.

This book argues that works by the *pieds-noirs* contribute to the edification of a collective memory for this community. Ella Shohat and Robert Stam, summarizing cultural theorist Frederic Jameson, describe "texts which metaphorize the public sphere even when narrating apparently private stories, and where 'the personal and the political, the private and the historical, become inextricably linked.'"[63] The apparently personal texts studied in the current book, which inevitably evoke the colonial past, similarly act as representative of the experiences and history of a wider *pied-noir* community. This study also draws on Nancy Wood's concept of collective memory as performative as it has some degree of social intent.[64] In this way, narratives and other cultural products become "vectors" or "conduits" of performativity.[65] Textual and on-screen representations discussed here are equally considered as conduits of performativity.

It is useful to point out at this juncture that genre is subordinate to function in the current book, as stories analyzed seek, without necessarily succeeding, to underline a communal identity. These narratives fall on a spectrum from autobiography to fiction. In some cases, authors (and their publishers) downplay autobiographical elements and present works as novels while in other fictionalized narratives, they foreground autobiographical elements and claim that the text is more accurate than history. In some instances, it is therefore appropriate to refer to the author, while in others it is more appropriate to refer to the narrator. The occasional possibility of slippage between author and narrator here is a reflection of the performance of some authors who seek to disguise their proximity to the events described, just as others seek to put forward their texts as a true reflection of their lived experience. The current study argues that the use of fiction permits myth making or the active construction of a public history and an associated identity. However, it also reveals the important role of fiction in unsettling conventional narratives.

The term *pied-noir* reveals ongoing myth making by the *pied-noir* community that is worth considering here. Some stories suggest that the barefoot indigenous population named the settlers on seeing the black boots worn by French soldiers. Others link the name to the wine-stained feet of industrious settlers. However, critics agree that these theories are unlikely. The true origins of the term remain in doubt, although its use in Algeria to designate Europeans originated in the mid-1950s and coincided with the designation of the indigenous population, rather than the settlers, as Algerian.[66] Moreover, a theory included in Andrea L. Smith's study suggests that metropolitan French citizens first used the term as a coded warning that the former settlers were not really white, as they had been "tainted" by their time in North Africa.[67] While the term originally had pejorative connotations, this study uses it as the *Français d'Algérie* have themselves reclaimed the name and it now commonly refers to a population that, under colonization, referred to itself as "Algérien" [Algerian]. Interestingly, a psychological study on the general health benefits of creating a narrative suggests that people "with a nonvisible identity" benefit "more when writing about being a member of the stigmatized group" as opposed to people with a visible, stigmatized identity, who benefit more "from writing about being a member of the general community."[68] Thus, in the specific case under examination here, the *pieds-noirs*, as a group with a nonvisible, initially stigmatized identity in France, benefited in the aftermath of the conflict from writing about being members of a *pied-noir* community or family.

V. TELLING TALES IN LITERATURE AND ON-SCREEN

Philip Dine has underlined the particular importance of the role of telling tales (*histoires*) both privately and publicly in the generation of France's complex history (*Histoire*) in Algeria.[69] Furthermore, Stora argues that books produced by different groups since the beginning of the conflict are extremely important vectors of knowledge that act as "*une archive à part entière*" [an archive in its own right], although historians tend to overlook such material.[70] The current book underlines the role of tales in the creation and preservation of a postindependence identity that is marked by the Algerian War or by an engagement with the real possibility of the end of colonial Algeria. It is useful to note that Janine de la Hogue (herself a *pied-noir*) dates the beginning of this body of writing to 1954.[71] Feminist French Algerian writer Marie Cardinal, however, considers World War II as a moment of simultaneous separation from and unification with France and thereby the defining moment for the birth of an as-yet-unnamed *pied-noir* identity.[72] Various representations of the *pieds-noirs* on-screen are also of interest to the current study, particularly since, as William B. Cohen notes, Algerian-related films in France have generally been "unable to create a consensual image."[73] Films or TV series targeted at national or even global audiences are thus another extremely effective means of creating memories with regard to the former colony.

Given the substantial corpus produced by the *pieds-noirs*, this book considers a broad selection that is reflective of the material available. In its examination of a variety of narratives aimed at a *pied-noir* audience and beyond, it examines over thirty canonical and noncanonical works. While it references works by others in passing, the main writers, screenwriters, and filmmakers examined are Albert Camus, Francine Dessaigne, Anne Loesch, Marie Elbe, Micheline Susini, Marie Cardinal, Brigitte Roüan, Hélène Cixous, Jules Roy, Emmanuel Roblès, Jean Pélégri, Gabriel Conesa, Daniel Saint-Hamont, Jean Sénac, Lucien Legrand, Élie-Georges Berreby, Hélène Gadal, Virginie Buisson, Jean-Noël Pancrazi, Brigitte Benkemoun, and Claire Messud.

Chapter 1 of this study focuses on arguably the most famous member of this community, Albert Camus. It reassesses his works, including the idealized mother figure, in light of Camus's Algerian background. It also examines the writer's attempts to construct a hybrid, macho masculinity that continues to influence current representations of the *pieds-noirs*. Chapter 2 investigates works by *pied-noir* women, whose voices emerged in the immediate aftermath of the war in texts and films that disrupt some narratives but also foreground certain themes and representations of gender. Chapter 3 considers conventional and nonconventional depictions of *pied-noir* masculinity including representations of homosexuality in the colony. Chapter 4 seeks to go beyond the narrow field of study on the subject of the *pieds-noirs* by comprehensively analyzing the popularity of child and adolescent narrators who can portray the *pieds-noirs* as innocent victims but may nonetheless produce a potentially fruitful liminal space from which to broach the subject of colonialism and represent alternative identities.

For Butler, trying fully to satisfy the norms of gender identity is a Sisyphean task.[74] Interestingly, Camus appears to have pointed to the performance of identity by arguing in his *Le Mythe de Sisyphe* [The Myth of Sisyphus] that "un homme se définit aussi bien par ses comédies que par ses élans sincères" [a man defines himself just as much for his playacting as for his sincere impulses].[75] In the same text, he suggests that "peut-être la grande oeuvre d'art a moins d'importance en elle-même que dans l'épreuve qu'elle exige d'un homme et l'occasion qu'elle lui fournit de surmonter ses fantômes et d'approcher d'un peu plus près sa réalité nue" [perhaps the great work of art is of lesser importance in its own right than for the test it requires of man and the opportunity it gives him to overcome his phantoms and to come a little bit closer to his naked reality].[76] Against this backdrop, chapter 1 examines Camus's attempts to work through a phantasmatic *pied-noir* identity in literature.

NOTES

1. Isabelle Ligner, "Pour des Algériens, le recours à une loi de 1955 est une 'provocation,'" AFP, November 8, 2005, LexisNexis.

2. Andrew Hussey, "The French Intifada: How the Arab banlieues are fighting the French state," *The Observer*, February 23, 2014.

3. Manu Saadia, "To understand the Paris 'Yellow Vests' riots, look to French Guiana," *The Washington Post*, December 4, 2018. Comparisons between rural France and the colonies are not new. Eugen Weber describes the Paris administration's "colonizing enterprise" that formed part of the "civilization" of rural France from 1870 to 1914 in his *Peasants into Frenchmen: The Modernization of Rural France 1870-1914* (London: Chatto & Windus, 1977), 490.

4. Ivan Rioufol, "Macron confronté à la France déchirée," *Le Figaro*, January 11, 2019. All translations are my own unless otherwise stated.

5. Maël Thierry, "Gilets jaunes: Je crains une forme de scission à l'intérieur du pays," *L'OBS*, December 3, 2018.

6. See, for example, an interview with historian Emmanuel Todd by Jean-Baptiste de Montvalon and Sylvia Zappi, "Ce que Sarkozy propose, c'est la haine de l'autre," *Le Monde*, December 27, 2009.

7. John Lichfield, "It's a French woman's duty to wear a bikini, says ex-minister; Islamophobia row as Sarkozy supporter hits out at Muslim on beach in headscarf," *The Independent*, August 19, 2014.

8. Houllebecq himself was born Michel Thomas in France's overseas territory of Réunion and lived in colonial Algeria for the first five years of his life. According to the author of his unauthorized biography, Denis Demonpion, Houllebecq's father and two paratroopers brought him to France in 1961. See Jérôme Dupuis, "Acte III: «Houellebecq a tout programmé depuis le premier jour»," *L'Express*, September 1, 2005.

9. French-born men in their twenties and thirties were among the perpetrators of both attacks. Further acts of terrorism carried out by French-born youth include the 2016 murder of a police officer and his partner at their home west of Paris, the 2016 murder of a priest near Rouen, and the 2018 Strasbourg Christmas market shooting.

10. See works such as Éric Savarèse, *L'Invention des pieds-noirs* (Paris: Séguier, 2002); Emmanuelle Comtat, *Les Pieds-Noirs et la politique: quarante ans après le retour* (Paris: Sciences Po, 2009); Claire Eldridge, *From Empire to Exile: History and Memory within the Pied-Noir and Harki Communities* (Manchester: Manchester University Press, 2016); Fiona Barclay, "Reporting on 1962: the evolution of *pied-noir* identity across fifty years of print media," *Modern & Contemporary* France 23, no. 2 (2015): 197–211 and Sung-Eun Choi, *Decolonization and the French of Algeria: Bringing the Settler Colony Home* (Basingstoke, UK: Palgrave Macmillan, 2016).

11. Martini, for example, suggests that *pied-noir* writers seek to show others "un portrait sincère" [a sincere portrait] of themselves. See Lucienne Martini, *Racines de papier: Essai sur l'expression littéraire de l'identité Pieds-Noirs* (Paris: Publisud, 1997), 87.

12. The Jewish community are also included in texts such as Emmanuel Roblès, ed., *Les Pieds-Noirs* (Paris: Philippe Lebaud, 1982).

13. In "Cours du 4 février 1976," Foucault refers to "l'effet de retour [. . .] de la pratique coloniale" [the rebound effect [. . .] of colonial practice], whereby colonial mechanisms of power were transported back to the West. See Michel Foucault, *«Il faut défendre la société»: Cours au collège de France (1975-1976)* (Paris: Gallimard, 1997), 89.

14. Andrea L. Smith, *Colonial Memory and Postcolonial Europe: Maltese Settlers in Algeria and France* (Bloomington, IN: Indiana University Press, 2006), 73.

15. Anne Loesch, *La Valise et le cercueil* (Paris: Plon, 1963).

16. Jean-Jacques Jordi, *Les Pieds-Noirs* (Paris: Le Cavalier Bleu, 2009), 91.

17. Ibid., 110–11. See also an interview with Jean-Jacques Jordi in Hélène Rouquette-Valeins, "L'apport des pieds-noirs," *Sud Ouest*, November 21, 2010.

18. Jordi, *Les Pieds-Noirs*, 86–88.

19. Richard L. Derderian, "Algeria as a *lieu de mémoire*: Ethnic Minority Memory and National Identity in Contemporary France," *Radical History Review*, no. 83 (Spring 2002): 29.

20. Etienne Achille, Charles Forsdick, and Lydie Moudileno, eds. *Postcolonial Realms of Memory: Sites and Symbols in Modern France* (Liverpool: Liverpool University Press, 2020).

21. Anonymous, "France Remembers the Algerian War, 50 Years On," France 24, http://www.france24.com/en/20120316-commemorations-mark-end-algerian-war-independence-france-evian-accords. Date accessed: February 24, 2014.

22. Antoine Fouchet, "Le souvenir de la guerre d'Algérie divise encore les parlementaires; La proposition de loi PS faisant du 19 mars le jour du souvenir de la guerre d'Algérie n'a pas fait l'unanimité, hier, au Sénat. Les associations de pieds-noirs et de harkis dénoncent le choix de cette date," *La Croix*, November 9, 2012.

23. The number of casualties and deaths for both incidents remains contested. For the Rue d'Isly incident, scholars generally cite the number of deaths as between forty and ninety. For the July 5, 1962, incident, the estimated number of deaths varies between several hundred and several thousand. Guy Pervillé's detailed research suggests that the number of victims was approximately 700. See Guy Pervillé, *Oran, 5 juillet 1962. Leçon d'histoire sur un massacre* (Paris: Vendémiaire, 2014).

24. Patrick Roger, "Colonisation: les propos inédits de Macron font polémique," *Le Monde*, February 16, 2017.

25. Jean-Paul Pelissier, "Polémique sur la colonisation: à Toulon, Macron ose un 'Je vous ai compris,'" *LeParisien.fr*, February 18, 2017.

26. Ibid.

27. Pascal Lachenaud, "Colonisation: Une association de Pieds-Noirs porte plainte contre Macron," *LeParisien.fr*, February 27, 2017. The usually nuanced colonial historian Guy Pervillé also criticized Macron's "Je vous ai compris" declaration and accused him of committing an anachronism by condemning the conquest as a crime against humanity. See Guy Pervillé, "Réponse à Emmanuel Macron (2017)," Guy Pervillé, http://guy.perville.free.fr/spip/article.php3?id_article=390. Date accessed: July 2, 2017.

28. Joseph Pérez, "E Macron: Une compassion bien selective," Communiqué CDHA, http://data.over-blog-kiwi.com/1/43/00/01/20180917/ob_26eb39_2018-09-1 3-communique-du-cdha1.pdf. Date accessed: September 13, 2018.

29. Philip Dine, "Reading and remembering *la guerre des mythes*: French literary representations of the Algerian war," *Modern & Contemporary France* 2, no. 2 (1994):143–44.

30. See, for example, Raphaëlle Branche, *La Guerre d'Algérie: une histoire apaisée?* (Paris: Seuil, 2005); Benjamin Stora, *La Gangrène et l'oubli: La mémoire de la guerre d'Algérie* (Paris: La Découverte, 1998); Jo McCormack, *Collective Memory: France and the Algerian War (1954-1962)* (Lanham, MD: Lexington, 2007).

31. Benjamin Stora, "Algérie-France, mémoires sous tension," *Le Monde*, March 18, 2012.

32. Frederick Cooper and Ann L. Stoler, "Between Metropole and Colony: Rethinking a Research Agenda," in *Tensions of Empire: Colonial Cultures in a Bourgeois World*, ed. Frederick Cooper and Ann L. Stoler (Berkeley, CA: University of California Press, 1997), 4.

33. Ibid., 37.

34. Ann L. Stoler, *Carnal Knowledge and Imperial Power: Race and the Intimate in Colonial Rule* (Berkeley, CA: University of California Press, 2002), 8.

35. Julia Clancy-Smith, "Islam, Gender, and Identities in the Making of French Algeria, 1830-1962," in *Domesticating the Empire: Race, Gender, and Family Life in French and Dutch Colonialism*, ed. Julia Clancy-Smith and Frances Gouda (Charlottesville, VA: University of Virginia Press, 1998), 158.

36. John Strachan, "Reshaping the Mythologies of Frenchness: Culture, History and Identity in European Algeria, 1870-1930" (unpublished PhD dissertation, University of Manchester, 2006). See Chapter 2, 87–131.

37. Ibid., 122–23.

38. Julia Clancy-Smith and Frances Gouda, "Introduction," in Clancy-Smith and Gouda, *Domesticating the Empire*, 9.

39. Patricia M. E. Lorcin, *Historicizing Colonial Nostalgia: European Women's Narratives of Algeria and Kenya 1900-Present* (Basingstoke: Palgrave Macmillan, 2012), 177.

40. Jordi, *Les Pieds-Noirs*, 130.

41. Clarisse Buono, *Pieds-noirs de père en fils* (Paris: Balland, 2004), 9, 29. Historian Joëlle Hureau evokes similar imagery in *La Mémoire des pieds-noirs: de 1830 à nos jours* (Paris: Perrin, 2010), 117, 102–3, where she describes the *pieds-noirs* as orphans of a scattered family on their repatriation, while France is as an abusive stepmother. See also *pied-noir* journalist Danielle Michel-Chich's description of an extended family unit in Algeria that, although fragmented by repatriation, remains a key element of identity, in her *Déracinés: les pieds-noirs aujourd'hui* (Paris: Plume, 1990), 104–6.

42. Maurice Benassayag, "Familles, je vous aime," in Roblès, *Les Pieds-Noirs*, 164.

43. Frantz Fanon, *L'An V de la révolution algérienne* (Paris: La Découverte, 2001), 106.

44. Hureau, *La Mémoire des pieds-noirs*, 159.

45. Richard M. Koubi, *Pieds-Noirs belle pointure: Onze portraits de famille* (Paris: L'Atlanthrope, 1979), 10.

46. Ibid., 195–219.

47. Hureau, *La Mémoire des pieds-noirs*, 332. David Prochaska has analyzed the influence of different languages on this dialect, known as *pataouète*, and its use in literature. See David Prochaska, *Making Algeria French: Colonialism in Bône, 1870-1920* (Cambridge: Cambridge University Press, 1990), 224–29. Baïlac's evocation of a unifying language spoken by a "new man" also recalls Camus's 1937 lecture on "La Nouvelle Culture Méditerrannéenne" [The New Mediterranean Culture] in which Islam and Arabic are elided while Christianity and linguistic unity are presented as unifying features in a new concept of the Mediterranean "famille" [family]. See Albert Camus, *Essais* (Paris: Gallimard, 2000), 1321–27.

48. Geneviève Baïlac, *La Famille Hernandez* (France: Films Etienne Baïlac, 1964).

49. Ibid.

50. Geneviève Baïlac, *La Famille Hernandez* (Théâtre du Gymnase Marie Bell, Paris: Antenne 2, 1987).

51. Judith Butler, *Gender Trouble: Feminism and the Subversion of Identity* (London: Routledge, 1999), xxv.

52. Ibid., 173. Butler's emphasis.

53. Ibid.

54. Michel Foucault, *L'Archéologie du savoir* (Paris: Gallimard, 1969), 106.

55. Sara Mills, *Michel Foucault* (London: Routledge, 2003), 55.

56. Butler, *Gender Trouble*, 180.

57. Ibid., 175, 176.

58. Judith Butler, *Bodies that Matter: On the Discursive Limits of 'Sex'* (New York: Routledge, 1993), 231. Butler's emphasis.

59. Nicholas Thomas, *Colonialism's Culture: Anthropology, Travel and Government* (Cambridge: Polity Press, 1994), 2. Cited in Philip Dine, "Big-Game Hunting in Algeria from Jules Gérard to *Tartarin de Tarascon*," *Moving Worlds: A Journal of Transcultural Writings* 12, no. 1 (2012): 48.

60. Butler, *Gender Trouble*, 174.

61. Benedict Anderson, *Imagined Communities: Reflections on the Origin and Spread of Nationalism* (London: Verso, 1991), 6.

62. Eric Hobsbawm, "Introduction: Inventing Traditions," in *The Invention of Tradition*, ed. Eric Hobsbawm and Terence Ranger (Cambridge: Cambridge University Press, 1996), 1.

63. Frederic Jameson, "Third World Literature in the Era of Multinational Capitalism," *Social Text*, no. 15 (Autumn 1986). Cited in Ella Shohat and Robert Stam, *Unthinking Eurocentrism: Multiculturalism and the Media* (London: Routledge, 1994), 230.

64. Nancy Wood, *Vectors of Memory: Legacies of Trauma in Postwar Europe* (Oxford: Berg, 1999), 2.

65. Ibid., 6, 2.

66. Xavier Yacono thoroughly examines the term in "Pourquoi pieds-noirs?," in Roblès, *Les Pieds-Noirs*, 15–19. He notes that it originally referred to the indigenous population of Algeria and finds evidence of its initial (although not widespread) use in reference to Europeans in the former French territories of West Africa as well as in Tunisia and Morocco from or before 1955.

67. Smith, *Colonial Memory and Postcolonial Europe*, 182.

68. James W. Pennebaker and Janel D. Seagal, "Forming a Story: The Health Benefits of Narrative," *Journal of Clinical Psychology* 55, no. 10 (1999): 1247.

69. See Dine, "Reading and remembering *la guerre des mythes*, 141–42.

70. Benjamin Stora, *Le Livre, mémoire de l'Histoire: Réflexions sur le livre et la guerre d'Algérie* (Paris: Le Préau des Collines, 2005), 7. Stora's emphasis.

71. Janine de la Hogue, "Les Livres comme patrie," in Roblès, *Les Pieds-Noirs*, 113.

72. Marie Cardinal, *Les Pieds-Noirs* (Paris: Belfond, 1988), 46, 72.

73. William B. Cohen, "The Algerian War and French Memory," *Contemporary European History* 9, no. 3 (November 2000): 490.

74. Judith Butler, *Trouble dans le genre (Gender Trouble): Le féminisme et la subversion de l'identité*, trans. Cynthia Kraus (Paris: La Découverte, 2005), 17. In his introduction, Éric Fassin sums up as follows: "Nouveau mythe de Sisyphe, malgré tous les efforts du monde, nul ne saurait satisfaire entièrement à la norme" [There is a new myth of Sisyphus: despite people's best efforts, no one could entirely satisfy the norm].

75. Camus, *Essais*, 106.

76. Ibid., 191.

Chapter 1

Camus, Meursault, Daru, Cormery

The First Pied-Noir *Men*

1.1 INTRODUCTION: CAMUS, CRIME, AND PUNISHMENT IN THE *PIED-NOIR* FAMILY

Albert Camus was the most famous writer of the *École d'Alger* [Algiers School]—a literary movement of the mid-1930s to the 1950s that focused on a united Mediterranean identity. Yet many critics have effectively ignored his Algerian origins in favor of universalist readings of his works.[1] Scholars have nonetheless periodically drawn attention to Camus's roots in harsh postcolonial critiques or analyses seeking to rehabilitate the author.[2] This chapter casts new light on Camus's Algerian origins and takes its place among contemporary studies that attempt to explore the writer's Algerian background from a nuanced viewpoint.[3] The current chapter, however, diverges from other studies by drawing on theories of performativity to make original findings about how the writer seeks to inform commemorative discourses about his community. Theories of performativity also make it possible to unravel ways in which Camus represents some of the identity challenges faced by the former settlers.

The author's stance on the Algerian War made him an unpopular figure before he died. Both *Français d'Algérie* protesters and Muslims greeted the writer with cries of "Camus à mort!" [Death to Camus] during his unsuccessful appeal for a civil truce in Algiers in 1956. On this occasion, FLN commandos protected him while *Algérie Française* militants threatened him with abduction.[4] These threats recall Judith Butler's assertion that "we regularly punish those who fail to do their gender right";[5] by implication, communities punish those who fail to perform their group's identity correctly. In this case, for many of his compatriots, the writer failed to "do" his identity as a member of the settler community.

Of particular interest is that Camus's legacy remains a source of contention in both France and Algeria, which signals the continued contested identity of the settlers more generally. In 2010, then French president Nicolas Sarkozy's proposal to rebury the author in the Pantheon along with other great French writers sparked heated controversy, and the author remains buried in a humble grave in the Provencal village of Lourmarin.[6] Moreover, plans to honor Camus in Algeria on the fiftieth anniversary of his death were either a "flop or invited hostility."[7] The centenary of Camus's birth also went largely unrecognized in both countries.[8] This said, an exhibition planned to take place in Aix-en-Provence for the centenary, in November 2013, sparked controversy when the celebrated Algerian War historian Benjamin Stora lost his role as its official curator to Michel Onfray, author of *L'Ordre libertaire: La vie philosophique d'Albert Camus* (2012) [*Libertarian Order: The Philosophical Life of Albert Camus*]. In this tome, Onfray laments what he sees as the neglect of Camus by philosophers in the second half of the twentieth century and contradicts what he calls a negative "fiction sartrienne" [Sartrian fiction] surrounding the author, in favor of a portrait of a hedonist, libertarian, anarchist, anti-colonial, and anti-totalitarian philosopher.[9] Some critics accused the right-wing mayor of Aix-en-Provence, Maryse Joissains, of courting a *pied-noir* electorate by supporting Onfray, whose rehabilitation of Camus had received considerable attention in the media.[10] Amidst the ensuing controversy, Onfray denied he was "le candidat [. . .] de l'extrême droite, de l'OAS, des petits blancs, du colonialisme, de l'Algérie française" [the candidate of [. . .] the far right, the OAS, poor white settlers, colonialism [or] French Algeria] and resigned from the project.[11] However, it went ahead from October 2013 until January 2014 (the anniversary of the author's death), this time organized by a team of historians and philosophers.[12] The resulting exhibition received disappointing reviews and seemed to have suffered due to its attempts to avoid further debate.[13] The new organizers' stated aim for the exhibition positioned Camus within a global family or "fraternité universelle" [universal fraternity], in a move that sidelined politics.[14]

Camus died before Algerian independence and the exodus of the majority of the *Français d'Algérie*, whose identity as *pieds-noirs* only became solidified on their arrival in France. His preoccupation with a *pied-noir* family is nevertheless undeniable. In 1957, the author explained his self-imposed public silence on the Algerian War to the secretary of the French teachers' union, Denis Forestier, in the following terms: "Je ne puis accepter personnellement de faire quoi que ce soit qui, même de loin, même indirectement, puisse justifier celui qui frappera les miens" [I cannot personally agree to do anything which might, even from afar, even indirectly, justify the person who will target my people].[15] A desire to protect his family would come to the fore publicly in 1957, when Camus won the Nobel Prize for literature. It was while in Sweden to accept the award that Camus replied to an Algerian student's question at Uppsala University by stating:

> J'ai toujours condamné la terreur. Je dois condamner aussi un terrorisme qui s'exerce, aveuglément, dans les rues d'Alger par exemple, et qui un jour peut frapper ma mère ou ma famille. Je crois à la justice, mais je défendrai ma mère avant la justice.[16]
>
> [I have always condemned terror. I must also condemn a terrorism which is blindly carried out on the streets of Algiers, for example, and which could strike my mother or my family one day. I believe in justice but I will defend my mother before justice.]

For some contemporary critics, this statement is an indication of Camus's belief that violent means cannot be justified.[17] Moreover, this chapter points to themes of familial attachment (and severing ties) as an engaged response to the prospect of decolonization. At the time, however, both sides, including French intellectuals Francis Jeanson and Jean-Paul Sartre, vilified Camus.

The rejection of Camus by a significant number of settlers during the Algerian War contrasts with the way in which the *pied-noir* community has reclaimed him postindependence. For Jean-Robert Henry, a literary family that is uniquely *pied-noir* has unified with the passage of time.[18] Consequently, writers like Camus "sont désormais revendiqués comme membres à part entière d'une famille, qui se reconnaît mieux qu'hier dans les grandes *sagas* historiques" [are henceforth claimed as fully fledged members of a family which recognizes itself more than ever in big historical sagas].[19] The writer's well-known love of soccer is significant in this regard, with one *pied-noir* interviewee emphasizing that the author's intellectual endeavors were, unlike Sartre's, offset by virile activities.[20] This particular interviewee thus concludes that Camus is his spiritual brother: "en vieillissant, Camus m'est devenu beaucoup plus fraternel, parce que je me suis aperçu qu'il y avait cette dualité chez Camus, que naturellement Sartre ne jouait pas au foot" [in later life, Camus became more fraternal to me because I realized that there was this duality with Camus, that, naturally, Sartre did not play soccer].[21] Olivier Todd also documents Camus's humble background, attachment to his mother, numerous affairs, and sense of "le code de l'honneur nord-africain, la parole donnée" [the North African code of honor, keeping your word].[22] From the author's life, a number of tropes are therefore visible. These would form cornerstones of a literary identity that encompasses modest origins, an attachment to the mother, and, by extension, distinctively Mediterranean honor codes. Camus evokes such codes in "L'Été à Alger" [Summer in Algiers], an essay in the collection *Noces* (1938) [Nuptials], where he describes "real" men who respect their mothers, wives, and pregnant women, and do not attack an adversary if their opponent is outnumbered.

Against this backdrop, the current chapter reveals the writer's developing construction of a French Algerian identity. It argues that by creating fictionalized narratives, Camus begins to engage with the impact of colonialism and with his own contested identity. It also analyzes the Camusian mother figure as part of the specifically colonial context in which Camus grew up. This chapter uncovers the construction of a masculinity that positions the writer as the *père spirituel* [spiritual father] of postindependence narratives by former settlers. It equally points to Camus's influence on traditionally opposing memory groups from the war.

The primary focus is on the male protagonists in Camus's first and last published novels—*L'Étranger* (1942) [The Outsider] and *Le Premier Homme* (1994) [The First Man]. The chapter also examines the short story "L'Hôte" [The Guest] from *L'Exil et le Royaume* (1957) [Exile and the Kingdom]. It additionally refers to Camus's *La Peste* (1947) [The Plague], although this story is largely regarded as a parable about the Occupation that could have been set anywhere, and to essays on Algeria contained in the aforementioned *Noces* and *L'Été* (1954) [Summer]. The stories studied stand apart from the writer's critical stance with regard to colonial injustice in essays such as those contained within *Actuelles, III: Chroniques algériennes, 1939–1958* (1958) [Actualities III: Algerian Chronicles, 1939–1958]. The use of fiction consequently facilitated Camus's elaboration of a sympathetic settler identity that would come to be known as *pied-noir*. To draw on Butler's view of gender norms as "phantasmatic," Camus, through fictional male characters, can represent a hypermasculinity that is impossible to embody in real life.[23] However, the writer's professed experience during a day trip to Tipasa is worth citing here:

> Il y a un sentiment que connaissent les acteurs lorsqu'ils ont conscience d'avoir bien rempli leur rôle, c'est-à-dire [. . .], d'avoir fait coïncider leurs gestes et ceux du personnage idéal qu'ils incarnent. [. . .] C'était précisément cela que je ressentais: j'avais bien joué mon rôle. J'avais fait mon métier d'homme.[24]

> [There is a feeling that actors get when they are aware of having done their job well, that is [. . .], they have made their gestures coincide with those of the ideal character they are embodying. [. . .] That was exactly how I felt: I had played my role well, I had done my job as a man.]

This leads to an examination of the protagonist of Camus's *L'Étranger* (1942).

1.2 CONSTRUCTING THE FRENCH ALGERIAN OUTSIDER

Camus had left Algeria for Paris two years before the publication of *L'Étranger*, which appeared in the context of World War II. His arrival in France in 1940 followed the collapse of his career as a journalist with the daily *Alger Républicain* [Republican Algiers] and its later incarnation, *Soir Républicain* [Republican Nightly], due to censorship by the authorities. However, the author undoubtedly remained preoccupied with his place of birth and would have suffered from a particular sense of isolation as a French Algerian writer based in metropolitan France. According to fellow French Algerian Jacques Derrida, the November 1942 Allied landings in North Africa sparked "la constitution d'une sorte de capitale littéraire de la France en exil à Alger" [the formation of a sort of literary capital of exiled France in Algiers][25]—a hub from which Camus was excluded. Furthermore, according to Conor Cruise O'Brien, Camus had begun working on *L'Étranger* in 1938, while still in Algeria.[26] In the same period, he wrote critical reports for *Alger Républicain*, denouncing conditions for the Berbers of Kabylia in essays such as his 1939 series "Misère de la Kabylie" [Misery in Kabylia]. Yet, Camus's wide-reaching novel published in multiple languages sits uneasily with his concern for social justice, as expressed in such essays, as it privileges the voice of the settler protagonist rather than the indigenous victim he murders. This study reconsiders the colonial context of Camus's foremost work of fiction in order to reveal the author's depiction of a unique settler identity.

Perhaps the most significant critics of *L'Étranger*'s colonialist viewpoint are O'Brien and Edward Said. O'Brien justifiably links the protagonist of the novel, Meursault, to Camus, who used this name as a journalist and who, like the protagonist, worked as a clerk.[27] His assertion that the novel presents a mythified colonial Algeria in which the court system does not give precedence to the colonizing population, thereby denying "the colonial reality" and sustaining "the colonial fiction," appears to be equally valid.[28] For Said, the very form of Camus's fiction forms part of "France's methodically constructed political geography of Algeria," which strives to "represent, inhabit, and possess the territory itself" by means of an "imperial gesture," which is "the realistic novel."[29] Literary reactions to the novel that privilege the Algerian viewpoint support this claim. Indeed, the consciously challenging form of Kateb Yacine's novel *Nedjma* (1956), in which the author's decision to write in French was hailed as "le fruit d'une bâtardise assumée" [the fruit of an accepted bastardy], can be considered a response to the deceptive formal simplicity of *L'Étranger*.[30] Kamel Daoud's *Meursault, Contre-enquête: roman* (2013) [*Meursault, Counter-Inquiry: a Novel*] is a more recent and overt response to the novel, this time using the traditional novel form. This study, however, diverges from critical stances that consider the novel a means to promote a Western, colonial, or explicitly French viewpoint. Instead, the concern of this section is to demonstrate that through Meursault, Camus develops a concept, furthered in later fictionalized narratives, of a specifically French Algerian, rather than French, identity, which places the dying mother(land) at its core.

L'Étranger famously begins with news of the death of Meursault's mother at a point in time that the protagonist is unable to determine precisely, apart from acknowledging that it occurred either that day or the day before.[31] What critics regard as Meursault's indifference to this news is not so clear-cut.[32] In fact, the narrator is eager to see his mother "tout de suite" [straightaway] when he initially arrives at the nursing home, although he later declines the opportunity to view her in her coffin (10). This recalls the ambivalence of a character from Camus's later novel set in Oran, *La Peste* (1947) [The Plague]. In the later text, the character Tarrou, who dies before the end of the novel, comments on the likeness between his friend Rieux's mother and his own, admitting with an air of detachment that simultaneously conveys maternal attachment: "Ma mère était ainsi [. . .] c'est elle que j'ai toujours voulu rejoindre. Il y a huit ans, je ne peux pas dire qu'elle soit morte" [My mother was like that [. . .] she is the one to whom I have always wanted to return. She may have died eight years ago, I cannot say].[33] A preoccupation with the settler mother is therefore evident in Camus's Algerian-based fictionalized works. It is also useful to note that descriptions of Meursault's mother silently gazing at him when she was alive (11) appear inspired by Camus's own mother, who was mute and displayed a "strange inertia."[34] The Camusian mother-son relationship is consequently worth considering with regard to the author's personal experience. The writer himself, as an existentialist philosopher who emphasized free choice, may not have approved of applying theories of human behavior to the individual. Nevertheless, psychoanalytical critiques of the mother as she appears in Camus's literature are illuminating.

For Geraldine F. Montgomery, Camus liberates himself from his mourning or depressed mother through artistic expression.[35] Such liberation is vital, according to Julia Kristeva, and may involve eroticizing the mother.[36] Kirsteen Anderson similarly discusses Camus's attempts to free himself from a voiceless mother figure who, in her analysis, suffers due to a patriarchal culture that encourages the son to become the "mothering protector of his own infantilized mother."[37] Such analyses are helpful but do not consider the colonial context, which is central to any examination of Camus's literary maternal figures. In fact, his idealized settler mother—in Meursault's case it is an elderly woman whom he vaguely believes to be in her sixties (37)—relates closely to the lifetime of conquered colonial Algeria—a theme that chapter 3 will show was taken up by several *pied-noir* writers postindependence. As a settler woman, Meursault's girlfriend Marie Cardona is also significant and his actions when he encounters her while swimming following his mother's funeral are suggestive of his desire to return to the sanctuary of the womb. At this point, he rests his head on her belly for some time, feeling "le ventre de Marie battre doucement" [Marie's gently pulsating belly] as they lie half-asleep (30). The absolute "contentement" [contentment] Meursault feels when swimming in the sea (la mer) with Marie is therefore suggestive of a short-lived return to its French homophone, the mother (la mère). Similarly, the sea is a site of brief contentment for Rieux and Tarrou at the height of their battle against the plague.[38] The sea and land also appear as feminized sources of joy in essays contained in both *Noces* and *L'Été*.[39] Moreover, Marie is associated with the sea, the landscape, and the indigenous population through references to her salty hair and body, "visage de fleur" [flower-like face], tanned skin, and sun-kissed face (31, 71, 49, 30, 154). In consequence, Meursault's union with the sea, which Marie facilitates, evokes a short-lived sexual liaison with the country, as the following scene suggests: "Marie m'a appris un jeu. Il fallait, en nageant, boire à la crête des vagues, accumuler dans sa bouche toute l'écume et se mettre ensuite sur le dos pour la projeter contre le ciel" (49–50) [Marie taught me a game. While swimming, you had to drink in on the crest of a wave, build up all the foam in your mouth and then lie on your back and eject it into the sky].

However, a question mark hangs over Marie's morality, as she and Meursault are judged at the murder trial as having had a "liaison irrégulière" [immoral liaison] and to have given in to "la débauche" [debauchery] (124, 126). This echoes Raymond's relationship with his Arab mistress, which is described as "une affaire de moeurs inqualifiable" [an affair of indecent morals] (127). The relationship that Meursault's mother has with her male companion, Thomas Pérez, equally points to a latent sexuality. As Christine Margerrison points out: "the threat of a treacherous sexual excess is one that taints all women. Only the dead woman may function as an immutable symbol of purity."[40] The resultant tension points to the instability inherent in colonial processes of domination, in particular fears of miscegenation and of the sexual potency of the colonized population. This uneasy atmosphere is captured when Meursault describes a group of Arabs silently staring at him, when he is in the company of Raymond and Marie, "à leur manière, ni plus ni moins que si nous étions des pierres ou des arbres morts" (67) [in their way, just as if we were rocks or dead trees]. More significantly, however, Meursault's mother, pure only in her death, points to the unrealizable ideal of the colony with which she is associated.

It is only on hearing details of how he neglected his mother that Meursault realizes he is guilty (119). His only means of returning to her is through his own death and his thoughts as this approaches are worth quoting here:

> Pour la première fois depuis bien longtemps, j'ai pensé à maman. Il m'a semblé que je comprenais pourquoi à la fin d'une vie elle avait pris un «fiancé», pourquoi elle avait joué à recommencer. [. . .] Si près de la mort, maman devait s'y sentir libérée et prête à tout revivre. Personne, personne n'avait le droit de pleurer sur elle. (158–59)

> [For the first time in a very long time, I thought of Mama. I thought I now understood why she had chosen a 'fiancé' at the end of her life, why she had played at starting again. [. . .] Mama must have felt liberated and ready to relive everything when so close to death. No one, no one at all had the right to cry over her.]

Said reads these lines as staunchly colonial: "We have done what we have done here, and so let us do it again."[41] However, Meursault's mother's death foreshadows the death of colonial Algeria, a distinct possibility that Camus worked out in fiction.

According to French Algerian sociologist Jacques Berque, the end of the colonial regime could be predicted from 1919 and even more so from 1930.[42] Berque contends that "Certains esprits perspicaces" [Some perceptive minds] recognized the imminent downfall of the French empire, which was evident from its apogee, in the early 1930s.[43] Similarly, Seth Graebner has convincingly shown that, while there was a hint of desperation behind "declarations of triumphalist colonialism" during the 1930 Centenary celebrations, anxiety about the future of colonialism was a significant issue for the French of Algeria by the late 1930s.[44] At this point, projects of political enfranchisement for the colonized population had failed, notably the Blum-Violette bill proposed by the Popular Front government in 1936. Furthermore, indigenous soldiers' fight for France in World War II coincided with the 1943 *Manifeste du Peuple Algérien* [Manifesto of the Algerian People], which demanded full political rights for all of the country's inhabitants. Nationalist riots at Sétif followed in May 1945, resulting in the massacre of thousands of Muslims as the authorities brutally repressed the rebellion. In consequence, Graebner notes that intellectuals of the *École d'Alger* knew that the colony was on the verge of failure or had already failed, and this led to a certain nostalgia in some of their works, as well as the realization that they had little cause for nostalgia.[45] Moreover, Graebner asserts that their works "contained an analysis of where French Algeria had gone wrong, and of what history they might construct as part of their effort to set it right."[46]

In Camus's case, despite publicly stated hopes about the future of Algeria (including in *Actuelles III*), he revealed his despair in a letter to Jean Grenier dated August 4, 1958:

> Je crois comme vous qu'il est sans doute trop tard pour l'Algérie. Je ne l'ai pas dit dans mon livre parce que lo peor no es siempre seguro [*sic*]—parce qu'il faut laisser ses chances au hasard historique—et parce qu'on n'écrit pas pour dire que tout est fichu. Dans ce cas-là, on se tait. Je m'y prepare.[47]
>
> [Like you I think that it is probably too late for Algeria. I did not say so in my book because the worst-case scenario does not always materialize—because we have to leave things to historical chance—and because you do not write to say that everything is doomed. In that case, you keep quiet. I am preparing for that.]

Although Camus wrote *L'Étranger* before this, it seems clear that the author knew that French Algeria was on the verge of extinction unless the indigenous population attained the same rights as the settlers. Indeed, as Said notes, Camus was "always surrounded by the signs of Franco-Algerian struggle" and the years when he worked on *L'Étranger* "were filled with numerous events punctuating Algerian nationalism's long and bloody resistance to the French."[48] Thus, through the fictional character of the motherless Meursault, Camus confronts his fears. His desire to return to the lost mother(land) also prefigures a nostalgia that would become part of a model of *pied-noir* identity that Meursault exemplifies.

In a preface included in the English-language edition of *L'Étranger* in 1956 (dated 1955), Camus stated that Meursault is condemned "because he doesn't play the game."[49] While his rebellion may be an existential bid to live authentically, Meursault also refuses to play the metropolitan French game. Before his mother's funeral, the caretaker at the nursing home contrasts funeral ceremonies in metropolitan France with those in Algeria. The heat in Algeria necessitates quick burials, whereas in France grieving family and friends can mourn for three or four days before the funeral: "A Paris, on reste avec le mort trois, quatre jours quelquefois. Ici on n'a pas le temps, on ne s'est pas fait à l'idée que déjà il faut courir derrière le corbillard" (15) [In Paris, they stay with the deceased for three or sometimes four days. Here we do not have the time; you are hardly used to the idea when it is already time to run behind the hearse]. An exaggerated description of this type of speedy burial also appears in *La Peste*, as the narrator (Rieux) notes: "ce qui caractérisait au début nos cérémonies [de l'enterrement] c'était la rapidité" [speed was what characterized our [burial] ceremonies at the beginning].[50] In his autobiographical *Les Oliviers de la justice* (1959) [The Olive Trees of Justice], French Algerian writer Jean Pélégri similarly mentions the speed with which his father is buried, noting that the ceremony was over by 11:00 a.m. on the day in question.[51] Similarly, Meursault buries his mother the day he hears about her death in a rapid ceremony that fits in with Muslim and Jewish practice (according to which burials take place as soon as possible) rather than with metropolitan French traditions. Furthermore, the Christian burial requested by Meursault's mother appears as a cultural, rather than religious, marker of identity. Thus, Meursault notes that his mother, while not an atheist, "n'avait jamais pensé de son vivant à la religion" (13) [had never thought of religion in her lifetime]. For his part, Meursault professes that he has never regretted anything (132) and that he does not want to waste time on God (155–56). Thus, time appears accelerated and the young, focused on life, bear no sentimentality toward the past or previous generations. Camus's views in essays in the collection *Noces* also illustrate this concept. In "Le vent à Djémila [The wind in Djémila]" and "L'Été à Alger," for example, the population appears as a *peuple jeune* [youthful people], which focuses on living life to the full in the present moment rather than dwelling on death in the distant future.[52] Camus further notes in "L'Été à Alger" that "On se dépêche de vivre" [People are in a hurry to live].[53] Indeed, he claims that in Algiers, "Tout ce qui touche à la mort est [. . .] ridicule ou odieux [Anything related to death is [. . .] ridiculous and odious].[54] Furthermore, he states in this text that cities in Algeria have no past or traditions, a claim he also makes in *L'Été*, most notably in the essay "Petit guide pour des villes sans passé" [Little guide for cities without a past].[55]

Meursault's apparent failure to mourn his mother's death takes place, therefore, within the context of this construction of "French Algerian time," which negates any need to dwell on the past, as is evident by the reaction of his boss, acquaintances, and friends. His boss is not pleased when he asks for two days' leave from work for the funeral, prompting him to justify his absence by exclaiming: "Ce n'est pas de ma faute" (9) [It is not my fault]. Marie is taken aback to hear his mother has just died but by that evening, "Marie avait tout oublié" (31) [Marie had forgotten everything]. After the funeral, his boss merely asks him how old his mother was, after which "c'était une affaire terminée" [the matter was closed], while his colleague Emmanuel engages in a fun-filled race with him during lunch (30). For his part, Céleste, the owner of the restaurant Meursault frequents, simply asks him if "ça allait quand même" (38) [he was o.k. anyway]. After a long conversation about his plans to exact revenge on his mistress, Raymond merely alludes to the death by saying: "c'était une chose qui devait arriver un jour ou l'autre" (47–48) [it was something which had to happen some day]. Furthermore, Raymond overtly draws attention to accelerated time, noting, "le temps passait vite" (47) [time was passing quickly]. Similarly, Marie later exclaims after lunch, following a morning spent swimming at the beach, that it is only 11:30 a.m. (72). Even Meursault, who bemoans the fact that days bleed into each other in prison, notes that in the end, "l'été a très vite remplacé l'été" (106, 109) [summer very quickly became summer again].

Meursault's decision to make the most of life's pleasures by living in the moment, refusing to dwell on the past or to apologize, is therefore a key part of his identity. Indeed, as Azzedine Haddour has pointed out, he sits trial for his "passion for life rather than his crime."[56] He is condemned for this passion "au nom du peuple français" (140) [in the name of the French people] by a judicial system put in place by metropolitan France. Furthermore, the administration denies him the right to participate in discussions about his fate, which is decided "sans qu'on prenne mon avis" (129) [without asking my opinion]. Yet, through his carefree swimming with Marie, as both enjoy the land, sea, sun, and sky (71), Meursault differentiates himself from officialdom and performs his identity as a member of the French Algerian race described by Camus in the essays cited above.[57] Indeed, his youthful concentration on physical activities calls to mind the observation of another one of Camus's French Algerian characters, Yvars, in the short story "Les Muets" [The Mute Men]: "L'eau profonde et claire, le fort soleil, les filles, la vie du corps, il n'y avait pas d'autre bonheur dans son pays. Et ce bonheur passait avec la jeunesse" [The deep, clear water, the strong sun, the girls, corporeal activities; there was no other form of happiness in his country and that happiness passed with youth].[58] This way of life contrasts with that of the pale-skinned Parisians evoked by Meursault in a negative description of the "sale" [dirty] capital of metropolitan France (60). However, the indigenous Algerian population does not appear to share this lifestyle either, as is seen by the way in which Meursault eradicates the Arab character from the beach in *L'Étranger*, an incident referenced again in *La Peste*.[59] Significantly, indigenous Algerians are also noticeably absent from descriptions in "L'Été à Alger" of "des joies saines" [healthy joys], such as swimming and sunbathing, which cause the transformation of white skin: "Quand on va pendant l'été aux bains du port, on prend conscience d'un passage simultané de toutes les peaux du blanc au doré, puis au brun, et pour finir à une couleur tabac."[60] [When you go to the baths at the port during the summer, you become aware of a simultaneous transformation of all skin from white to golden, then brown and finally a tobacco color].

Thus, although Camus maintained that Meursault is executed "pour n'avoir pas pleuré à l'enterrement de sa mère" [for not crying at his mother's funeral],[61] it seems that he is judged not only as an existential outsider but also specifically as a character who performs French Algerian identity as conceived by the author.

Meursault's actions equally reveal the construction of a macho identity, which other details of the narrative elucidate. For example, a police officer chastises Raymond, not for beating his allegedly unfaithful Arab mistress, but for trembling as a result of his alcohol intake (53). Raymond beats his mistress's brother, initially described as "l'autre" [the other], for questioning his masculinity (42) and confides in Meursault about the episode as he regards the latter as "un homme" (42) [a man]. The tolerance of casual violence in this world evokes myths surrounding pioneering culture.[62] Moreover, the novel gives the impression that men fight for their honor from a position of equality. Indeed, the initial fight between Raymond and his mistress's brother near the tramway seems quite civilized. Having exchanged blows and kicks, Raymond asks his opponent if he has had enough, to which the latter replies in the affirmative (42). Raymond also minimizes his behavior by attributing his reaction to his quick temper, claiming: "c'est pas que je suis méchant, mais je suis vif" (42) [It's not that I'm mean, it's that I'm hot-tempered]. Meursault takes this quarrel to its conclusion by shooting his friend's opponent on the beach but the attack does not seem personal and his Arab prison mates do not appear to hold it against him (97). By blaming his murder of the Arab on the sun, he then casts himself as a victim of circumstances, while violence in the colonies appears the result of a culture influenced by a hot climate rather than politics or history.[63] Furthermore, Meursault projects virility through his interactions with Marie and various other women whose faces come back to haunt him in his prison cell (103). Other significant character traits include honesty, as exemplified by his refusal to lie during the trial, and loyalty to those in his circle—traits that allow the reader to forget his act of murder.

The trial appears as a performance, with each lawyer trying to outdo the other, but crucially, Meursault also performs his gender as a European settler of Algeria. It is useful to note here that anthropologist Andrea L. Smith reports that the former settlers of Algeria often do not consider repatriates from Tunisia to be real *pieds-noirs*, as they did not suffer from the same trauma of a prolonged war and consequently going back to Tunisia has been easier for them.[64] Meursault, in contrast, suffers from his imprisonment:

> Au début de ma détention [. . .] ce qui a été le plus dur, c'est que j'avais des pensées d'homme libre. Par exemple, l'envie me prenait d'être sur une plage et de descendre vers la mer. A imaginer le bruit des premières vagues sous la plante de mes pieds, l'entrée du corps dans l'eau et la délivrance que j'y trouvais, je sentais tout d'un coup combien les murs de ma prison étaient rapprochés. (101–2)

[At the beginning of my imprisonment [. . .] what was hardest was that I had a free man's thoughts. For example, I would feel like being on a beach and heading down to the sea. When I imagined the sound of the first waves under the soles of my feet, my body entering the water and the release I found in it, I would suddenly feel the walls of my prison closing in.]

Furthermore, as Amy Hubbell points out, by remembering every detail of his apartment from his cell, he can reconnect to the "lost limb" of a country from which he is separated, a technique that connects this character to subsequent *pied-noir* writers.[65] Indeed, his final wish is for "Une vie où je pourrais me souvenir de celle-ci" (155) [A life where I could remember this one]. By recording his story, Meursault ensures the perpetuation of this life—an example that many real-life settlers would later follow. He can therefore pass as an "authentic" *pied-noir* man—living in the present, generous, virile, victimized, and exiled—before the term *pied-noir* came into common usage. Moreover, Smith notes that due to their "double migration" (from Europe to Algeria and back, as in the case of Camus's Spanish ancestors), the *pieds-noirs* she interviewed in France "saw themselves as more 'immigrant' than any other group in contemporary French society," while most of those she interviewed were "outsiders" who were isolated from "true" French people.[66] Meursault's rejection by a French judicial system to which he refuses to conform makes him the original *pied-noir* outsider.

Meursault's final lines show him to be at one with the world for the first time: "je m'ouvrais pour la première fois à la tendre indifférence du monde. De l'éprouver si pareil à moi, si fraternel enfin, j'ai senti que j'avais été heureux, et que je l'étais encore" (159) [For the first time, I opened myself up to the tender indifference of the world. Sensing that it was so like me, so fraternal finally, I felt I had been happy and that I still was]. The "fraternal" feeling he alludes to with regard to his surroundings points to the concept of settler hybridity. In this way, the protagonist of *L'Étranger* is receptive toward both the metropolitan French and the indigenous Algerian population. After talks with his lawyer and the judge, both of whom represent the French authorities, Meursault has "l'impression ridicule de «faire partie de la famille" (95) [the ridiculous impression of being "a member" of the family]. The Arab prisoners also treat him as one of the family; despite laughing at him when he first arrives and falling silent when he initially tells them he has killed an Arab, they soon help him make up his bed when night falls (97). Thus, he appears trapped between the two sides from the beginning of the novel, when the nurse hints at his mother's funeral that there is no way out of his broader predicament: "Si on va doucement, on risque une insolation. Mais si on va trop vite, on est en transpiration et dans l'église on attrape un chaud et froid" (27) [If you move slowly, you run the risk of getting sunstroke. But if you move too quickly, you sweat and you catch a cold in the church]. While in prison, he confronts the idea that the nurse's statement at his mother's funeral was correct: "il n'y avait pas d'issue" (108) [there was no way out].

Meursault's apparent desire to return to his mother also positions his story as an Oedipal drama that is doomed to end in disaster. Indeed, Meursault has been called the "tragic hero" of a "secular tragedy" by John Fletcher, who interprets the novel as an Oedipal tale (by a Greek scholar) in which the sea is a mother figure with which Meursault has a sexual union, as opposed to a dominant, hostile father-figure sun.[67] References in the story to a mother who kills her son with the help of her daughter, and to a son who kills his father, also evoke the universality of familial feuds (106, 109, 133). By performing as a member of a flawed family, Meursault becomes a sympathetic character.[68] He is both an outsider and a member of what would, twenty years later, become an exiled *pied-noir* community. He also performs as a victim, to whom the majority will not listen. Indeed, Camus went so far as to call Mersault "the only Christ we deserve" in his preface to the 1956 English-language edition of his work.[69] This statement links this fictional character to that of Tarrou in *La Peste*, who dies as an innocent victim of a plague that he has done his best to combat, in his desire to be a "saint sans Dieu" [a saint without god].[70]

Thanks to the creation of a character such as Meursault, many of the former settlers have accepted Camus as a member of a wider *pied-noir* family. His final remark, "et qu'ils m'accueillent avec des cris de haine" (159) [and may they welcome me with cries of hatred], was subsequently used as the title of an autobiographical book in which Henri Martinez details his involvement in the OAS.[71] Martinez's allusion to Camus's novel forms part of a broader appropriation of the author by both *pied-noir* militants and those who criticize the OAS, such as the *Association nationale des Pieds-Noirs progressistes et leurs amis* [National Association of Progressive *Pieds-Noirs* and their Friends]. The latter association, in seeking reconciliation and solidarity with all sides, cites Camus as an exemplar who, by his "origines familiales et son parcours" [family origins and career], shows that the French of Algeria were not all "des colonialistes exploiteurs" [colonist exploiters].[72]

Furthermore, Camus (perhaps unconsciously) created a prototype of settler masculinity. Historian Pierre Nora certainly interpreted Meursault as a typical *pied-noir*, noting of the murder scene:

> ce tête à tête, un dimanche, sur la plage écrasée de soleil [. . .] libère une agressivité latente, apparente [. . .] le héros [. . .] à tout Français en Algérie. Et la condamnation à mort que Camus inflige pour finir à Meursault, loin d'évoquer on ne sait quel procès kafkéen devient alors l'aveu troublant d'une culpabilité historique et prend les allures d'une anticipation.[73]

[this one-to-one encounter, one Sunday on the sun-drenched beach [. . .] releases a latent aggression, links [. . .] the hero [. . .] to every French person in Algeria. And the death sentence that Camus finally inflicts on Meursault, far from evoking some sort of Kafkaesque trial, therefore becomes the disturbing admission of a historic guilt and begins to look like a prediction.]

Nora's analysis fails to credit Camus with working through the death of his beloved mother(land). However, his consideration of Meursault as representative of a French Algerian man strikingly reveals the legacy of Camus's protagonist. In a letter to Nora, Camus's compatriot Derrida praises the historian's reading of the novel, noting:

J'ai toujours lu ce livre comme un livre algérien, et tout l'appareil critico-philosophique que Sartre a plaqué sur lui m'a toujours paru, en effet, diminuer son sens et son originalité "historiques," les dissimuler, et d'abord, peut-être aux yeux de Camus lui-même.[74]

[I have always read this book as an Algerian book, and indeed it always seemed to me that the whole critical-philosophical apparatus that Sartre pinned onto it diminished its "historical" meaning and originality and concealed them, perhaps first and foremost, from Camus himself.]

It is worth noting here that in this letter to Nora, written in 1961 but not published until 2012, Derrida, who names himself a member of the *Français d'Algérie* community here, does come to Camus's defense.[75] More generally, he praises Camus's intentions and criticizes Nora's treatise for its aggressive tone, selective examples, and failure to give due consideration to the French administration's role in colonization.[76] However, renowned British historian Alistair Horne would subsequently note that *L'Étranger* "perhaps personifies the *pied noir* mentality better than any other fictional character."[77] Consequently, the novel's contribution to the shaping of collective memory must not be underestimated. Nonetheless, a later fictional character, Daru, forms part of Camus's literary development of French Algerian masculinity.

1.3 DARU—THE PERFECT HOST

Camus's collection of short stories *L'Exil et le Royaume* was published in 1957, the year after his unsuccessful appeal for a civil truce, when the writer was struggling for acceptance from either side in the Algerian War. This section discusses the character of Daru in the story "L'Hôte" [The Guest].[78] Ambiguities in the text, not least the significance of the title's reference to either Daru or the unnamed Arab as either a host or a guest in colonial Algeria, have caused disagreement among critics. Philip Dine, for example, considers descriptions of the indigenous character as indicative of Camus's colonialist thought while for Andy Stafford, the writer is attempting to show "the voice of the settler 'idiolecte' [idiolect] used by elements of the French population, *pieds-noirs* or not, to designate, in a condescending and stereotyping fashion, every Algerian as 'Arabe'" [Arab].[79]

Daru, whose place in Algeria appears as his birthright, reveals traits that are part of Camus's model of settler masculinity. The narrator informs us that he was born in the territory and that "Partout ailleurs, il se sentait exilé" (83) [He felt exiled everywhere else]. His role as an educator of poverty-stricken indigenous Algerian children, to whom he also distributes food, further justifies his presence. Far from being an exploitative colonist, he lives a simple, quasi-monastic existence, "content [. . .] du peu qu'il avait" (83) [content with what little he had]. Daru also embodies the limitless generosity and natural hospitality that Camus believed marked out his community from the French.[80] In his analysis of the *Français d'Algérie*, Pierre Nora viewed this apparent hospitality with mistrust.[81] Nora's mistrust notwithstanding, Emmanuel Roblès also highlighted a "sens de l'hospitalité" [sense of hospitality] twenty years after Algerian independence as "une des vertus les plus foncières des pieds-noirs" [one of the most fundamental virtues of the *pieds-noirs*].[82] For his compatriot Derrida, a form of "hospitalité pure et hyperbolique" [pure and hyperbolic hospitality] is necessary to inspire the fairest legislation, which is nevertheless always to some extent exclusionary with regard to outsiders.[83] Derrida's particular position as a Jewish French Algerian influenced his thought: he lost his French citizenship under the Vichy regime, before the authorities belatedly restored the Jewish population's rights in 1943.[84] His concept is nevertheless worth quoting in the context of Daru's actions: "L'hospitalité pure consiste à accueillir l'arrivant avant de lui poser des conditions, avant de savoir et de demander quoi que ce soit" [Pure hospitality involves welcoming the newcomer before laying down conditions, before knowing or asking anything].[85] Daru appears to conform to this pure form of hospitality as, when the policeman, Balducci, and his Arab prisoner unexpectedly arrive, he offers to heat the classroom to ensure that they are "plus à l'aise" (84) [more at ease], serves tea to both men, and unties the prisoner before asking about the reasons for their arrival (85). Later, he cooks for his prisoner, eats with him, and sleeps beside him, while the next day he provides the man with money and food and grants him his freedom by leaving him on a plateau (91–93, 98–99). Through such acts of generosity, Daru recalls another French Algerian character from the same volume, the previously cited Yvars in "Les Muets," who shares his lunch with his Arab coworker, Saïd, in a moment of fraternal solidarity.[86] Daru's decision not to hand over the prisoner reveals his subscription to a distinctively Mediterranean masculine code of honor: "le livrer était contraire à l'honneur: d'y penser seulement le rendait fou d'humiliation" (96) [turning him in was dishonorable: he felt completely humiliated just thinking about it]. His strength and courage are evident here by his certainty that "s'il le fallait, il casserait en deux son adversaire" (93–94) [if necessary, he would break his opponent in two].

Balducci also demonstrates generosity of spirit and subscribes to a similar code of honor. He advances up the slope slowly on his horse, "pour ne pas blesser l'Arabe" [so as not to injure the Arab], who is walking alongside him (84). The reader later discovers that the Arab has slit his cousin's throat in a family quarrel (87). Thus, Balducci, in the opening scene, looks down on his prisoner, whom he magnanimously agrees to untie after the journey (85), from the physical as well as the moral high ground. He also gives Daru a revolver (which Daru accepts, despite his professed abhorrence of violence) and admits his shame at tying up any man (89). Furthermore, he informs Daru that he will not denounce him if he fails to deliver the prisoner. Balducci sums up his confidence in Daru's honesty, should the authorities question him, as follows: "Tu es d'ici, tu es un homme" (89) [You are from here; you are a man]. In this way, both Daru's and Balducci's performance of their masculinity places a value on honesty, generosity, honor, and thus, by implication, shame.

The most significant feature of these characters' identities, however, is that they appear as innocent victims of an administrative system that they cannot control. Despite Balducci's admitted shame at tying up the prisoner, he must follow orders as the prisoner has committed murder and "on ne peut pas les laisser faire" [we cannot just leave them to it] (89). Similarly, Daru is obliged to accept the prisoner but serves as a more striking example of a tragic destiny. Having deviated from his official duty by freeing the prisoner, he returns to find a threatening message on the blackboard of his classroom: "Tu as livré notre frère. Tu paieras" (99) [You turned in our brother. You will pay]. This message, presumably left by the Algerian nationalists alluded to in Balduccci's reference to war, stands in stark contrast to the earlier image on Daru's blackboard of the four rivers of metropolitan France (86, 81). Despite Daru's good intentions regarding his pupils and his prisoner, he therefore ends up an outsider, like Camus at this time, who alienates both the French authorities and the indigenous Algerian population. In this way, Daru represents a level of estrangement that moves beyond that of Meursault, who maintains cordial relations with his indigenous Algerian cellmates.

While Daru appears as a tragic victim of circumstance, the narrator describes the prisoner in less than flattering terms as having stereotypically big lips and a "bouche animale" (92) [animal-like mouth]. He is also guilty of murder. This act is perhaps mitigated by Daru's outlook on the desert as a place where men "s'aimaient ou se mordaient à la gorge, puis mouraient" (91) [loved each other or sank their teeth into each other's throats, then died]. As in *L'Étranger*, however, casual violence, including by extension that of Algerian nationalists, seems more related to the natural environment than to the consequences of colonization. Furthermore, the prisoner's agency is in doubt as, when freed, he walks toward the police station rather than to freedom. Andy Stafford usefully draws a parallel between this narrative and Frank O'Connor's 1931 short story on the Irish anti-colonial struggle, "Guests of the Nation," in his collection of the same name.[87] Yet, there is an important difference between these texts. While the nationalists in O'Connor's story, Noble and Bonaparte (the narrator), bond with their British army prisoners, Belcher and Hawkins, and wish to let them go at the end of the story, they do not and are unequivocally responsible for their deaths.[88] Daru, however, is culpable neither for the Arab prisoner's unhappy fate nor for colonization as a whole. Indeed, despite Daru's ambivalent attitude toward the indigenous Algerian prisoner, David Carroll views his offer of shelter to the anonymous murderer as "an *absolute* form of hospitality,"—an analysis that echoes the pure hospitality reflected on by Derrida.[89] In this way, the protagonist's actions are, in Carroll's view, "outside or beyond self-interest, sociopolitical differences, political disputes—and even or especially armed conflict," in a gesture that is "antithetical to colonialism."[90] Camus therefore lays the foundations here for the public commemoration of a blameless *pied-noir* masculinity, which, as we shall see, he later developed in *Le Premier Homme*.

1.4 BECOMING THE FIRST MAN

A preface by Camus's daughter Catherine to *Le Premier Homme*, published in 1994, explains that her father's unfinished manuscript of the novel was in his satchel on January 4, 1960, the date of his death in a car accident.[91] In an expanded foreword to the English-language edition, Catherine Camus explains some of the reasons behind the decision not to publish at the time:

> In advocating a multi-cultural Algeria where both communities would enjoy the same rights, Camus antagonized both the right and the left. At the time of his tragic death he was very much isolated and subject to attacks from all sides designed to destroy the man and the artist so that his ideas would have no impact. In these circumstances, to have published an unfinished manuscript [. . .] might well have given ammunition to those who were saying Camus was finished as a writer.[92]

This section considers the story of Jacques Cormery as a means for the author to work through his own contested identity in a personal story that also seeks to represent the settlers more generally. This unfinished story, centering largely on a man's memories of his youth, is largely autobiographical. Jacques's mother Lucie is also called Catherine (the name of the author's mother) or "Vve Camus" [Widow Camus] in the text. She is also similarly partially deaf and mute. Jacques's teacher M. [Mr.] Bernard also appears as "M. Germain," at certain points of the novel (224, 164)—the name of Camus's own teacher—and the protagonist's surname was Camus's paternal grandmother's maiden name.[93] Elements of fiction, however, allow the novel's protagonist to appear as an idealized model of French Algerian masculinity.

In his analysis of machismo or "the cult of the male," Richard Basham describes "socially expected" behavioral ideals for men in Latin countries, where a typical macho man is "primarily identified with his mother."[94] Basham's description of the conventional view of women in such societies is worth considering:

> The natural place of the woman is in the home. [. . .] At marriage she must be a virgin. [. . .] As a married woman in her role of mother and wife, the woman is expected to be the binding force within the family. She must be absolutely faithful to her husband. She should, however, expect her husband to be unfaithful to her and must overlook it for the sake of the continuity of the family.[95]

In keeping with such codes, Jacques feels "amour désespéré" [desperate love] for his mother (189). He also believes that his loves should be virgins not only with regard to men but, in keeping with the colonial theme of virginal lands, also with regard to the implicitly political and historical past: "Amours: il aurait voulu qu'elles fussent toutes vierges de passé et d'hommes" (359) [Loves: he would have liked them all unsullied by the past and men]. While, according to Basham, macho men project an image of their own sexual prowess, wives and mothers "are enveloped in complex patterns designed to deny their sexuality."[96] By the same token, Jacques has numerous affairs with women but is reluctant to acknowledge his mother's sexuality by admitting that his older brother was conceived out of wedlock (335).

The ideal macho man also "suffers no injustice without response, and [. . .] above all, never evinces fear."[97] This corresponds with how Jacques must behave from a young age. He describes how, at school, "une injure rituelle [. . .] entraînait immédiatement la bataille, l'insulte à la mère et aux morts étant de toute éternité la plus grave sur les bords de la Méditerranée" (170) [a ritual insult [. . .] immediately led to combat, insulting the mother and the dead being, from time immemorial, the most serious insults on the shores of the Mediterranean]. Before the ensuing duels or "donnades," the boys must affect "le calme et la résolution propres à la virilité" [the composure and resolve that are specific to virility], despite their anxiety (171). Jacques's memories also convey his childhood love of tales of honor and courage (86) and his participation in traditionally male-oriented activities. Soccer is described as "son royaume" (99) [his kingdom], while he and his best friend Pierre often run to school "en se passant un des cartables comme un ballon de rugby" (229) [passing one of their satchels back and forth like a rugby ball]. Hunting is a particularly important part of masculine identity as Jacques, who hunts with his uncle, informs us that all the male workers in the area engaged in this activity (160). This particular sport evokes the archetypally heroic colonial pioneer who, for both the British and the French of the nineteenth century, furthered the imperial project by symbolizing a "viripotent masculinity which reflected and sustained a natural hierarchical order of superordinate and subordinate masculinities."[98] Jacques's identity therefore goes beyond stereotypical Latin machismo and coheres with a pioneering tradition. In consequence, his childhood efforts to be courageous have an added impetus—he believes he is following in the footsteps of heroic French Algerian settlers. Thus, when Jacques's older brother Louis refuses to fetch a hen in the dark, his grandmother draws on the mythic bravery of past settlers: "La grand-mère avait ricané et vitupéré ces enfants de riches qui n'étaient pas comme ceux de son temps, au fin fond du bled, et qui n'avaient peur de rien" (250) [Their grandmother had sniggered and railed against these rich kids who were not like children of her time, who in the deepest darkest scrubland, were afraid of nothing]. Jacques consequently feels obliged to complete the task, thereby proving that he is "viril" (253) [manly].

Jacques demonstrates aspects of the mythical Mediterranean identity promoted by the *École d'Alger*, as suggested by a reference to his "tribu" [tribe] being "comme tous les Méditerranéens" (70) [like all Mediterraneans].[99] However, Camus's approach to this identity, as revealed in his 1937 speech on a new Mediterranean culture, ignored Arabic and Islam and instead focused on Latin and Christianity, in particular Catholicism.[100] John Strachan's analysis is revealing in this regard. He draws attention to Jacques's conflicting experiences of learning the catechism in his free time and his school education, where his teacher, Monsieur Bernard, disapproves of religion.[101] Strachan equally notes that there was "limited enthusiasm for *laïcité* [secularism] and for the political culture of the Republic" among the settlers, although the Ferry Laws, enacted in Algeria between 1883 and 1888, established "the basic principles of compulsory, free and increasingly secular education."[102] A particularly striking representation of this apparent divide between the Christian leanings of the French Algerian settlers as opposed to secular metropolitan educators appears in *La Famille Hernandez* (1964), which is worth mentioning here. At this film's dénouement, its settler protagonists go into a church to pray. A metropolitan teacher follows the group and begins to recite the Lord's Prayer, despite his claim that he would be ridiculed if his colleagues could see him, "moi qui suis de l'école laïque" [me who is from the secular school].[103] In this case, following a close-up of a statue of the Virgin Mary, the characters' prayers are answered, leading to a happy ending for all.

It is important to note, however, that the Christianity exhibited by Jacques and his family appears unique to the colonial context. Although Jacques makes his Holy Communion, and his initials "J. C." (39) evoke Christ, he states that he and his family have little time for religion (181). Instead, they follow the religion of life, living in the present like Meursault: "Elle [Catherine Cormery] ne parlait jamais de Dieu. Ce mot-là, à vrai dire, Jacques ne l'avait jamais entendu prononcer pendant toute son enfance, et lui-même ne s'en inquiétait pas. La vie, mystérieuse et éclatante, suffisait à le remplir tout entier" (183) [She [Catherine Cormery] never spoke of God. If truth be told, Jacques had never heard that word mentioned throughout his whole childhood, and he himself did not worry about it. Life, mysterious and dazzling as it was, was enough to occupy him fully]. This recalls Camus's 1937 essay, in which he sees Mediterranean culture as facilitating the transformation of Catholicism into a "hymne à la nature et à la joie naïve" [hymn to nature and to naïve joy], as opposed to Protestantism, which he considers to be "le catholicisme arraché à la Méditerranée et à son influence à la fois néfaste et exaltante" [Catholicism snatched from the Mediterranean and from its influence that is harmful and thrilling in equal measure].[104] While Jacques and his family are not religious, like Meursault's mother, Catholic practices nevertheless form part of their identity: "C'est que la religion faisait partie pour eux, comme pour la majorité des Algériens, de la vie sociale et d'elle seulement. On était catholique comme on est français, cela oblige à un certain nombre de rites" (183) [Religion, for them and for the majority of Algerians, was just a part of one's social life and nothing more. They were Catholic in the same way people are French—it requires a certain number of rituals]. The settlers also evoke the suffering of Christ. Jacques's birth, after his parents' long journey by horse-drawn cart, and his humble laundry-basket cradle, echo the nativity scene, positioning him as one who must eventually suffer for the sins of others. His outsider status, his alienation from "l'enfance dont il n'avait jamais guéri" (53) [the childhood he never got over], and his tortured realization that he feels "solidaire des bourreaux" (353) [solidarity with the persecutors] are all proof of this destiny and appear to make him, like Meursault and Camus himself, an authentic French Algerian man.[105]

Desirable features of manhood in the colonized community also feature as a key part of this French Algerian identity. In her discussion of varieties of masculinity in Islamic societies, Linda Jones evokes idealized traits such as courage, loyalty, generosity, truthfulness, and mastery of one's emotions, including showing emotion at appropriate moments (such as being moved to tears by a poem),[106] qualities that are also foregrounded in *Le Premier Homme*. Jacques, like Meursault, is loyal, telling his good friend Malan that he would willingly give him all his possessions (44). His generosity is also evident from the chambermaid's surprise, at a hotel in Saint-Brieuc, when he tips her (31). The settlers take a dim view of penny-pinching, as is evident when Jacques's uncle Étienne deems his other uncle Joséphin to be tight-fisted (133). Étienne punishes Joséphin for his behavior and he only dares to return to the family home when Étienne is not there. Honesty equally features as an identity trait. Thus, the young Jacques feels "un bouleversement de honte" (103) [a searing shame] when he steals a two franc coin from his grandmother and is reluctant to lie to get a summer job (285). Mastery of his emotions, exemplified at its most extreme by Meursault's air of indifference, is also important to Jacques, as he and some of his classmates refuse to cry when punished by Monsieur Bernard (169). When he hears the ending of Roland Dorgelès's fictionalized account of World War I in *Les Croix de bois* [Wooden Crosses], however, Jacques is not afraid to show his feelings at the "correct" time: "il [M. Bernard] vit Jacques au premier rang qui le regardait fixement, le visage couvert de larmes, secoué de sanglots interminables, qui semblaient ne devoir jamais s'arrêter" (167) [He [M. Bernard] saw Jacques, who was gazing at him from the front row, his face wet with tears, shaking from interminable sobs, which seemed like they would never stop].

Moreover, like Meursault, Jacques's community has no inclination to spend long periods in mourning. Instead, it aims to forget death or treat it with humor, such as when Jacques's grandmother declares that a dead man "ne pétera plus" (181–82) [will fart no more]. Indeed, for settlers like Jacques's grandmother, mourning is out of the question as "la nécessité du présent était trop forte pour elle plus encore que pour les Algériens en général, privés par leurs préoccupations et par leur destin collectif de cette piété funéraire qui fleurit au sommet des civilisations" (182) [the needs of the present were too pressing for her, even more so than for Algerians in general, whose concerns and collective destiny deprived them of that funereal piety which flourishes at the height of civilizations]. Jacques is therefore neither wholly inclined to secularism nor a conventional Catholic; he is neither French nor an indigenous Algerian, and yet he is influenced by idealized markers of Arab masculinity. In this way, he embodies a French Algerian man for whom, like Meursault, living in the moment is a religion. Jacques's "appétit dévorant de la vie" (299) [all-consuming zest for life] echoes Meursault's behavior, as does his desire for nothing but "tout ce que la vie a de bon, de mystérieux et qui ne s'achète ni ne s'achètera jamais" (299–300) [everything good and mysterious that life has to offer, which money cannot and will never buy].

In addition to working through a model of masculinity, the author strives to come to terms with the demise of colonial Algeria, which is associated with femininity. Jacques's relationship with a feminine sea again evokes its French homophone, mother, in addition to an erotic union between the settlers and the territory: "La mer était douce, tiède, le soleil léger maintenant sur les têtes mouillées, et la gloire de la lumière emplissait ces jeunes corps d'une joie qui les faisait crier sans arrêt" (64) [The sea was gentle and warm. The sun was mild on damp heads and the splendor of the sunlight filled these young bodies with a joy that made them cry out continuously]. It also recalls Camus's description of his personal relationship with a feminized landscape and sea in his essay "Noces à Tipasa" [Nuptials in Tipasa] (*Noces*):

> Il me faut être nu et puis plonger dans la mer, encore tout parfumé des essences de la terre, laver celles-ci dans celle-là, et nouer sur ma peau l'étreinte pour laquelle soupirent lèvres à lèvres depuis si longtemps la terre et la mer.[107]

> [I need to be naked and then plunge into the sea, while still fully perfumed with the scents of the land, wash those scents in it and link, with my skin, the embrace for which land and sea, lip to lip, have pined for so long.]

Yet the presence of indigenous women undermines the concept of a stable, consenting union with the motherland. Along with their male counterparts, they appear symbolic of the menacing threat of "the other" both to Jacques himself and to the colonial system:

> ils [les colonisés] se retiraient pourtant dans leurs maisons inconnues, où l'on ne pénétrait jamais, barricadées aussi avec leurs femmes qu'on ne voyait jamais ou, si on les voyait dans la rue, on ne savait pas qui elles étaient, avec leur voile à mi-visage et leurs beaux yeux sensuels et doux au-dessus du linge blanc, et ils étaient si nombreux dans les quartiers où ils étaient concentrés, si nombreux que par leur seul nombre, bien que résignés et fatigués, ils faisaient planer une menace invisible. (302)

> [Yet, they [the colonized] would withdraw into their unknown houses, which we never penetrated, barricaded in with their wives too, whom we never saw or, if we saw them on the street, we did not know who they were, with their veils covering half their faces and their beautiful, sensuous, seductive eyes underneath the white linen. And there were so many of them in the areas in which they were concentrated, so many of them that by their volume alone, although they were resigned and fatigued, they caused an invisible sense of menace to linger.]

The way these women perform their femininity by failing to engage with the colonizer suggests that colonialism is doomed to fail, as observed by Berque.[108]

Jacques unquestionably associates his elderly mother, who was born in 1882 (74), with the lifespan of the colony. This conflation is evident from his desire to "se mêler à ce que la terre avait de plus chaud, ce que sans le savoir il attendait de sa mère" (304) [mingle with the hottest part of the land, with what he was unknowingly waiting for from his mother]. Catherine is gentle yet mysterious and inaccessible, and therefore slightly threatening, as the following extract suggests:

> Il allait dire: «Tu es très belle» et s'arrêta. [. . .] c'eût été franchir la barrière invisible derrière laquelle toute sa vie il l'avait vue retranchée—douce, polie, conciliante, passive même, et cependant jamais conquise par rien ni personne, isolée dans sa demi-surdité, ses difficultés de langage, belle certainement mais à peu près inaccessible. (71)

> [He was going to say: "You are very beautiful" but stopped himself [. . .] it would have meant breaking through the invisible barrier which he had always seen her retreat behind—gentle, polite, conciliatory, even passive and yet, never conquered by anything or anyone, isolated in her semi-deafness, her language difficulties; beautiful, certainly, but more or less inaccessible.]

Although Jacques desperately wants to communicate his feelings to her, he fails to do so, but this appears, at least in part, to be her fault. For example, when trying to comfort her after his grandmother calls her a "putain" [whore], Jacques tells his mother she looks beautiful but failing to hear him, she waves him away (137). Although Catherine is an unearthly Madonna figure, Jacques questions her virginal status before marriage and the attention of a male suitor exposes her sexuality. Her performance of femininity therefore fails to live up to Jacques's image of perfection and like Meursault's mother in *L'Étranger*, she can only become pure in death, a prospect he imagines by conjuring up images of her "visage [. . .] d'agonisante" (89, 213) [face of a dying woman], although it is agony in turn for him so to do. It is true that, as Alison Rice observes, when Jacques returns home as an adult and embraces Catherine, "The body of his mother is like a country, opening up to the son who comes back to find himself."[109] Yet she represents his childhood and his past: "Chez la mère. Suite de l'enfance—il retrouve l'enfance et non le père" (311) [At his mother's. Continuation of childhood—he rediscovers his childhood and not his father].

Significantly, however, Jacques associates his father Henri with France and with adulthood. Henri died as a soldier in World War I and Jacques visits his grave there aged forty. Jacques becomes father to his own father on seeing Henri's grave and realizing that, having died aged twenty-nine, Henri is now "plus jeune que lui" (34) [younger than him]. For Anthony Rizzuto, this moment is significant as "the son resurrects his father and symbolically kills him in order to achieve independence."[110] In this Oedipal analysis, Jacques, like Meursault, then "rejoins his mother in death" by returning to her in Algeria.[111] However, Jacques gives no indication that he plans to stay with his mother or to withdraw from the world. In fact, given the traumatic circumstances of the Algerian War, he invites her to accompany him to France, but she refuses, adding that she is old and wants to stay "chez nous" (89) [at home]. Jacques consequently begins to face the prospect of his mother's eventual death. He is thus unlike Meursault in that he does not reject France, where he lives, and liberates himself more successfully from the mother and, by extension, the motherland. While Meursault focuses on the motherland and Daru is isolated from both sides, this later character's ability to look toward France is therefore noteworthy in terms of character development and Camus's engagement with the colony's imminent demise.

While the fictionalized character of Jacques is significant with regard to confronting the end of colonialism and associated concerns surrounding identity for the author on a personal level, the protagonist also stands as a metaphor for his community. In this way, the novel acts as a *lieu de mémoire* [site of memory] or a conduit of collective memory, written when a peaceful resolution to the conflict looked increasingly unlikely.[112] A note states that Jacques will seek to "Arracher cette famille pauvre au destin des pauvres qui est de disparaître de l'histoire sans laisser des traces. Les Muets" (338) [wrest this impoverished family from the destiny of the poor, which is to disappear from history without leaving a trace. The Mute Ones], thereby positioning the text as a key forerunner to the postindependence texts that sought to bring the history of the *pieds-noirs* to light, often with a positive slant.[113] The reference to a poor, mute family recalls the coopers of modest means in Camus's short story "Les Muets," thus reiterating a theme of physical and psychological impoverishment, which, as Strachan has persuasively shown, is a significant feature of representations of the *pieds-noirs* by themselves and others.[114] In this way, the reader is encouraged to sympathize with the settlers. A desire to represent Jacques Cormery's story in a certain light is also clear from notes in the manuscript, which show that the author was eager to portray the protagonist as a monstrous outsider (29, 219). This can, at least in part, be attributed to his status as a colonizer who will never be accepted as Algerian by the colonized population and who is a "corps étranger" (53) [foreign body] in France. Barbara Creed, in her analysis of the monstrous feminine, draws on Julia Kristeva to point out that "historically, it has been the function of religion to purify the abject but with the disintegration of the 'historical forms' of religion, the work of purification now rests solely with 'that catharsis par excellence called art.'"[115] Following on from Creed, this study suggests that Camus's description of yet another French Algerian outsider is an attempt to facilitate the purification of his community through a cathartic narrative. In fact, the author leaves a public legacy regarding the *pieds-noirs* that places little emphasis on settler culpability. It is useful to note here that Butler considers the performance of gender as "a strategy of survival within compulsory systems" which has "cultural survival at its end."[116] In a similar manner, the novel facilitates the cultural survival of a settler population that would soon become exiled *pieds-noirs*.

An important strategy in Camus's construction of a collective narrative is the depiction of the colonial history of Algeria as a family drama. Carroll notes that, although Camus's father's ancestors "were among the earliest French colonialists in Algeria," the writer "seems to have believed" that this part of the family "consisted exclusively of Alsatians who had chosen to emigrate to Algeria in 1871, after the French defeat in the Franco-Prussian war, rather than live in an Alsace occupied by Germany."[117] Jacques equally appears as the descendant of a long line of settlers whose presence in Algeria is justified in a similar manner. His father's family originally came from Alsace as they were fleeing "des ennemis appelés Allemands" [enemies called Germans], while his mother's family came from Mahon in Menorca "parce qu'ils crevaient de faim" (80) [because they were dying of hunger].

Significantly, Jacques's family is linked to a wider colonizing "family" as a settler called Veillard and the local doctor recount the story of the foundation of Jacques's birthplace, Solferino, by Parisian settlers following the 1848 revolution (202–5). As Edward Hughes notes, an emphasis on their emigration and on the difficult circumstances of their arrival "accords authority to the act of settlement by spelling out the misery of the early European settlers."[118] The deaths of two-thirds of these settlers who were encouraged to emigrate by France, "sans avoir touché la pioche et la charrue" [without having touched the pickaxe and the plough], recalls Jacques's father's death in equally alien surroundings shortly after his call-up to fight for that same country (208, 324). Furthermore, Jacques pictures his father's arrival in Solferino as part of the same pioneering movement of emigrants, despite the fact that his father was born in Algeria:

Il voyait son père qu'il n'avait jamais vu [. . .] sur ce quai de Bône parmi les émigrants, pendant que les palans descendaient les pauvres meubles qui avaient survécu au voyage [. . .] et après tout n'était-ce pas la même route qu'il avait prise de Bône à Solferino, près de quarante ans plus tôt, à bord de la carriole, sous le même ciel d'automne? (205–6)

[He saw the father he had never seen [. . .] among the emigrants on that quay in Bône while the hoists lowered the shabby furniture which had survived the journey [. . .] and, after all, was this not the same road that he had taken from

Bône to Solferino almost forty years earlier, aboard the cart, under the same Autumn sky?]

In another conflation, Jacques imagines his mother as part of this same group of emigrant settlers with a tragic destiny:

> et pourquoi Jacques pensait-il à sa mère pendant que l'avion montait et redescendait maintenant? En revoyant ce char embourbé sur la route de Bône, où les colons avaient laissé une femme enceinte pour aller chercher de l'aide et où ils retrouveraient la femme le ventre ouvert et les seins coupés. (209)

> [and why was Jacques now thinking about his mother as the plane ascended and descended? On thinking again of that wagon stuck in the mud on the road to Bône, where the colonists had left a pregnant woman in order to get help and where they would find the woman again with her stomach slit and her breasts cut off.]

Although Catherine Cormery, whom Jacques reimagines as one of the first settlers, notes on her arrival in Solferino that "Il n'y a personne" (16) [There is no one here], Herbert Lottman pains a more realistic picture:

> Si la vie était dure pour les nouveaux venus à la colonie, elle l'était encore davantage pour la population musulmane indigène. Confronté à une mentalité de ruée vers l'or, le gouvernement français avait souvent autant de mal à protéger les musulmans et leurs terres qu'à encourager la colonisation par les Européens.[119]

> [If life was hard for the new-comers to the colony, it was even more so for the indigenous Muslim population. The French government, faced with a gold rush mentality, often had as much difficulty protecting Muslims and their lands as encouraging colonization by the Europeans.]

In *Le Premier Homme*, however, there is little emphasis on colonial violence, apart from an allusion to the "persécutés-persécuteurs" [persecuted persecutors] who were given the lands of indigenous rebels—"des insurgés de 71, tués ou emprisonnés" (210) [killed or imprisoned insurgents from '71]. The story of the Solferino settlers therefore encourages the reader to sympathize with the colonizing population, whose arduous five-week journey on "*Le Labrador*" (205, Camus's emphasis) evokes the Mayflower passengers on their way to the New World. Camus had previously used comparisons between French Algeria and America to justify the French Algerian presence, as the following quotation from "Petit guide pour des villes sans passé" (*L'Été*) demonstrates: "Les Français d'Algérie sont une race bâtarde, faite de mélanges imprévus. Espagnols et Alsaciens, Italiens, Maltais, Juifs, Grecs enfin s'y sont rencontrés. Ces croisements brutaux ont donné, comme en Amérique, d'heureux résultats" [The French of Algeria are a bastard race, made up of unexpected combinations. Spanish and Alsatians, Italians, Maltese, Jews, finally Greeks, encountered each other there. This sudden mingling, as in America, produced fruitful results].[120] Moreover, his reference to "Le Labrador" in *Le Premier Homme* evokes Acadian settlers, specifically Jacques Cartier's alleged description of the Labrador coast as "the land God gave to Cain."[121] In addition to this allusion, explicit references to Cain date violence in Algeria back to this first criminal (209, 345). Thus, the Algerian War appears as a family feud, which, perhaps like the first murderer and the first farmer, Cain, created, or has the potential to create, something positive.

In *Le Premier Homme*, Jacques is thus an internal member of the settler community, while the Arabo-Berber population is part of an extended family going back to the dawn of time. Conversations between Jacques and an Arab friend, Saddock, during the Algerian War, position the latter as a "frère" [brother], from whom Jacques is separated by the tragic circumstances of war, but to whom he shows hospitality, in a gesture that echoes Daru's: "il accueille S., le droit d'asile étant sacré" (325) [he welcomes S, the right to asylum being sacred].[122] Other limited references to the indigenous population in the text similarly allude to a fraternal bond between the colonizer and colonized (21, 142, 258).[123] Furthermore, despite Jacques's reference to xenophobic men, their behavior is apparently the result of unemployment, which affects both the settler and indigenous populations as individuals compete to find work (278). Thus, the author casts the relationship between both groups as a familial one in which fighting brothers, particularly in the context of the Algerian War, will eventually reconcile. As the elder farmer Veillard states:

> On est fait pour s'entendre. Aussi bêtes et brutes que nous, mais le même sang d'homme. On va encore un peu se tuer, se couper les couilles et se torturer un brin. Et puis on recommencera à vivre entre hommes. C'est le pays qui veut ça. (199)

> [We were made to get along. [They are] as simple and as rough as us, but with the same blood of men. We will kill each other a little longer, cut off each other's balls and torture each other a bit. And then we will start to live again between men. It is the country that wants that.]

Even if, as Carroll argues, Veillard is not Camus's mouthpiece,[124] this statement, along with other examples of fraternity in the text, leaves the reader with an overall impression of the war as an unfortunate familial falling-out.

The depiction of members of Jacques's immediate family, who appear as representatives for their community, bolsters this family narrative. His poverty-stricken mother and uncle are elderly victims of a war they do not understand. It is thus revealing that Camus considered calling the novel "Adam," presumably in reference to Jacques's uncle Étienne, who has an "innocence adamique" (116) [Adamic innocence].[125] The following question put by Étienne to Jacques underlines his bewilderment: "Dis, les bandits, c'est bien? [. . .] Bon, j'ai dit à ta mère les patrons trop durs [sic]. [. . .] mais les bandits c'est pas possible" (145) [Say, the bandits—are they good? Well, I said to your mother—the bosses: too hard. [. . .] but the bandits—that can't be right]. Moreover, his family (and presumably his Algerian "family" at large) is prone to feuds for no apparent reason, just like the Arab's mysterious act of murder in "L'Hôte" or Meursault's unplanned annihilation of the Arab on the beach:

> D'obscures querelles divisaient parfois sa famille, et personne en vérité n'eût été capable d'en débrouiller les origines, et d'autant moins que, la mémoire manquant à tous, ils ne se souvenaient plus des causes, se bornant à entretenir mécaniquement l'effet une fois pour toute accepté et ruminé. (134)

> [Obscure quarrels sometimes divided his family, and in truth, no one would have been able to unravel the origins of them, even less so since they were all lacking in memory, so they no longer remembered the causes and contented themselves with mechanically maintaining its effect once it had been accepted and brooded over.]

Indeed, a type of casual violence pervades this macho culture, in which the young Jacques witnesses a man dying of a gunshot wound to his head inflicted by a restaurant owner (150) and a barber cuts an Arab's throat (282).

As in *L'Étranger*, this community also has a unique relationship with time, as seen through members of Jacques's family, who are "naturellement largement en avance, comme le sont toujours les pauvres qui ont peu d'obligations sociales et de plaisirs, et qui craignent de n'y être point exacts" (273–74) [naturally largely ahead of time, as the poor always are, having few social obligations and pleasures and fearing not being exactly on time for those they have]. While Nancy Wood suggests that public memory seeks to produce "a consciousness of an identity through time," Jacques implies a break between his people and linear time, pointing to the cyclical nature of "les empires et les peuples" (13) [empires and peoples] that have previously passed through Algeria.[126] This trope legitimizes the French presence and implies an affinity with what the unnamed editors of Kateb's *Nedjma* refer to (in a potentially essentializing way) as circular Arab thought as opposed to Western linearity.[127] Thus, each generation of French Algerians become the first men, consigning the previous generation to "l'immense oubli qui était la patrie définitive des hommes de sa race" (212) [the immense oblivion that was the definitive homeland of men of his race].

Paradoxically, Veillard's and the doctor's accounts of the settlers show that they have not forgotten previous generations. Veillard tells Jacques that he knows nothing about his father Henri: "Ici, on ne garde rien. On abat et on reconstruit. On pense à l'avenir et on oublie le reste" (197) [Here, we keep nothing. We destroy and we rebuild. We think of the future and forget the rest]. Yet, the doctor later tells Jacques about his parents' arrival and about his birth, which is recorded in the "livre d'état civil" (202) [register of births, marriages and deaths]. Camus's representation of an apparent break between generations of French Algerians and historical time therefore appears consciously constructed and the novel becomes a way of remembering a community of which Jacques is a sympathetic representative.

Characters such as Jacques, Daru, and Meursault thus appear in a positive light as part of a French Algerian family, which extends to include the indigenous population and the whole world as an alternately united and divided family, dating from Cain and Abel. The key role of the maternal figure adds to this impression of familial affiliation. Due to the universal appeal of such narratives, readers from notably diverse backgrounds have claimed Camus as one of their own. In particular since Algeria's *décennie noire* [dark decade] of increased terrorist violence in the 1990s, Camus's influence is evident in works by Algerian writers such as Assia Djebar, Maissa Bey, Salim Bachi, Kamel Daoud, Hamid Grine, and Boualem Sansal.[128] As Emily Apter notes, the writer has now become "a code-name for the promulgation of an international democracy movement that would heal the breach between the Islamic world and the west."[129] In another example of Camus's wide appeal and in spite of the absence of developed female characters in his fiction, Elizabeth Ann Bartlett uses his works to give an insight into feminism—citing, for example, Camus's advocacy of resistance to oppression and his affirmation of "human dignity, solidarity, friendship, justice, liberation and beauty."[130]

Camus's variety of masculinity, with its emphasis on the mother and motherland, has also earned him admittance into the *pied-noir* community. A statement by one of his readers illustrates this:

> On était des frères de Camus, je pense que c'est cela qu'il a voulu rendre, l'Algérie, c'est ma mère, c'est sa mère, mais il faut voir au-déla, il y a un lien charnel qui nous attachait au pays et qui échappe à toute notion politique.[131]
>
> [We were Camus's brothers, I think that is what he wanted to portray—Algeria is my mother, it is his mother but you have to see beyond that, there is a corporeal link which attached us to the country and which eludes all political concepts.]

The following chapters point to Camus's influence on diverse *pied-noir* writers. Moreover, they reveal the key role of writing in developing postwar concepts of *pied-noir* memory and identity.

NOTES

1. As Germaine Bree noted in 1960, a legend surrounding the author has tended to transform him into "une sorte de saint laïque" [a kind of secular saint]. See Germaine Bree, "Camus," *The French Review* 33, no. 6 (May 1960): 542.

2. Camus's most famous postcolonial critics include Albert Memmi, Conor Cruise-O'Brien, and Edward Said. Arguments against such critiques include those by John Foley and Michel Onfray. See Albert Memmi, "Camus ou le colonisateur de bonne volonté," *La Nef* 12 (December 1957): 95–96. Cited in Philip Dine, "Fighting and writing the war without a name: polemics and the French-Algerian conflict," *Aurifex*, no. 2 (2002), http://www.goldsmiths.ac.uk/aurifex/issue2/dine.html. Date accessed: February 17, 2014. See also Conor Cruise O'Brien, *Camus* (London: Fontana, 1970); Edward W. Said, *Culture and Imperialism* (London: Chatto & Windus, 1993); John Foley, *Albert Camus: From the Absurd to Revolt* (Montreal: McGill-Queen's University Press, 2008); and Michel Onfray, *L'Ordre libertaire: La vie philosophique d'Albert Camus* (Paris: Flammarion, 2012).

3. See David Carroll, *Albert Camus the Algerian: Colonialism, Terrorism, Justice* (New York: Columbia University Press, 2007) and Aicha Kassoul and Mohamed-Lakhdar Maougal, *The Algerian Destiny of Albert Camus*, trans. Philip Beitchman (Bethesda, MD: Academica Press, 2006).

4. Emmanuel Roblès, *Camus, frère de soleil* (Paris: Seuil, 1995), 111, 84. Roblès states that the OAS threatened Camus with abduction at this time, although the group did not officially form until 1961, in response to Charles de Gaulle's national referendum that approved the principle of self-determination in Algeria. This slippage is perhaps indicative of the author's desire to frame the past in terms of clearly defined sides (OAS and FLN) with Camus in the middle.

5. Judith Butler, *Gender Trouble: Feminism and the Subversion of Identity* (London: Routledge, 1999), 178.

6. See, for example, John Lichfield, "Why Sarkozy won't let Camus rest in peace: France's right-wing leader stands accused of political bodysnatching with a plan to move the author's remains to the Pantheon—burial place of the country's establishment," *The Independent*, January 5, 2010.

7. Peter Beaumont, "Albert Camus, the outsider, is still dividing opinion in Algeria 50 years after his death," *The Observer*, February 28, 2010.

8. John Dugdale, "Albert Camus centenary goes without much honour at home. Neither France nor Algeria pay much attention to 100th anniversary, leaving job to Google," *The Guardian*, November 7, 2013.

9. Onfray, *L'Ordre libertaire*, 25.

10. As an article in *La Croix* put it, "Soupçonnée d'avoir voulu ménager son électorat pied-noir, la mairie UMP aixoise se tourne alors vers le philosophe Michel Onfray" [Suspected of seeking to please its *pied-noir* electorate, the Mayor's (rightwing) UMP Party turns to the philosopher Michel Onfray]. See Corinne Boyer, "Aix-en-Provence tient absolument à une exposition Camus; Les organisateurs de Marseille-Provence 2013 ont renoncé à une exposition consacré au prix Nobel de littérature. La ville d'Aix-en-Provence reprend le projet dans un contexte chaotique," *La Croix*, October 18, 2012.

11. Anonymous, "Michel Onfray ne sera pas le commissaire de l'exposition Camus à Aix," AFP, September 15, 2012, LexisNexis.

12. Anonymous, "Aix-en-Provence: hommage à Camus, un an après la polémique," *Libération*, October 6, 2013.

13. Macha Séry, "Exposition: Albert Camus à Aix-en-Provence: autopsie d'un gâchis," *Le Monde*, October 8, 2013. The journalist notes that the exhibition contains "Rien qui fâche" [Nothing to spark anger].

14. Anonymous, "Aix-en-Provence: hommage à Camus."

15. Olivier Todd, *Albert Camus: une vie* (Paris: Gallimard, 1996), 935.

16. Ibid., 965.

17. See, for example, Carroll, *Albert Camus the Algerian*, 97, 104 and Mark Orme, *The Development of Albert Camus's Concern for Social and Political Justice: "Justice pour un juste"* (Madison, NJ: Fairleigh Dickinson University Press, 2007), 194.

18. See Jean-Robert Henry's preface to Lucienne Martini's *Racines de papier: Essai sur l'expression littéraire de l'identité Pieds-Noirs* (Paris: Publisud, 1997), 3.

19. Ibid.

20. Cited by Jeannine Verdès-Leroux, *Les Français d'Algérie de 1830 à aujourd'hui* (Paris: Fayard, 2001), 340–41.

21. Ibid.

22. Todd, *Albert Camus*, 587.

23. For Butler, no one can internalize constructions of gender completely as gender norms are "phantasmatic, impossible to embody." See Butler, *Gender Trouble*, 179.

24. Albert Camus, *Essais* (Paris: Gallimard, 2000), 60. This extract is from "Noces à Tipasa" (*Noces*).

25. Jacques Derrida, *Le Monolinguisme de l'autre ou la prothèse d'origine* (Paris: Galilée, 1996), 83–84. *L'Étranger* went on sale in June 1942, just a few months before the Allied landings.

26. Conor Cruise O'Brien, *Camus* (London: Fontana, 1970), 31. O'Brien notes that the novel was finished before the Occupation of France in 1940.

27. O'Brien, *Camus*.

28. Ibid., 23.

29. Said, *Culture and Imperialism*, 213.

30. See the preface to *Nedjma* by Gilles Carpentier in Kateb Yacine, *Nedjma* (Paris: Seuil, 1996), v.

31. Albert Camus, *L'Étranger* (Paris: Gallimard, 1942), 10. All subsequent references to this and other primary sources cited are in parentheses in the main body of the text.
32. See, for example, Colin Wilson, *The Outsider* (London: Indigo, 1997), Chapter 2, 27–46. Wilson argues that Meursault is completely indifferent to life due to a sense of unreality, but that his imminent death awakens him, albeit too late, to a sense of freedom.
33. Albert Camus, *La Peste* (Paris: Gallimard, 1947), 250.
34. Orme, *The Development of Albert Camus's Concern*, 27.
35. Geraldine F. Montgomery, "La Mère Sacrée dans *Le Premier Homme*," in *Albert Camus 20: 'Le Premier homme' en perspective*, ed. Raymond Gay-Crosier (Paris: Lettres Modernes Minard, 2004), 73.
36. Ibid., 72. Montgomery cites Julia Kristeva, *Soleil Noir – dépression et mélancolie* (Paris: Gallimard, 1987), 38.
37. Kirsteen H. R. Anderson, "La Première Femme: The Mother's Ressurrection in the Work of Camus and Irigaray," *Society for French Studies* 56, no. 1 (2002): 32–33.
38. Camus, *La Peste*, 231–32.
39. Camus, *Essais*. See, for example, "Noces à Tipasa," 55–60, "L'Été à Alger," 67–78, and "Petit guide pour des villes sans passé," 845–50, in which Camus writes of his "liaison" with the Algerian land, 848.
40. Christine Margerrison, "The Dark Continent of Camus's *L'Étranger*," *Society for French Studies* 55, no. 1 (2001), 72.
41. Said, *Culture and Imperialism*, 224.
42. Jacques Berque, *Le Maghreb entre deux guerres* (Paris: Seuil, 1962), 417.
43. Ibid., 418–19.
44. Seth Graebner, *History's Place: Nostalgia and the City in French Algerian Literature* (Lanham, MD: Lexington, 2007), 191.
45. Ibid., 192.
46. Ibid.
47. Albert Camus and Jean Grenier, *Correspondance: 1932–1960* (Paris: Gallimard, 1981), 222.
48. Said, *Culture and Imperialism*, 215–16.
49. Albert Camus, *The Outsider*, trans. Joseph Laredo (London: Penguin, 1982), 118.
50. Camus, *La Peste*, 160.
51. Jean Pélégri, *Les Oliviers de la justice* (Paris: Gallimard, 1959), 168, 181.
52. Camus, *Essais*, 61–76.
53. Ibid., 74.
54. Ibid., 73.
55. Ibid., 74, 847–50.
56. Azzedine Haddour, *Colonial Myths: History and Narrative* (Manchester: Manchester University Press, 2000), 44.
57. In "Noces à Tipasa" (*Noces*), for example, Camus describes "une race née du soleil et de la mer" [a race born of the sun and the sea]. See Camus, *Essais*, 60.

58. Albert Camus, *L'Exil et le Royaume* (Paris: Gallimard, 2003), 62.

59. Grand witnesses a conversation about "un jeune employé de commerce qui avait tué un Arabe sur une plage" [a young salesman who had killed an Arab on a beach]. See Camus, *La Peste*, 57.

60. Camus, *Essais*, 68–69.

61. Cited by John Fletcher, "Interpreting *L'Etranger*," *The French Review* 1(Winter 1970): 163.

62. Similarly, Krin Gabbard links American gun culture to concepts of masculinity and a destiny dating from "myths of the frontier." See Krin Gabbard, "Men In Film," in *Debating Masculinity*, ed. Josep M. Armengol and Àngels Carabí (Harriman, TN: Men's Studies Press, 2009), 55.

63. Richard C. Keller notes that psychiatrists considered excessive heat and light to be dangerous for human minds in the colonies and underlines the perceived "relationship between race, climate, and madness" since the origins of the psychiatric profession. See Richard C. Keller, *Colonial Madness: Psychiatry in French North Africa* (Chicago: University of Chicago Press, 2007), 124. The word "doolally," which originated in the British army camp in the town of Deolali in India, where Indian summers and monsoon season were believed to send soldiers mad, is further evidence of the perceived links between mental illness and climate. For more on this, see Maj Martin, "The Madness at Deolali," *Royal Army Medical Corps* 152, no. 2 (2006): 94–95.

64. Andrea L. Smith, *Colonial Memory and Postcolonial Europe: Maltese Settlers in Algeria and France* (Bloomington, IN: Indiana University Press, 2006), 165.

65. Amy L. Hubbell, *Remembering French Algeria: Pieds-Noirs, Identity and Exile*. (Nebraska: University of Nebraska Press, 2015), 215.

66. Smith, *Colonial Memory and Postcolonial Europe*, 135, 15.

67. Fletcher, "Interpreting *L'Etranger*," 166–67.

68. Roger Shattuck views the novel as a fable about a citizen who yields to outside pressures to commit an inhuman act, while the sympathetic reader unwittingly becomes a collaborator in this act. While Shattuck's interpretation of the novel involves the Soviet Union and Nazi Germany rather than colonialism, it seems appropriate here to note that the reader is encouraged to sympathize with Meursault and is unlikely, therefore, to blame him (or the *pieds-noirs* in general) for colonialism. See Roger Shattuck, "Guilt, Justice, and Empathy in Melville and Camus," *Partisan Review*, 63, no. 3, (1996): 448. Cited in Mangesh Kulkarni, "The Ambiguous Fate of a *Pied-Noir*: Albert Camus and Colonialism," *Economic and Political Weekly* 32, no. 26 (June 28–July 4, 1997): 1530.

69. Camus, *The Outsider*, 119.

70. Camus, *La Peste*, 230.

71. Henri Martinez, *Et qu'ils m'accueillent avec des cris de haine: Oran 1962* (Paris: Robert Laffont, 1982).

72. Anonymous, "Il y a 50 ans mourait Albert Camus," L'Association nationale des Pieds Noirs progressistes et leurs amis, http://www.anpnpa.org/?p=166. Date accessed: October 6, 2013.

73. Pierre Nora, *Les Français d'Algérie* (Paris: Julliard, 1961), 190–91. For Nora, the text may be seen as "l'exact reflet du sentiment vécu de la présence française en Algérie" [the exact reflection of the feelings experienced by the French presence in Algeria], although he suggests that Camus was an exception who could see a truth that his compatriots could not.

74. Pierre Nora, *Les Français d'Algérie: Édition revue et augmentée, précédée de «Cinquante ans après» et suivie d'un document inédit de Jacques Derrida, «Mon cher Nora . . .»* (Paris: Christian Bourgois, 2012), 292.

75. Ibid., 274, 292.

76. Ibid., 271–99. For example, Derrida comments on stereotypes of land-obsessed settlers, stating that most lived in cities, and emphasizes, as did many of the *pieds-noirs* in postindependence narratives, that the average income of most settlers was lower than the average income of the metropolitan French.

77. Alistair Horne, *A Savage War of Peace: Algeria 1954-1962* (New York: New York Review Books, 2006), 52.

78. Camus, *L'Exil et le Royaume*, 81–99.

79. Andy Stafford, "Ambivalence and Ambiguity of the Short Story in Albert Camus's 'L'Hôte' and Mohammed Dib's 'La Fin,'" in *Postcolonial Poetics: Genre and Form*, ed. Patrick Crowley and Jane Hiddleston (Liverpool: Liverpool University Press, 2011), 232. Stafford's argument that Daru's voice is not necessarily Camus's contrasts with Dine's view that Daru is Camus's "mouthpiece." See Philip Dine, *Images of the Algerian War: French Fiction and Film, 1954-1992* (Oxford: Oxford University Press, 1994), 105.

80. See "Petit Guide pour des villes sans passé" *(L'Été)*, in *Camus, Essais*, 850.

81. Nora considers his experience of "l'hospitalité aggressive" [the aggressive hospitality] of the French of Algeria as a deliberate ploy: "Se prête-t-on, tant soit peu, à ces embrassades, on est immédiatement incorporé, à peu de frais initié, dévoré et bientôt digéré" [If you give in, even slightly, to these embraces, you are immediately recruited, cheaply initiated, devoured and soon swallowed up]. See the 1961 edition of Nora, *Les Français d'Algérie*, 44.

82. Emmanuel Roblès, "Préface," in *Les Pieds-Noirs*, ed. Emmanuel Roblès (Paris: Philippe Lebaud, 1982), 12.

83. See Derrida's interview on concepts of hospitality as they relate to immigration and citizenship in Dominique Dhombres, "Il n'y a pas de culture ni de lien social sans un principe d'hospitalité; ce penseur estime que c'est au nom de ce principe, pris absolument, qu'il faut inventer les meilleures mesures en matière d'immigration," *Le Monde*, December 2, 1997.

84. Derrida discusses this formative experience in *Le Monolinguisme de l'autre ou la prothèse d'origine* (Paris: Galilée, 1996).

85. Dominique Dhombres, "Il n'y a pas de culture."

86. Camus, *L'Exil et le Royaume*, 72–73.

87. Stafford, "Ambivalence and Ambiguity," 230.

88. Tellingly, the guilt from this episode stays with Bonaparte forever, as the last lines of the story tell us: "And anything that ever happened me after I never felt the

same about again." See Frank O'Connor, *Guests of the Nation* (London: Macmillan, 1931), 19.

89. Carroll, *Albert Camus the Algerian*, 75. Carroll's emphasis.

90. Ibid.

91. Albert Camus, *Le Premier Homme* (Paris: Gallimard, 1994), 9.

92. Albert Camus, *The First Man*, trans. David Hapgood (London: Hamish Hamilton, 1995), vi.

93. Herbert R. Lottman, *Albert Camus* (Paris: Seuil, 1978), 20.

94. Richard Basham, "Machismo," *Frontiers: A Journal of Women Studies* 1, no. 2 (Spring 1976): 126–27.

95. Ibid., 128–29.

96. Ibid., 129.

97. Ibid., 127.

98. J. A. Mangan and Callum McKenzie, "Prologue: Statement," in "'Blooding' the Martial Male: The Officer Hunter, Field Sports and Big Game Hunting," special issue, *International Journal of the History of Sport* 25, no. 9 (August 2008): 1057–79 (1062). This quotation refers to the British context but Dine confirms its relevance for Algeria. Cited in Philip Dine, "Big-Game Hunting in Algeria from Jules Gérard to *Tartarin de Tarascon*," *Moving Worlds: A Journal of Transcultural Writings* 12, no. 1 (2012): 48.

99. For more on this identity, see Dunwoodie, who draws attention to the École d'Alger's cultural construction of a "'Mediterranean man' [. . .] as a geographically and culturally redrawn figure cutting across (imperialist) national and cultural boundaries." Peter Dunwoodie, *Writing French Algeria* (Oxford: Oxford University Press, 1998), 176.

100. Camus, *Essais*, 1321–27.

101. John Strachan, "Between History, Memory, and Mythology: The Algerian Education of Albert Camus," in *France's Lost Empires*, ed. Kate Marsh and Nicola Frith (Lanham, MD: Lexington, 2011), 57.

102. Ibid., 58.

103. Geneviève Baïlac, *La Famille Hernandez* (France: Films Etienne Baïlac, 1964).

104. Camus, *Essais*, 1323.

105. The latter quotation also calls to mind the artist Jonas from the eponymous short story in *L'Exil et le Royaume*, whose choice is to remain "*solitaire* ou *solidaire*" (Camus's emphasis) [solitary or in solidarity]. See Camus, *L'Exil et le Royaume*, 139.

106. Linda Jones, "Islamic Masculinities," in *Debating Masculinity*, 93–112.

107. Camus, *Essais*, 57.

108. Berque suggests that "l'hypothèse coloniale se révèle avoir été sterile à terme" [the colonial hypothesis proved to have been be fruitless over time] due to the colonized population's ability to turn lessons learned from the colonizers against them in order to revolt. See Berque, *Le Maghreb entre deux guerres*, 412–14.

109. Alison Rice, *Polygraphies: Francophone Women Writing Algeria* (Charlottesville, VA: University of Virginia Press, 2012), 93.

110. Anthony Rizzuto, *Camus: Love and Sexuality* (Gainesville, FL: University Press of Florida, 1998), 121.

111. Ibid., 113.

112. As Strachan points out, "Three weeks after his [Camus's] death, on the streets of Algiers, *pied-noir* 'ultras' erected barricades, killed more than a dozen *gendarmes*, and marked the final, irrevocable separation of French Algeria from metropolitan France." See Strachan, "Between History, Memory, and Mythology," 55.

113. Daniel Leconte, for example, invokes Camus in his appeal for recognition of what he sees as the positive aspects of colonialism as well as its faults: "Soyons donc «camusiens» et tentons, alors que l'histoire a désormais tranché, de fabriquer une mémoire commune qui permette aux uns et aux autres de trouver leur compte et de vivre ensemble" [Therefore let us be "Camusian" and try, even though history has thus far stopped short, to forge a communal memory which may allow everyone to find their tale and to live together]. See Leconte, *Camus, si tu savais . . . suivi de Les Pieds-Noirs* (Paris: Seuil, 2006), xli.

114. John Strachan, "From Poverty to Wretchedness: Albert Camus and the psychology of the *pieds-noirs*," *Journal of Colonialism and Colonial History* 14, no. 2 (Summer 2013), Project Muse.

115. Barbara Creed, "Horror and the Monstrous Feminine: An Imaginary Abjection," *Screen* 27, no. 1 (1986): 53. Creed cites Julia Kristeva, *Powers of Horror: An Essay on Abjection* (New York: Columbia University Press, 1982), 17.

116. Butler, *Gender Trouble*, 178, 177.

117. Carroll, *Albert Camus the Algerian*, 1–2. Lottman, *Albert Camus*, 19–20, notes that while Jean Grenier, in his book on Camus, claimed that the local authorities in Algeria did not have the information Camus needed to research his ancestry, such information is readily available to all French citizens in state archives.

118. Edward J. Hughes, "Building the Colonial Archive: The Case of Camus's *Le premier homme*," *Research in African Literatures* 30, no. 3 (1999):178.

119. Lottman, *Albert Camus*, 21.

120. See Camus, *Essais*, 848.

121. Laurel Sefton MacDowell, *An Environmental History of Canada* (Vancouver: UBC Press, 2012), 25. Dunwoodie, *Writing French Algeria*, 273, notes that *Le Labrador* was the name of the ship on which impoverished Paris volunteers traveled to Mondovi in 1848.

122. The name of this character recalls Mohamed Ben Sadock, former vice president of the Algerian assembly and FLN member. Camus privately interceded for Ben Sadock in 1957, as he awaited the death penalty, by writing to the judge in question. As Foley notes, however, Camus withdrew his support for Ben Saddok (as Foley spells it) when details of his intercession appeared in the press. See Foley, *Albert Camus*, 162.

123. Several critics have discussed the absence of the indigenous population in Camus's novels, including, for example, Emily Apter, who contends that the real "First Man" is missing from this novel—"he is an Algerian native, the novel's aborted character *par excellence*." See Emily Apter, "Out of Character: Camus's French Algerian Subjects," *MLN French Issue* 112, no. 4 (September 1997): 513–14.

124. Carroll, *Albert Camus the Algerian*, 172.

125. Lottman, *Albert Camus*, 19.

126. Nancy Wood, *Vectors of Memory: Legacies of Trauma in Postwar Europe* (Oxford: Berg, 1999), 3. Wood argues that Camus shows settlers who deliberately turned their backs on past acts of violence (see pages 159–60). However, the author himself elides these acts of aggression in the novel.

127. For this 1956 preface by the editors, which is absent from some later editions, see Anonymous, "Avertissement," http://www.limag.refer.org/Documents/AvertissementNedjma1956.pdf. Date accessed: February 5, 2014

128. See, for example, Assia Djebar, *Le Blanc de l'Algérie: récit* (Paris: Albin Michel, 1995); Maissa Bey, *L'ombre d'un homme qui marche au soleil: Réflexions sur Albert Camus* (Montpellier: Chèvre-feuille étoilée, 2004); Boualem Sansal's preface in Jacques Ferrandez, *L'Hôte: d'après l'œuvre d'Albert Camus, tirée de L'Exil et le royaume* (Paris: Gallimard, 2009); Hamid Grine, *Camus dans le narguilé* (Paris: Éditions Après la lune, 2011); Salim Bachi, *Le dernier été d'un jeune homme* (Paris: Flammarion, 2013); Kamel Daoud, *Meursault, Contre-enquête: roman* (Arles: Actes Sud, 2014).

129. Apter, "Out of Character," 501.

130. Elizabeth Ann Bartlett, *Rebellious Feminism: Camus's Ethic of Rebellion and Feminist Thought* (New York: Palgrave Macmillan, 2004), 1. Todd in *Albert Camus*, 1020, notes that Camus's plan for *Le Premier Homme*, which he professed to Jean-Claude Brisville, was that it would be his first book in which women, heretofore "mythiques" [mythical] in his works, would have a major role.

131. Cited by Verdès-Leroux, *Les Français d'Algérie*, 339.

Chapter 2

Performing French Algerian Femininity

2.1 INTRODUCTION: (UNDER)STUDYING WOMEN IN THE COLONIES

Traditionally, narratives of colonialism have been male-centered. This chapter builds on significant contemporary research that reveals the centrality of women to the gendered dynamics of colonial processes and the connections between colonialism, sexuality, and performances of gender.[1] Discourses surrounding femininity in Algeria have been the subject of some critical studies.[2] To date, however, settler women's performance of femininity remains underexplored. With regard to the French context, Janet R. Horne's analysis of women in metropolitan France and the colonies in the late nineteenth and early twentieth centuries suggests that women's role overseas was to aid France's *mission civilisatrice* [civilizing mission] by preserving tradition and morality within the family while also bringing modernity, hygiene, and childcare techniques to native homes.[3] Against the backdrop of this tradition-modernity dichotomy, the current chapter examines the stories put forward by *pied-noir* women themselves in works that are frequently semi-fictional. By focusing on female voices, it continues the corrective work of Patricia Lorcin's 2009 comparative study on the subject of colonial nostalgia.[4] Lorcin's research reveals European women's embellishment of their lived experience in narratives that were maintained throughout colonialism and afterward. The significance of this type of nostalgia becomes clear from the fact that it is not solely the preserve of the *pieds-noirs*, but encompasses a wider nostalgia for an exoticism centered on a romantic view of the past, gleaned from writers such as Elissa Rhaïs (1876–1940) and Isabelle Eberhardt (1877–1904).[5] Lorcin's study supports Benjamin Stora's suggestion that women may be responsible for the phenomenon of widespread nostalgia or *nostalgérie* [nostalgeria] for an idealized lost homeland within the settler community.[6] This chapter reiterates the powerful role of settler women in telling tales about the colony. By adopting a focus on the feminine, it uncovers the heretofore largely ignored contribution of women to the creation of postindependence *pied-noir* memory and identity.

As metropolitan France prepared for decolonization, settler women became an absent presence in the nation's narrative. Todd Shepard suggests that the authorities linked OAS violence to a lack of femininity in the colony, while for historian Pierre Nora, women, when they did appear, were a destructive force.[7] By early 1962, therefore, "new left journalists presented an Algeria where women were never seen, heard, or even interviewed."[8] In Nora's assessment, meanwhile, the settler woman was a "parasite du rapport colonial" [parasite of the colonial relationship] who was "généralement plus raciste que l'homme" [generally more racist than men].[9] A desire to respond to such preconceptions must in part have influenced *pied-noir* women's writing from this time. Moreover, Stora suggests that the *pieds-noirs* have been the most prolific of all the women writing in French about the war.[10] His analysis of the significance of this literature is worth citing here:

> Dans la période 1963–1981, la France semble désormais occupée à effacer les traces d'une guerre perdue et de sa présence en Algérie; à liquider des concepts («intégration», «pacification», «assimilation» . . .); à mettre entre parenthèses ses «années algériennes». C'est le moment où, dans la faible production d'ouvrages consacrés à la guerre d'Algérie, émerge, en force, la parole des femmes pieds-noires.[11]

> [Between 1963 and 1981, France seemed preoccupied with erasing traces of a lost war and its presence in Algeria from that point on, seeking to liquidate concepts ("integration," "pacification," "assimilation") and to put its "Algerian years" behind it. This was the period when, during the low output of works dedicated to the Algerian War, the voices of *pied-noir* women emerged in force.]

Women's early accounts of the war are therefore of particular significance regarding conceptions of *pied-noir* identity after 1962. For Stora, this writing is also noteworthy as women are largely observers rather than participants in war, and are therefore in a unique position to transgress boundaries and confront different perspectives.[12] This chapter questions the notion that settler women use their writing to challenge different sides of the memorial divide in any broad sense. In fact, the current analysis argues that apparently private works published in the immediate aftermath of the war are conduits of performativity specifically for the *pieds-noirs*. In this way, women are considered as "especially adept at colonizing the mind,"[13] both during and after colonization, as their role as partners, mothers, and custodians of narratives about their particular communities continued.

In the face of a general avoidance of colonial history, texts by settler women consciously organized representations of the past and sought to influence the way readers remember it. Female narrators appear concerned with the personal, rather than the political. However, the intimate inevitably becomes political in colonial encounters. In this way, the current chapter brings to light the development of myths surrounding the naming of the settler community, a pioneering tradition and unique suffering, all of which take on a political dimension. This chapter also reveals that in shaping a *pied-noir* identity, early texts by women emphasize hyperfemininity and the "beautification" of women, which exposes gender as performative. Much later narratives sustain this emphasis on a unique hyperfeminine identity. Consequently, stories seek to influence the performance of gender among settlers in a way that differentiates them from the colonized population and from the metropolitan French. Yet, female narrators also evoke apparent similarities with the colonized population in narratives that emphasize a privileged relationship with a feminized Algeria, thereby naturalizing their presence in the territory. Crucially, this chapter also recognizes the fallacious nature of the concept of a unified or uniform *pied-noir* population that many of these stories emphasize. For some women, growing up as part of the settler community inspired a feminist stance and encouraged critical thinking with regard to both the performance of gender and the inequalities fostered by the colonial system. The chapter focuses on a broad range of both lesser-known and well-known women from the settler community, namely Francine Dessaigne, Anne Loesch, Marie Elbe, Micheline Susini, Marie Cardinal, Brigitte Roüan, and Hélène Cixous. In this way, it uncovers some of the typical narratives perpetuated by women, in addition to works that challenge the status quo.

2.2 WOMEN'S EARLY NARRATIVES— CONDUITS OF COLLECTIVE MEMORY

Many of the personal stories published during France's perceived historiographical silence on the subject of the Algerian conflict serve as metaphors for the *pied-noir* community and therefore influence a collective memory that is performative with regard to the themes privileged or elided. Francine Dessaigne's 1962 memoir, *Journal d'une mère de famille pied-noir* [Diary of a *pied-noir* mother], is a striking example in this regard. Dessaigne positions herself as a potentially Camusian mother figure within a specifically *pied-noir* family, despite the fact that she was actually born in France, a fact that reveals her conscious performance.[14] In her preface to the 1972 edition, Dessaigne acts as a spokesperson for the *pieds-noirs*, who appear as part of a wider family with similar memories:

> En écrivant ce que je voyais, ce que j'entendais, ce qui m'étreignait le cœur, je devenais, sans m'en douter, les yeux, les oreilles, les cœurs de tous les autres pris par la tourmente au même moment. Mon journal était tellement chargé d'humbles vérités qu'il était celui que chaque mère de famille aurait voulu écrire, le livre où chaque famille française [en Algérie] se retrouvait. (i)

> [By writing what I was seeing, what I was hearing, what tormented my heart, I was unwittingly becoming the eyes, the ears, the hearts of all the others who were caught up in turmoil at the same time. My diary was so full of simple truths that it was what every mother would have liked to write, the book with which every French family [in Algeria] identified.]

According to this quotation, all *pieds-noirs* have suffered, but mothers appear as custodians of such memories. In this manner, the author casts women as guardians of a "true" *pied-noir* identity, which is at risk as her community is "loin de la sérénité de l'Histoire et encore plus de la vérité du témoignage" (v) [far from the impartiality of history and even further from the truth of testimony].[15] Although she denies that she originally intended to publish the diary (7), her decision to do so sets it apart from other wartime journals such as that of Anne Frank, famously published posthumously. The author's admission that she decided to insert into her diary a text written in Paris (where she lived from 1954 to 1956), which retrospectively describes life in Algeria from 1946 to 1954 (14), underlines the selection process at work in this apparently private story.

Dessaigne states openly in her preface that she wishes to give a voice to her community's memories, as ignoring them in favor of political or polemical debates distorts reality. By seeking to remove politics from discussions about the end of colonial Algeria, however, the author casts decolonization as a tragedy. At one point, she likens the situation to classic tragedies by Pierre Corneille and Jean Racine (78), thereby suggesting that the *pieds-noirs* were victims of destiny, who were subsequently rejected by their metropolitan French brothers and sisters: "En métropole, seuls quelques amis nous ont ouvert les bras. Notre malheur aurait eu besoin d'un grand élan fraternel de nos compatriots" (ii) [In metropolitan France, only a few friends welcomed us with open arms. Our misfortune would have needed a great surge of fraternal feeling from our compatriots]. In this way, she depicts the *pieds-noirs* as forgotten victims in a familial drama. Grievances include Dessaigne's claim that "Un grand nombre des nôtres est mort d'insurmontables difficultés matérielles, de chagrin, de déracinement" (ii) [many of our people died from insurmountable financial difficulties from grief, from being uprooted], as well as a lack of recognition of, or reparation for, a traumatic departure from "la terre natale perdue" (iv) [the lost native land]. This public advancement of apparently shared misfortunes makes a significant contribution to the constitution of a *pied-noir* identity in exile despite a generalized official silence on the war.

References in the text to Algeria's Roman occupiers (71) reiterate some of the markers of settler identity, such as what Philip Dine calls the "myth of *pied-noir* latinity" and the "myth of the eternal Mediterranean"—key tropes reinforced throughout colonization by the likes of Louis Bertrand, which are still evoked today.[16] Dessaigne also continues a familiar articulation of the benefits of France's *mission civilisatrice* through descriptions of, for example, the primitive dwellings of inhabitants of Kabylia (27–28), in contrast to her husband's construction work, which she believes will bring prosperity to the region (20). However, she develops further markers of a *pied-noir* identity in exile, most notably with regard to the naming of the former settlers. Despite stating in her 1972 preface that the term *pied-noir* was relatively new when she first published the text, she suggests at the beginning of the diary proper that it originated in 1830, when the French soldiers' black military boots surprised the barefoot or Turkish slipper-wearing native population (8). This explanation for the term would resurface frequently in interviews with the *pieds-noirs*.[17]

Dessaigne also elaborates on the myth of "pioneering creation," considered a key trope with regard to representations of the settlers,[18] as she notes that ancestors of the *pieds-noirs* went ahead of French troops and suffered to make Algeria the country it became: "Allant de l'avant, devançant même les troupes, les colons se répandent autour des villes, défrichent, assèchent les marécages pestilentiels, souffrent et meurent" (73) [Forging ahead, even arriving ahead of the troops, the settlers spread out around the towns, cleared the land, drained the pestilent swamps, suffered and died]. Éric Savarèse's study is worth referencing here as he suggests that the *pieds-noirs* invented the pioneering tradition after Algerian independence in order to unite their community in the face of hostile and pejorative images of the settlers in metropolitan France.[19] This invented tradition places Algeria ahead of France regarding education, infrastructure, agriculture, and wine production.[20] Many of these early texts by women further this narrative by depicting the *pieds-noirs* as pioneers, not only in colonial Algeria but also in France. In Dessaigne's case, she herself appears as a type of pioneering and specifically reformist historian:

> Ce passé que l'on veut effacer, je vais essayer [. . .] de le rendre vivant. Je vais le faire en redonnant leur sens aux mots qu'on n'ose plus employer: colon,

conquête, entre autres. On a voulu en faire des injures, je vais tenter de les
réhabiliter. Je le fais parce que je me refuse à rayer des mémoires et de l'histoire
la plus belle œuvre française, une œuvre unique dans le monde. (71)

[I am going to try [. . .] to bring the past that people wish to erase back to life. I
am going to do so by giving back meaning to words that people no longer dare
to use, including colonist and conquest. People wanted to turn these words into
insults; I am going to try to rehabilitate them. I am doing so because I refuse to
expunge, from memories and from history, the most beautiful of French endeavors, an endeavor that is unique in the world.]

A postindependence *pied-noir* identity is associated with suffering—that of pioneering ancestors, but also that associated with the war and subsequent exodus. References to FLN bombs feature (10), as do references to other massacres of Europeans (10, 19, 46, 64–65, 68, 202).[21] However, violence perpetrated by French Algerians, including racist attacks or "ratonnades" against the indigenous population (77), appears as a response to guerrilla violence and as a manifestation of excessive love for their homeland—another theme that resurfaces in subsequent discussions of the *pieds-noirs*.[22] Although Dessaigne does not condemn torture used by the army against the FLN during the Battle of Algiers, she raises the issue of its use against those suspected of OAS membership. She thus portrays the massacre of such French torturers as a necessary form of decontamination ("assainissement") by the OAS (138). Moreover, she depicts the suffering of the *pieds-noirs* as worse than anything experienced by the metropolitan French, including Delphine Renard, the iconic four-year-old victim of an OAS explosion near Paris:[23]

Les journaux de métropole étalent de gros titres. Toutes les consciences
se révoltent et les mots cinglants tombent sur «le plastiqueur» de la petite
Delphine. Nous n'avons pas été habitués à de tels déchaînements pour les pauvres petits massacrés ici depuis sept ans. La rancœur submerge la pitié. Nous
voudrions pouvoir dire aux journalistes: Et les nôtres? Depuis sept ans, le F.L.N.
tue, mutile des enfants volontairement visés par les grenades, les balles ou le
couteau, qu'ils soient Français de souche ou Musulmans. (146)

[Metropolitan French newspapers rolled out headlines. Everyone was outraged
and scathing words were reserved for little Delphine's "plastic explosives
bomber." We were not used to such an outcry for the poor little ones who had
been massacred here for seven years. Bitterness overwhelmed pity. We wanted
to be able to say to journalists: And what about our people? For seven years, the
FLN has killed and mutilated children who were deliberately targeted with grenades, bullets or knives, whether they were native-born French or Muslims.][24]

The text also commemorates specific sites of suffering, which are worth discussing here. The most striking example is a heart-rending description of the shooting of pro-*Algérie française* protestors by the French army on the Rue d'Isly in Algiers on March 26, 1962, during a protest in support of OAS activists who gained control of the European neighborhood of Bab-el-Oued before the army surrounded the area. Specialists know of the Rue d'Isly episode because the first works on Algeria published after independence described it.[25] However, it retains a central place in the memory of the *pied-noir* community,[26] and the writings of female authors in the early days of Algerian independence therefore played a significant part in this. In her testimony, Dessaigne positions herself as a protector, both of other people and of the truth, as she posits herself as a reliable witness to atrocities committed by French soldiers on the Rue d'Isly who were trying to "clean up"[27] the street by wiping out the *pieds-noirs*:

> L'armée française, portant l'uniforme français, vise et tire sur des civils couchés. J'ai vu, je peux donc témoigner de cette honte. [. . .] Je suis couchée dans du sang. [. . .] Les soldats, tournés vers la rue d'Isly, l'arrosent systématiquement sur toute sa largeur. Je vois les mitraillettes aller de droite à gauche pour nettoyer la rue. [. . .] Jamais nous n'aurions cru possible que l'armée tire sur des civils. [. . .] J'en porte le témoignage, comme je témoigne que l'armée a tiré sur nous alors que nous étions aplatis sur sol. (166–68)

> [The French army, wearing the French uniform, aimed and shot at civilians who were lying on the ground. I saw, I am able, therefore, to bear witness to this shameful act. [. . .] I lay down in the blood. [. . .] The soldiers, facing Rue d'Isly, systematically sprayed the full width of the street. I saw the submachine guns going from right to left to clear the street. [. . .] We would never have thought it possible that the army would shoot at civilians. [. . .] I am bearing witness to this, just as I am bearing witness to the fact that the army shot at us while we were lying flat on the ground.]

The author describes the "pèlerinage" [pilgrimage] that she and her husband, along with many others, undertake the day after the shooting, by returning to the Rue d'Isly where they look for traces of bullets and blood. This street, subsequently renamed in honor of murdered independence activist Larbi Ben M'Hidi, therefore becomes a place of not only private but also public memory (169) for the *pied-noir* community.

The diary's focus on some sites is revealingly selective. For example, despite the brutally repressed 1945 riots at Sétif, which left thousands of indigenous Algerians dead,[28] references to this massacre are noticeably absent, as she describes the town as having been created and made rich by colonization (36). The author also presents the working-class area of Bab-el-Oued in a positive light, as did Baïlac in her *La Famille Hernandez*, discussed in the introduction to this book and in chapter 1. Thus, it emerges as the home of an extroverted Mediterranean community whose "origines diverses se sont fondues en un magma coloré qui travaille, crie, s'agite, s'invective et complote dans l'exubérance du tempérament méditerranéen" (173) [diverse origins dissolved into a colorful jumble of people who work, shout, bustle about, hurl abuse at each other and plot with the exuberance of the Mediterranean temperament]. The Bab-el-Oued community appears as a true family with a biblical sense of justice: "Ce quartier populaire a le sens du clan et le goût du talion" (68) [This working-class area has a clannishness and an "eye for an eye" mentality]. In consequence, any violence perpetrated by its inhabitants is the result of frustrations built up over the course of a long war as the community explodes from having "trop comprimé leur chagrin et leur indignation" (80) [suppressed their grief and indignation for too long].

This work makes an important contribution to the association of *nostalgérie* with a *pied-noir* identity, as the author expresses her desire to forget her more traumatic memories of her homeland by freezing her positive memories (15), before regretfully describing the sights, sounds, and smells of Algiers (17–18). Perhaps more significantly, it leaves an impression that the *pieds-noirs* are a unified population with a "Vocabulaire commun" [common vocabulary] and an "angoisse commune" [common anxiety] (64). Repeated references to the suffering of this community, particularly children, respond to negative portrayals of the settlers, as the author consciously seeks to "susciter [. . .] un peu d'amitié pour les «Pieds-Noirs»" (8) [spark a bit of friendship for the *pieds-noirs*]. The apparently private memories discussed here therefore "perform, produce, and sustain" a narrative of identity,[29] which feeds into the public sphere via a text read by a largely *pied-noir* audience.

Other texts published by women in the immediate aftermath of the war are similarly significant conduits of collective memory. Anne Loesch's *La Valise et le cercueil* (1963) [The Suitcase and the Coffin] is noteworthy for the title's memorialization of the slogan that prompted many of the settlers to leave Algeria in 1962 ("the suitcase or the coffin")—adapted here to signify the death of a settler identity. It is also striking as an early attempt to rehabilitate the image of an OAS activist, in this case her former boyfriend Jean Sarradet who, along with his parents, had died from asphyxiation caused by a faulty gas heater in France in December 1962. Twenty years later, it would be the task of another woman, Micheline Susini, to attempt to rehabilitate the image of her husband Jean-Jacques Susini, a controversial OAS militant. It is also worth noting that Susini's text, *De Soleil et de larmes* (1982) [Of Sunshine and Tears], at times appears as a response to Loesch's *La Valise et le cercueil*, particularly as the former casts Jean Sarradet as a traitor.[30]

In the manner of Dessaigne's *Journal d'une mère de famille pied-noir*, Loesch presents her text as a series of private diary entries, in this case written retrospectively with "la fidélité que laissent les souvenirs brûlants" [the faithfulness of searing memories].[31] J.-R. Tournoux, a specialist in "secret" history, also states on the front cover that it is "un témoignage bouleversant sur le peuple 'pied-noir': *un document historique de premier ordre*" (Tournoux's emphasis) [a deeply moving testimony about the "pied-noir" people: *a historical document of the first order*]. However, it is important to point out that Loesch uses fiction as there are two narrative voices—that of her deceased boyfriend Jean and that of Anne. Of particular interest for the present analysis is a discussion of a *pied-noir* state that, although it never came to fruition, existed in the imagination of Jean, Anne, and their supporters, who lobbied for Algeria to become a federation divided into Muslim, Jewish, and *pied-noir* territories. Their vision, including plans for a constitution and flag for their *Algérie pied-noir* (125) [*Pied-Noir* Algeria], recalls Benedict Anderson's analysis of communities as essentially imagined.[32] This imagined federation that might have been suggests a development of the pioneering tradition and the continuation of what Dine labels the myths of "missed opportunities" that settlers used as a self-protective response to the Algerian War.[33] Following independence, however, a *pied-noir* pioneering spirit takes root in France, as Anne describes poverty-stricken, semi-abandoned villages inhabited by country bumpkins and notes her desire to shout at her compatriots: "*Colonisez donc la France, elle se meurt*" (265, Loesch's emphasis) [*Therefore colonize France; she is dying*]. A further evocation of this pioneering spirit simultaneously constructs a unified *pied-noir* community:

> Nous fabriquerons notre valeur par nos efforts, par notre rectitude morale scrupuleuse, par notre dynamisme, par nos œuvres. Nous nous plierons à une discipline d'acier pour ne jamais avoir à rougir de notre race. En France, nous travaillerons, nous construirons pour la France. Mais jamais nous n'oublierons que nous sommes pieds-noirs, tous unis, tous solidaires les uns des autres—tous semblables. (259)

> [We will realize our worth with our efforts, our scrupulous moral rectitude, our dynamism, our endeavors. We will submit to a discipline of steel so as never to bring shame on our race. In France, we will work, we will build for France but we will never forget that we are *pied-noir*, all united, all in solidarity with each other, all alike.]

Another aspect of this early vision of a *pied-noir* community is the resemblance it bears to Camus's evocation of a *peuple jeune* [youthful people], although France appears here as a bad parent, which is noteworthy as it continues to feature as a "marâtre" [stepmother] in discussions with the *pieds-noirs*.[34] The *pieds-noirs* are thus, "les fils d'une race au sang vif qui a un goût de la violence que vous avez eu vous aussi, Français, mais il y a bien longtemps, car vous êtes très vieux et ils sont jeunes" (167–68) [the sons of a hot-blooded race which has a taste for violence, which you French also had, but a very long time ago, as you are very old and they are young]. Here, the Algerian War is again portrayed as a family drama in which France acts as "parents impérieux et bornés" (168) [imperious and narrow-minded parents]. In this case, however, while the colonized population may be part of the family, they are not portrayed as brothers, but rather as an infantilized spouse who should have obtained independence "Plus tard, devenu adulte" (23) [later, as an adult].

The 1963 novel by Marie Elbe, the pseudonym of journalist Jeanine Plantié, *Et à l'heure de notre mort* [And at the hour of our death],[35] is an equally significant early contribution about the *pieds-noirs* to the public sphere. Unlike the aforementioned texts, this story is clearly a "roman" [novel]. Yet an expanded 1992 edition rather implausibly suggests that Elbe drew on "une mémoire intacte" [an intact memory] of events,[36] thereby presenting the novel as true to life. Furthermore, Elbe has stated that her main purpose was to "témoigner au nom des siens avec la rigueur et la crédibilité du journaliste"[37] [bear witness in the name of her people with a journalist's precision and credibility]. The novel's epigraph also alludes to this aim by quoting Roberto Pazzi, a writer who blends history and fiction: "Les étiquettes glissent et il ne reste que la vérité" [labels slip and only truth remains].

Like Elbe, the narrator, Emmanuelle Soria, is a journalist from Affreville, suggesting a strongly autobiographical approach. Emmanuelle recounts her own experiences and those of her friend Jeanne Fromenti, interspersed with the stories she overhears passengers telling each other as she waits to board a ship to metropolitan France in June 1962. This structure allows the author to privilege the traumatic departure of the *Français d'Algérie* from Algeria as well as their stories of suffering during the war, all of which become associated with a *pied-noir* identity. References to those who died at the Rue d'Isly shooting on March 26, 1962, evoke the death of French Algeria and, by extension, the death of a settler identity (15, 17). Descriptions of this shooting also engage with concepts such as the aforementioned myth of Algeria as part of an "eternal Mediterranean,"[38] with the suggestion that it was like a "corrida" [bull-fight] featuring "Des femmes, des vieux, des gosses" (17) [women, the elderly and kids]. France, however, does not necessarily form part of this Mediterranean identity and is instead "la mère marâtre" (294) [the step-mother]. Moreover, the immediacy of the stories recounted by the passengers, as they casually converse and interrupt each other, positions the reader among them and elicits sympathy for their situation. Lucienne Martini praises this technique and compares the passengers' anonymous voices to the chorus in a Greek tragedy, which evokes a common destiny in an authentically *"pied-noir"* manner, through colorful vocabulary and a sense of humor and optimism.[39] However, the positioning of the Algerian War as a tragedy undoubtedly seeks to leave a particular public record and shape collective memory.

Women seem to become involved in the conflict for largely personal reasons, thereby allowing them to evacuate politics from accounts of colonization and the Algerian War, with the latter becoming an unexplained and unexplainable tragedy.[40] It is worth noting here that this focus appears personally helpful to the writers involved. Stora suggests that for *pied-noir* women, "Before the malaise became too strong, perhaps it was necessary to attenuate the shock of exile through writing, to fill the void left by the disappearance of the native land, to soften the anguish of vertigo."[41] This comment is particularly apt since clinical psychologists have shown that writing about personal experiences in an emotional way (rather than about nonaffective topics) brings about improvements in mental and physical health, as "constructing stories [. . .] helps individuals to understand their experiences and themselves."[42] Psychologists note that the story constructed "can be in the form of an autobiography or even a third-person narrative," which underscores the benefits of writing for these female authors.[43] Furthermore, studies conducted by anthropologist Andrea L. Smith and French academic Anne Roche reveal that *pied-noir* women tended to recount personal experiences from the war by focusing on emotions, trauma, and the everyday, rather than on the political.[44] Apart from the personal benefits of these early texts, however, this study argues that they shaped perceptions of history and identity for their largely *pied-noir* audiences. This leads to an examination of the values foregrounded with regard to the performance of *pied-noir* femininity.

2.3 HIGHLIGHTING HYPERFEMININITY

A particularly striking aspect of Elbe's *À l'heure de notre mort* is the way in which characters describe femininity. They frequently evoke heels and make-up, "the armoury of femininity most typically associated with 'straight' women,"[45] as well as the importance of elegant dress despite the difficult circumstances of a brutal war. This struggle to attain beauty is particularly pertinent in light of suggestions that settler society lacked femininity.

For example, in a poignant description of an explosion that blows a sixteen-year-old girl's legs off, the teenager, who is ignorant of her plight, keeps asking, "Maman, et mes escarpins?"[Mama, what about my pumps?], having begged her mother for months for permission to go dancing in high heels (24). Another story details the fate of Espérance [Hope] and her best friend, Liberté [Liberty]. FLN gunshots fatally wound Liberté at the age of fourteen, when she is trying to buy thread in Bab-el-Oued in order to finish sewing silk dresses that she and Espérance had planned to wear to their first party that evening (193–94). The silk dress symbolizes a rite of passage for the girls, whose parents named them in honor of the Allied landings in 1942. Tragically, however, Liberté never has the opportunity to transition to womanhood and is buried in her dress, while Espérance's mental health suffers (194–95). Moreover, an OAS activist, Gripfix, breaks down on seeing his friend Jeanne's red high heels, as they remind him of his dead sister who "avait la folie des souliers, comme toutes les filles de Bab-el-Oued.—Comme toutes les filles d'Alger. [. . .]—Comme toutes les belles filles" (264) [had shoe mania, like all the girls of Bab-el-Oued, like all the girls of Algiers, like all pretty girls]. The importance the narrator's friend Jeanne attaches to her appearance is evident as she polishes her toenails in the aftermath of witnessing her friend Martine die in the Rue d'Isly shooting. Her observation, "Le vernis, ça fait soigné. [. . .] Une petite pied-noir aux ongles roses! [. . .] Il faut se préparer à mourir en beauté" (249–50) [polish gives the impression that you are well-groomed. [. . .] A little *pied-noir* with pink nails! One must be ready to die looking beautiful], weaves together her identity as a *pied-noir* and as a self-consciously feminine woman in an exaggerated performance, which reveals itself as imitative. As sociologist Éric Fassin notes in the preface to the French edition of *Gender Trouble*,

> au fond, l'homme qui surjoue (quelque peu) sa masculinité, ou bien la femme qui en rajoute (à peine) dans la féminité ne révèlent-ils pas, tout autant que la folle la plus extravagante, ou la *butch* la plus affirmée, le jeu du genre, et le jeu dans le genre?[46]

> [deep down, the man who overplays (somewhat) his masculinity, or else the woman who overdoes it (barely) in femininity, do they not reveal just as much as the most extravagant queen or the most assured butch, the game of gender and the game in gender?]

Further incidents during the war similarly reveal gender as performative. Thus, passengers waiting to board a ship describe OAS commandos' escape from the French *gendarmes mobiles* [military police] during a siege at Bab-el-Oued by dressing as women, with one man using a wig, cushions, and dressing gown to pretend he is pregnant, while another pretends to be his midwife (26).[47] However, just as Judith Butler has stated that potentially "denaturalizing parodies" such as drag can "reidealize heterosexual norms *without* calling them into question,"[48] this inescapably pantomime drag is far from subversive in its exposure of the performativity of gender. In fact, the scene underlines the unusual nature of these men's performance while reinstating *pied-noir* women's idealized role as mothers and caregivers. Stephanie Brown's theorizing of women's performance of femininity in terms of kitsch appears justified here. In analyzing the artifice associated with the "beautification" of women as opposed to perceptions that men are more "natural," Brown argues that "women have a certain look (one which, to be sure, connotes to-be-looked-at-ness) while men are supposed to just appear, like the inspired art work that springs ex nihilo from the artist's consciousness."[49] In this way, masculinity, like "True" art, appears transparent and effortless, whereas femininity is "always outside the realm of 'art,' limited by its (always presumed) artifice."[50] In this analysis, drag by men can become a camp, "sly celebration of bad taste and vulgarity from a position of privilege," since they can "enjoy a hegemonic superiority that enables them to impersonate the female while remaining male."[51] Conversley, like kitsch objects that are similarly adorned, femininity is "desirous of attaining true beauty, but inevitably unable to do so [. . .] constantly struggling not to parody itself but to be itself."[52]

Anne-Marie Fortier notes that "cultural specificity is viewed as best expressed in practices that emphasize gender differences."[53] Indeed, the performance of gender and of femininity in particular (in cases where it embodies "the threshold of identity/difference") is a "key stabilizing principle" of a fragmented community.[54] In consequence, an exaggerated performance of femininity appears as a means of demonstrating, by contrast, the exaggerated masculinity of *pied-noir* men. Gripfix, one of the central male *pied-noir* characters in Elbe's narrative, provides an example of a macho French Algerian man. Indeed, Martini identifies Jeanne and Gripfix as typical representatives of *pied-noir* masculinity and femininity.[55] Thus, while women consciously perform femininity through their "beautification," Gripfix's performance as a French Algerian man appears effortless. He has the colors of what would become the Algerian flag mapped onto his body, along with traits typically considered as Mediterranean:

> Quand il était petit, il avait pas assez de globules rouges, il était blanc comme la colle Gripfix. [. . .] En grandissant, il a pris une tête de toréador, verte un peu, et maigre avec des yeux comme des olives noires. Quand il est rentré à l'OAS, il avait l'air du toréador en colère. (63)
>
> [When he was little, he didn't have enough red blood cells; he was as white as Gripfix glue. As he grew up, his face took on the look of a bullfighter: a bit green and lean with eyes like black olives. When he went into the OAS, he looked like an angry bullfighter.]

Gripfix's mission is to avenge the rape and murder of his sister—the evocatively named Angèle—by *barbouzes* [counterterrorist secret agents].

Pied-noir women, therefore, become the guardians of a morality that men must protect from forces outside their community. The story even suggests that with the arrival of American troops in Affreville during World War II, "les pères prirent leurs pétoires pour défendre l'honneur des filles" [fathers took out their rusty old rifles to defend their daughters' honor], until they realized that the soldiers' ancestors were also settlers in the 1800s (42).

As symbols of morality, the performance of *pied-noir* women's femininity is differentiated from politically engaged female FLN activists such as Djamila Bouhired, who become "des mouques [mouquères—generic, pejorative term for indigenous servant women], ces garces, qui venaient les poser les bombes, dans leurs sacs de bain" (21) [Charwomen, these bitches, who used to come and plant bombs in their beach bags]. Moreover, this description of indigenous women serves to foreground men as both protectors of *pied-noir* women's honor and as virile beings who can conquer willing native women and, by extension, native lands:

> Tu la vois pas, la Djamila Bouhired, en train de venir se risquer dans un milk-bar de Bab-el-Oued?—Elle pouvait rentrer peut-être! Mais avec la bande de bâtards qui traînaient là-bas, elle ressortait plus. Y z'auraient commencé à te la mettre en boîte, à rigoler, à lui faire des propositions. (21–22)

> [Can you imagine Djamila Bouhired venturing into a milk bar in Bab-el-Oued? She might have been able to get in but with the crowd of bastards that hung around in there, she wouldn't have been able to get out again! They would have started teasing her, kidding around, propositioning her.]

Pied-noir men's "authentic" masculinity also contrasts with that of Arab and Berber men who commit acts of violence in the name of independence, such as Saadi Yacef, the FLN leader immortalized in the film *La Bataille d'Alger* (1966).[56] Such men are feminized or their masculinity is questioned (196, 134). Male *pied-noir* activists, by contrast, are distinguishable by Camusian descriptions of "leur santé, leurs muscles, [. . .] leurs poitrines bronzées" [their health, their muscles, [. . .] their bronzed chests] and the story suggests they are "jeunes bêtes vigoureuses et rigolardes" (222) [strong young fun-loving beasts]. Later, however, some characters facing exile from Algeria portray members of the OAS as emasculated by their defeat. They suggest that the OAS decided to "baisser le pantalon" [drop their trousers] to the FLN (270) and that talks between both organizations signaled the beginning of unhealthy "épousailles OAS-FLN sur le cadavre de l'Algérie" (276) [OAS-FLN nuptials over the dead body of Algeria]. The idea of an unhealthy marriage links with Kristin Ross's observation that decolonization was frequently evoked as a divorce in metropolitan France at the time, with the former colony now viewed as a wife who was capable of evicting the French, although a "free union" between both countries should instead be encouraged.⁵⁷ This concept is also mirrored by Anne's and Jean's desire, in *La Valise et le cercueil*, to separate from both France and the indigenous population by creating an *Algérie pied-noir* as Anne claims that a forced marriage between the settlers and the indigenous population would end in tragic divorce (168).

Thus, in such literary works published by *pied-noir* women in the wake of Algerian independence, the performance of gender takes on symbolic significance, as texts ensure the cultural survival of an imagined *pied-noir* family. Other evocations of an exaggerated femininity in these early postindependence texts are worth citing here. Anne in *La Valise et le cercueil*, for example, describes a particularly stressful week spent looking for an OAS activist's body (that of Michel Leroy) as having left her "dans un tailleur devenu poisseux, courant sur des talons éculés" (151) [in a suit that had become dusty, running in worn-down heels]—clearly a deviation from her normal dress code. By the same token, two anecdotes from Dessaigne's *Journal d'une mère de famille pied-noir* suggest an exaggerated femininity. A fashion show attended by elegant young women goes ahead in September 1961, although boutiques in the same spot must close the following day to let the storm of violence pass (97), and a client carefully chooses gloves in a shop owned by a friend of the narrator, although fighting is taking place just meters away (140). The perpetuation of this emphasis on exaggerated femininity stands out very noticeably in Susini's *De Soleil et de larmes*, published twenty years later. Micheline notes of her time in the OAS, for example, "Tant que je peux être coquette, je ne vais pas me trimbaler en treillis et en pataugas parce que j'essaie de me battre" [As long as I can be well turned-out, I am not going to go around in fatigues and hiking boots just because I'm trying to fight] (176). She even causes her husband Jean-Jacques to be late for an OAS meeting as she insists on applying her make-up before driving him (231). A distinctive femininity is equally striking in Marie Cardinal's introduction to her 1988 illustrated text, *Les Pieds-Noirs*. Cardinal describes the dress code for the *pieds-noirs* as a complicated art form, which is less about an inherent elegance than about a desire to show "les parties de son anatomie qui le méritaient et à dissimuler ou maquiller les autres" [the parts of one's anatomy which merited it and to hide or apply make-up to the other parts].⁵⁸ She explains that women would practice the "technique" of their walk by examining their reflections in shop windows (28). Cardinal suggests a conscious performance and an adoption of artifice that recalls Brown's discussion of the "production of 'feminine' beauty" in terms of kitsch.⁵⁹ She describes how girls sought to move their posterior in exactly the right way in order not to appear as either a "fille de rien" [a woman of easy virtue], a "bourrique" [an ass], or a woman "qui ne trouvera pas de mari ou alors un Francaoui [Français] qui lui fera des enfants prétentieux" (28) [who will not find a husband or else will find a metropolitan French frog who will give her pretentious children]. The continued reiteration of this exaggerated femininity is also evident in a contemporary interview, in which a *pied-noir* woman talks with pride of the beautiful outfit she wore to the demonstration on the day of the Rue d'Isly shooting, noting: "Il faut être bien habillé" [One must be well-dressed].[60] Another contemporary memoir, meanwhile, links women's efforts to attain beauty to a virginal purity that is unique to *pied-noir* women. In this narrative, Marie Gil describes spending hours putting on make-up as a young woman, although her brother discourages any potential suitor as "chez nous, c'était mirar y no tocar" [with us, it was a question of look but don't touch].[61] The author's use of the Spanish "mirar y no tocar" draws attention to the presence of large numbers of settlers of Spanish origin in her birthplace, Oran, and here points to a European-Mediterranean identity that is shaped by the North African context.

2.4 ORIENTING EUROPEAN IDENTITIES

This section investigates ways in which *pied-noir* women have depicted apparent similarities with the Arabo-Berber population as a singular aspect of their identity, making them, once exiled, appear as "Femmes [. . .] orientales en Europe" [Oriental women in Europe].[62] Stora suggests that both colonizing and colonized women's role in Algeria was restricted to the familial, domestic sphere.[63] This recalls Eugène Delacroix's famous 1834 painting of indigenous Algerian women, "Femmes d'Alger dans leur appartement" [Women of Algiers in their Apartment], as well as Assia Djebar's response to the artist's "compulsion fétichiste" [fetishist compulsion] in her 1980 novel of the same title.[64] In reality, however, colonizing women's way of life may not have been as different from that of metropolitan French women as their written testimonies suggest. Stora considers the Algerian War as the "instant du dégagement de l'emprise familiale" [moment of release from family control] for women and describes Susini's *De Soleil et de larmes* as "l'histoire d'une émancipation familiale et d'un engagement politique, doublée d'un roman d'amour" [the story of emancipation from a family and of political engagement as well as a love story].[65] The novel certainly recounts a woman's personal tale of emancipation from her family, but it also appears as a metaphor for a male-oriented society influenced by the colonized population, thereby setting her community apart once more from the metropolitan French.

Susini's evocation of the subversive nature of her political engagement as an OAS activist echoes that of Anne Loesch in *La Valise et le cercueil*, which provides a useful point of reference here. In descriptions reminiscent of the iconic scene from Gillo Pontecorvo's *La Bataille d'Alger*, in which Algerian women become objects of the viewer's gaze as they disguise themselves as Europeans before going outside to plant bombs,[66] Anne evokes moving from the domestic to the public sphere when Jean asks for her help (46). As she sets out on her first mission, people stare at this young woman in her twenties walking through the town (48). When she later arrives at Jean's hideout she describes "des Arabes immobiles, [qui] nous observent fixement" [motionless Arabs who stare at us] and claims she has the "Sensation d'avoir à évoluer devant un public" (54) [sensation of having to progress in front of an audience]. In this way, Anne becomes the object of the colonized populations' gaze and therefore appears divested of power, making her determined actions seem all the more courageous.

In *De Soleil et de larmes*, Micheline similarly evokes colonizing women as disempowered, claiming that a composite macho Mediterranean and Arab culture, which values the chastity of women, taught her to be submissive: "Pour les familles arabes, les adolescentes représentent un avoir. [. . .] Les pieds-noirs ne vendent pas leur fille, mais ils exigent la même soumission. Notre virginité est le meilleur capital pour le placement" (10) [For Arab families, female adolescents are the equivalent of a possession. [. . .] The *pieds-noirs* do not sell their daughters, but they demand the same submission. Our virginity is the best capital for investment]. While this statement problematically points to indigenous women who need "saving" from an inferior status imposed on them by colonized men, it also suggests that a reluctance to emancipate *pied-noir* women arises, at least partly, from the influence of Arabo-Berber Algerians over the settlers. Micheline further associates her identity with the colonized population as she states that her apprenticeship as a woman began at the age of seven. It was at this point that she began to miss the world of the street, which she associates with indigenous Algerian children in a manner that elides the inequalities that existed between the colonizing and colonized populations:

> A mesure que je grandissais, je regrettais les années où je pouvais jouer dans la rue. [. . .] On se battait de temps en temps avec les Arabes, à coups de cailloux, mais les périodes de trêve étaient préférables. Dans ces moments, on pouvait jouer à la cachette chez eux. (19)

> [As I grew up, I missed the years when I was able to play in the street. [. . .] We used to have fights with the Arabs from time to time, by throwing pebbles, but the truce times were better. Then we were able to play hide and seek in their homes.]

Her situation appears as both similar and superior to that of indigenous women as she mentions that a man to whom she is briefly engaged at the age of seventeen expresses his regret "de ne pas pouvoir me boucler comme les femmes arabes" (25) [not to be able to lock me away like Arab women]. Given her restricted life, therefore, Micheline claims she enjoys the imposition of a curfew during the Algerian War as it sometimes allows her to stay away from home at night: "Pour la plupart d'entre nous, nous tenons l'échappatoire rêvée, tant les familles nous oppressent. *Inch'Allah* les bombes!" (46–47) [For most of us, we have the dreamed-of way out, since our families oppress us so much. God bless the bombs!][67]

It is worth noting at this point that the life the narrator leads stands in opposition to the societal constraints that she highlights. Despite her emphasis on the seclusion of settler women, their submissive role, and the value placed on their chastity, Micheline actively participates in the war. Her first act of engagement involves smuggling guns past police and out of government buildings taken over by partisans of French Algeria on May 13, 1958, during the *coup* that led to the return of Charles de Gaulle as president (58). While waiting to return the guns to their owners, she loses her virginity to an acquaintance called Robert, whose reaction undermines her insistence on the chastity of settler women: "Je ne pouvais pas deviner que tu étais vierge à vingt-trois ans!" (59) [I couldn't have guessed that you were a virgin at the age of twenty-three!]. She later joins the OAS, transporting documents and weapons and acting as secretary and driver to one of its leaders, Jean-Jacques Susini. Moreover, she chooses to have a relationship with Jean-Jacques, a married man.

Thus, Micheline's performance of femininity initially appears as subversive. Her active role in the public sphere and her choice of lovers (including a Frenchman whom she visits in Cannes) suggest that she is far from submissive or secluded. As a result of her personal rebellion, in particular her relationship with Jean-Jacques, she is beaten, evicted from her family home, and called a "fille perdue" [fallen woman] by her mother (133). However, punishment for not "doing" her femininity correctly is not long-lasting, in that her actions do not permanently damage her familial relations and she later moves back home for two to three nights per week (157). There is also a suggestion that societal rules lose their importance for those engaged in the war (192), and Micheline alludes to the fluidity of gender roles during the conflict in general. Consequently, Arab men use veils to disguise themselves as women (92), while indigenous Algerian girls plant bombs, which spurs her into action on her own first mission: "j'ai eu tellement peur qu'il m'a fallu songer aux filles arabes qui plaçaient les bombes, pour que la rage me submerge et balaie l'angoisse" (107) [I got so frightened that I had to think of the Arab girls who were planting bombs, so that I would be overcome with a rage which would banish my anxiety]. Her descriptions of missions that involve hiding messages in her underwear and her swimsuit (106, 119–20) echo Arabo-Berber girls' apparent use of their femininity to avoid capture by dressing up as European women. Hence, the narrator's performance of her femininity appears, on closer inspection, as an anomaly while she continues to espouse traditional femininity. Despite her actions, for example, she claims she is insulted when a *parachutiste* [paratrooper] with whom she has a brief relationship offers to rent her an apartment with a view to getting married later: "Tu ne connais pas les filles pieds-noirs: ton offre séduisante pour tes métropolitaines est une insulte pour nous" (67) [You do not know *pied-noir* girls. Your offer is attractive to your metropolitan French girls but an insult to us]. Moreover, she continues in a domestic role as partner to Jean-Jacques, although one of the "recipes" she now learns is for a Molotov cocktail (110). Micheline's evocation of an affinity with recipes here, coupled with descriptions of settler women who continue to keep house under increasingly difficult conditions (213, 243–44), echoes the suggestion in a volume by *pied-noir* writers that "La cuisine, c'était et c'est encore pour certaines femmes pieds-noirs la justification de leur existence et le moyen d'affirmer un talent" [Cooking was and still is, for certain *pied-noir* women, their reason for being and the way to prove a talent].[68]

Significantly, descriptions of French Algerian femininity do not differ vastly from expected performances of metropolitan femininity at the time. Susan Weiner has outlined the emphasis on feminine domesticity in France during the period in question as well as wives' submission to their husbands under the Napoleonic *Code Civil*.[69] She has also pointed out that French women were accorded the right to vote by the government in exile in Algiers in March 1944 "well after most of their European counterparts, just months before the Liberation," while in France during the 1950s, "feminism was deemed obsolete since women had acquired the vote, a view Beauvoir herself espoused in *Le Deuxième sexe*" [The Second Sex].[70] Ross has also shown that the advent of household appliances linked women in France during the late 1950s and early 1960s to interior space and to the idea of "reenfolding inward—back onto the authentic French life [. . .] and the private interiority of the domestic."[71] Scholars have equally documented France's pronatalist policies throughout its modern history to the present time.[72] Conversely, Lorcin suggests, "As settler society developed, women took opportunities to move into the public sphere where, in the metropole, they might have been less likely to do so."[73] Her study reveals that colonizing women came to the fore during World War I and "consciously moved into the public sphere using the opportunities the colonial situation provided" in the interwar period.[74] Thus, while there were certainly strict divisions in colonial Algeria, women "could attain wider social recognition in the colony" than in the metropole for the limited positions on offer.[75]

Nevertheless, the portrayal of a femininity influenced by Islam in Susini's text and others suggests a privileged relationship with the colonized population that can work to naturalize the colonial presence in Algeria. Indigenous women are largely absent from Susini's narrative but she implies a certain complicity between them and *pied-noir* women against male power when she describes European women borrowing their maids' veils in order to follow wayward husbands (22). Similarly, Anne's femininity in *La Valise et le cercueil* allows a maternal relationship with her servant, whose name is tellingly interchangeable—Mélanie/Zorah (205). Elbe's *À l'heure de notre mort* goes further in its evocation of a shared feminine pain as the narrator, Emmanuelle, describes visiting cloistered women following the loss of loved ones on both sides during World War II (41). In the same novel, the following scene at an Algiers morgue in the wake of continued violence following the Algerian War's cease-fire, sums up this sorority, which recalls Veillard's allusion to fraternal conflict in *Le Premier Homme*:[76]

> Une Européenne s'est évanouie devant le corps de son fils, à côté d'une mauresque qui n'avait pas encore trouvé le sien. Elle a attrapé la Française, l'a portée dans ses bras jusqu'à un banc, et l'a aidée à revenir à elle. C'est à voir, je vous jure, cette dernière fraternisation! (241–42)

> [A European woman fainted on seeing her son's body, beside a Moorish woman who had not yet found her own son. She caught hold of the French woman, took her in her arms to a bench and helped her to come around. Honestly, it has to be seen to be believed, this latest fraternization!][77]

Moreover, the trauma of the war provokes an archetypally feminine pain. An extract from Dessaigne's *Journal d'une mère de famille pied-noir* is worth quoting in this regard:

> Je n'écris pas un roman, j'en suis incapable. Mais j'écris mon angoisse et c'est elle qui est «utérine». Elle est fondamentale, pleine comme une attente, lancinante comme des douleurs. Elle hurle en moi lorsque je crois mes enfants, beaux, vigoureux et sains, tués ou amputés, déchiquetés par une bombe ou transpercés par une lame. (78)

> [I am not writing a novel; I am incapable of that. However, I am writing about my anguish and that is what is "uterine." It is elemental, full as when expecting, shooting like labor pains. It howls in me when I imagine my beautiful, strong, healthy children killed or amputated, ripped apart by a bomb or pierced by a blade.]

Anne in *La Valise et le cercueil* manifests similar pain when her sister's death causes her to bleed (193),[78] while her closeness to her mother country allows her to describe the departure of her community as a personally painful abortion: "notre race a été avortée avant même que d'avoir vécu" (12) [our race was aborted before it even lived].

Thus, settler women appear to have a unique relationship with a feminized Algeria. In *De Soleil et de larmes,* Micheline Susini emphasizes the sun and sea, in which she swims every day, thereby evoking a youthful people who, like Micheline, are fighting for a land with which they have a privileged relationship: "Je me battrai pour mon soleil, pour la mer parce qu'ailleurs je ne pourrai pas vivre" (13) [I will fight for my sun and for the sea because I will not be able to live elsewhere]. Furthermore, the narrator depoliticizes this privileged relationship with Algeria when she wonders: "Pourquoi faut-il payer si chèrement ce ciel bleu?" (222) [Why must we pay so dearly for this blue sky?]. Elbe's *À l'heure de notre mort* is similarly Camusian in this regard, as women offer themselves up as sacrifices to the sun (34, 175), which appears as a male character called Kadour (97). Moreover, it is Jeanne, rather than indigenous Algerians, who embodies Algeria in this novel. Thus, Parisian journalist Julien loves Algeria through her and, in problematic evocations of her that ignore the presence of indigenous women, Jeanne has, "Comme toutes les femmes d'Alger [. . .] la chair mi-pâle mi ensoleillée dessinée par les traces de son bikini" (72, 81) [Like all the women of Algiers [. . .] half-pale, half radiant skin outlined by the marks of her bikini]. *Alger la Blanche* [Algiers the White (City)], the settlers' popular nickname for Algiers, which evokes its sparkling white buildings, therefore lives up to its nickname in every sense as it unequivocally relates to French Algerian femininity. Hence, Jeanne has a privileged relationship with Algiers that allows her to predict its (and her own) death when she leaves for France:

> «Alger . . . qu'est-ce que tu deviendras, quand nous serons partis . . . Ma belle grande ville, comme nous avons souffert et espéré ensemble, comme tu vas être seule, comme ils vont t'abîmer . . .». Je lui demande pardon de partir, de la laisser mourir derrière nous . . . Je me demande si je ne préférais pas mourir maintenant, tiens, couchée contre elle, sur un trottoir. (120)

> ["Algiers . . . what will become of you when we leave . . . My beautiful big city, how we have suffered and hoped together, how lonely you will be, how they will ruin you" I ask her forgiveness for leaving, for leaving her behind to die . . . You know, I wonder if I might prefer to die now, stretched out beside her on a sidewalk.]

Private postindependence narratives, therefore, not only distinguish *pied-noir* women's identities from the indigenous population but also highlight similarities in a way that naturalizes their presence in Algeria and differentiates them from the metropolitan population. Later volumes on the *pieds-noirs* echo such evocations of *pied-noir* femininity. Maurice Benassayag, for example, notes the "étrange mélange" [strange mix] that resulted from Europeans living with Arabs and suggests that while metropolitan women were regarded in Algeria as "des putes" [whores], settler women would have refused an emperor's advances without the promise of marriage.[79] An interviewee in Danielle Michel-Chich's study, meanwhile, contends that:

> Les femmes pieds-noirs sont plus émancipées que leurs voisines algériennes, néanmoins elles vivent dans un monde très oriental. [. . .] Les moeurs d'Alger ne sont pas celles de Paris et la jeune fille pied-noir ne quitte l'autorité de son père et de son frère que pour se soumettre à celle de son mari.[80]

> [*Pied-noir* women were more emancipated than their female Algerian neighbors. Nevertheless, they lived in a very Oriental world. [. . .] The mores in Algiers were not the same as in Paris and young *pied-noir* women only forsook their father's and brother's authority when submitting to that of their husband.]

Similarly, female *pieds-noirs* more recently have spoken of their restricted position as women in Algeria, which is naturalized by one as the result of the fact that Muslim men kept women, described in this case generically as "la Fatma," in the home.[81] Marie Cardinal, recalling Mediterranean stereotypes, has also described colonial Algeria as a world where "La vertu des filles, c'était quelque chose, ce n'était pas la rigolade! Et pas seulement pour les musulmanes. Pour les catholiques et les juives c'était pareil" [Girls' virtue meant something; it was no laughing matter. And this wasn't just for Muslim women—it was the same for Catholic and Jewish women].[82] The next section considers women whose background in colonial Algeria prompts efforts to analyze rather than idealize patriarchal social structures. The writers examined—Cardinal, Brigitte Roüan, and Hélène Cixous—have used fictionalized memories of their ambiguous position in colonial Algeria to attempt to interrogate dominant narratives.

2.5 FINDING FEMINISM AND CRITIQUING COLONIALISM?

Critics tend to overlook Marie Cardinal's status as a member of the colonizing community.[83] However, feminist readings of her works, including arguably her most famous work, *Les Mots pour le dire* (1975) [The Words to Say it], can benefit significantly from a consideration of her background in

Algeria. This text contains few references to the Algerian War and instead draws on Cardinal's real-life psychotherapy sessions in Paris. It is therefore of interest as an apparent counterpoint to the previously examined narratives by *pied-noir* women. It has also been far more commercially successful and reached a wider audience than the texts studied above.[84] As an autobiographical novel, however, it features descriptions of the author/narrator's childhood in Algeria that require further consideration.[85] It equally merits an examination of its central focus on the mother in light of Cardinal's status as a settler woman, while the key theme of mental illness is particularly pertinent to the colonial context.

The narrator's evocation of her journey from insanity to sanity recalls her position as a member of the colonizing population and the work of psychiatrists Frantz Fanon and Bernard Sigg on the trauma caused to both victims and perpetrators of violence within the colonial system.[86] She also has suicidal feelings from adolescence,[87] which is again suggestive of colonizing identities more generally. It useful to note here that for Butler, all sexual identities are melancholic due to the excluded aspect of them (namely homosexuality) created by laws and taboos. Drawing on Butler's work in *Gender Trouble*, Vikki Bell explains: "The homosexual becomes thereby 'encrypted' within the heterosexual. [. . .] This encrypting is melancholic in that it carries the lost or 'forbidden' object with it."[88] Applying this paradigm to the gendered colonial context is helpful here. Indeed, Butler has suggested that "a culturally instituted melancholia" results from racial taboos on miscegenation, as a class of people "are constituted essentially as the unthinkable, the unloveable, the ungrievable, and that then institutes a form of melancholia which is culturally pervasive, a strange ungrievability."[89] The narrators of many of the aforementioned texts allude to a melancholy or grief that, in this light, recalls what will forever be unavailable to them—an Arabo-Berber identity that would ultimately legitimize their presence in Algeria.[90]

The narrator of Cardinal's text certainly evokes the indigenous population, which she cannot emulate, in the following description of her performance of femininity:

Je les enviais. Je me sentais capable de faire tout ce qu'ils faisaient. Mais je ne le pouvais pas, ce n'était pas des jeux de filles, alors, avec les autres «pisseuses» (comme disait Kader), je cueillais des fleurs et j'arrangeais les cabanes. (67)

[I envied them. I felt capable of doing everything they did. Yet, I could not— their games were not for girls—so with the other "wee-wee girls," as Kader used to say, I picked flowers and tidied the huts.]

Furthermore, as the narrator reaches young adulthood, her mother's expectations point to the performance of an identity that will separate her definitively from the colonized community: "tu ne devras plus jamais rester seule avec un garçon et encore moins avec un homme. Toi qui aimes bien les jeux de garçons il faudra te contrôler. Finies les cavalcades dans la forêt avec les fils de Barded!" (75) [you must never again remain alone with a boy, much less with a man. You, liking boys' games as you do, will have to be kept in check. No more stampeding through the forest with Barded's sons!]

Restrictions imposed on the narrator in her position as a settler girl are revealed by a recurring dream from her youth featuring a horseman who smelt of vetiver—a tall tropical grass—as well as of "cuir et [. . .] crottin" (110) [leather and dung]. Although the horseman never looks at her, she admits: "Je le trouvais extrêmement séduisant et je savais qu'il connaissait ma présence" (110) [I found him extremely attractive and I knew he was aware of my presence]. She wishes to jump onto the horse behind the man but the dream turns into a frightening nightmare when, feeling paralyzed, she is unable to do so. She also realizes: "J'étais incapable d'identifier le cavalier qui n'avait pas de visage pour moi puisqu'il n'avait pas de regard" (110–11) [I was unable to identify the horseman who for me had no face because he had no eyes]. The narrator concludes, when reliving this suppressed dream in therapy, that it is about two worlds: the countryside that forms the backdrop to the dream represents the indoor world, "l'univers de ma mère: sans danger, agréable, un peu ennuyeux, un peu triste, sage, convenable, harmonieux, plat" (111) [the world of my mother: safe, pleasant, a bit boring, a bit dreary, restrained, respectable, harmonious, dull]. She decides that the horseman, however, represents "l'univers de la rue" [the world of the street], a world she unconsciously desired, "celui de l'aventure, de l'homme, du sexe" (111) [that of adventure, men, sex].

This faceless horseman, with whom she can never fraternize, appears as, not just a symbol of masculinity, but of indigenous Algerian manhood. Indeed, Éric Savarèse believes that fear of a faceless *fellagha* [rebel], who was physically absent from all posters and propaganda promoting French Algeria during the war, encouraged many *pieds-noirs* to form an ambivalent perception of Arabs, as they were unable to distinguish between those who formed part of daily life and the enemy.[91] In this light, another nightmare, in which the narrator dreams that she joins a group of women, including her mother, in an apartment that three such independence fighters invade, appears especially significant. The narrator is not frightened at first as she favors independence (157). In spite of her wish to talk to the men, however, she finds that destiny ties her to the other women, who drag her back and pray for salvation (157). She begins to feel their fear and remembers stories of "femmes violées et éventrées" (157) [women raped and disemboweled]. As she tries to escape, she realizes that the men are chasing her. One almost strangles her and brings a knife to her neck before she wakes up. The narrator connects this dream to a childhood memory of a man who tried to rape her when she was walking home from school. Yet she mentions that this man had "des yeux bleus et des cheveux blondasses" [blue eyes and dirty blond hair], which suggests he was of European origin (159). For the narrator, the dream represents a fear of male power and, more specifically, of the vulnerability of the female body (163). However, the specific context of the dream suggests that wartime propaganda and colonial discourse, casting native men as untrustworthy, deeply affected the narrator.

This said, it appears that, on leaving Algeria and undergoing therapy in Paris, the narrator liberates herself from colonial and patriarchal discourses, which allows her to understand that she grew up in an unjust and unequal society and that the conflict was more than a (Greek) tragedy:

> C'est maintenant seulement que je me rendais compte que [. . .] j'avais pris la guerre d'Algérie pour une affaire sentimentale, une triste histoire de famille digne des Atrides. Et pourquoi cela? Parce que je n'avais aucun rôle à jouer dans cette société où j'étais devenue folle. Aucun rôle sinon donner des garçons pour faire marcher les guerres et les gouvernements et des filles pour faire, à leur tour, des garçons aux garçons. Trente-sept ans de soumission absolue. Trente-sept ans à accepter l'inégalité et l'injustice sans broncher, sans même les voir ! (166)

> [I was only now realizing that [. . .] I had considered the Algerian War as a matter of the heart, a sad family story worthy of the Atreids [family from Greek mythology]. And why? Because I had no role to play in the society in which I had gone mad. No role except to produce boys to make wars and governments and daughters to make boys for the boys in turn. Thirty-seven years of absolute submission. Thirty-seven years accepting inequality and injustice without turning a hair, without even seeing it!][92]

The inequalities inherent in colonialism therefore appear to have played a role in Cardinal's inspiration for her feminism, as the narrator vows to ensure that power is divided between herself, her husband, and her children in order to create a microcosm of the society she desires (168).

Nevertheless, the above quotation appears to minimize her own and women's role more generally in colonialism. Recalling the current book's previous study of Camus and later *pied-noir* writers, the narrator also has a unique relationship with a feminized colonial Algeria. Indeed, the country becomes her "vraie mère" (59) [true mother], following her biological mother's admission that she tried to abort her (126). The narrator's trauma because of this attempted abortion, coupled with the feminization of her birthplace, echoes Loesch's description of her abortion from Algeria. In Cardinal's novel, although leaving French Algeria appears liberating, the end of the colony provokes an equally traumatic rupture: "Il me semble que la chose [la folie] a pris racine en moi d'une façon permanente, quand j'ai compris que nous allions assassiner l'Algérie" (59) [It seems to me that the thing [madness] took root in me permanently when I understood that we were going to assassinate Algeria]. Moreover, although the narrator links her subsequent psychosomatic bleeding (again evocative of Anne in *La Valise et le cercueil*) to her mother's admission of her attempted abortion, her symptoms did not strike until years after this admission. Developmental psychologist Bruno Bettelheim notes that the narrator's incessant bleeding began aged twenty-seven—the age of Cardinal's mother when she became pregnant—thereby suggesting that "the daughter's symptoms were the result of her identification with her mother."[93] However, her statement that colonial Algeria was her true mother puts a new slant on the identification process. Cardinal left Algeria in the 1950s, only to return for a visit twenty-five years later, as documented in her 1980 memoir *Au pays de mes racines* [To the country of my roots]. In this light, her continuous bleeding in her late twenties corresponds with the trauma of the loss of her mother country due to the circumstances of war.[94]

Furthermore, the sea again appears as a Camusian mother or lover. When the narrator discovers her husband has been to the beach with another woman, it is the thought of him swimming in the sea—a pastime she has introduced him to—that troubles her:

> Il a cru que c'était l'idée de cette femme qui me blessait. Mais il se trompait. Ce qui me bouleversait c'était d'imaginer le plaisir qu'il avait pris à entrer dans les vagues, à nager au large, à se laisser sécher au soleil, à sentir le sable sous ses pieds nus. C'est moi qui lui avais appris la mer, la plage, le vent chaud, la liberté du corps qui se donne à l'eau, se laisse caresser et porter par elle. Il était d'un pays froid où l'océan est un terrain de sport, j'étais d'un pays chaud où il est volupté. (139)

> [He thought that I was hurt by the idea of this woman. But he was wrong. What overwhelmed me was imagining the pleasure he had taken from stepping into the waves, swimming offshore, letting himself dry in the sun, feeling the sand under his bare feet. I was the one who had taught him about the sea, the beach, the warm wind, the freedom of the body which gives itself up to the water, lets itself be caressed and carried by her. He was from a cold country where the ocean is a sports facility; I was from a hot country where it is a sensual pleasure.]

She also describes her reconciliation with her husband in terms of a union with the sea:

> Nous allons entrer dans les vagues. Je connais un passage de sable blanc où tu ne te blesseras pas, où tu n'auras qu'à te laisser aller. Rappelle-toi, mon doux, mon

beau, que la mer est bonne si tu ne la crains pas. Elle ne veut que te lécher, te caresser, te porter, te bercer, permets-lui de le faire et elle te plaira encore. (143)

[We are going to enter the waves. I know a passageway of white sand where you will not get hurt, where all you will have to do is let yourself go. Remember my sweet, handsome love that the sea is kind if you do not fear her. She only wants to lap against you, caress you, carry you, cradle you. Allow her to do that and she will give you more pleasure.

The narrator, therefore, seems to have a privileged relationship with the sea in contrast to her French husband. Perhaps surprisingly then, given Cardinal's apparent support for Algerian independence, representations of a feminized land and sea repeat the often-nostalgic Camusian tropes used by the women writers analyzed above. Indeed, several of the narrator's memories of her childhood in Algeria are similarly infused with nostalgia, with the forest where she played described as "un paradis" [a paradise], for example (66). Descriptions of a farmhouse built by her ancestor in 1837 (57), and her emphasis on the hard work of "les premiers colons" [the first colonists] on "cette terre arrachée à la stérilité" (83) [this land wrested from sterility], also reiterate the pioneering tradition and suggest a natural continuity of generations that was broken in 1962.

Moreover, while colonial Algeria emerges as a site of limitation for women, including the narrator's mother (127), it is important to remember the role of the colony as a "means of social, cultural, or indirectly political fulfilment that was not readily available in the metropole."[95] Cardinal's emphasis on women's restricted role minimizes their complicity in the colonial system, while her portrayal of a privileged relationship with Algeria simultaneously validates their presence there as members of its family. In fact, Cardinal justifies her decision not to discuss the Algerian War publicly by stating in *Les Pieds-Noirs* that "Les histoires de famille se règlent en famille" [Family matters are settled within the family].[96]

Another possible counterpoint to the above texts is provided by Brigitte Roüan's 1990 semiautobiographical film, *Outremer (Les enfants du désarroi)* [Overseas (The Children of Turmoil)], which centers on *pied-noir* women.[97] As a film described as feminist and anti-colonial in its depiction of three sisters, it is worth considering here.[98] Alison Murray contends that, "In part, the story of the syndrome of empire is being written in French contemporary cinema, a site where problems of historical consciousness are worked out, and as such, [. . .] [are] both reflective and constitutive of collective memory."[99] The same is true of films representing the *pieds-noirs*, which often reach a more diverse audience than texts on the subject. Roüan's film is especially significant as it won an award at Cannes Film Festival and reached an international audience. It is also worth noting the spectator's role while viewing films. Drawing on Butler, Bell points to the gaze as "an historical deployment that does not innocently respond to visual cues, but that operates as part of a wider *dispositif* that enables cues to be seen as such."[100] What Bell terms the "politics of seeing"[101] is especially valid in the case of films featuring the contentious subject of the Algerian War and the *pieds-noirs*. Laura Mulvey's theories on "scopophilia" or the visual pleasure offered by cinema, particularly with the woman as object of the male gaze, and the viewer's narcissistic identification with this gaze ("ego libido") are also useful in this regard.[102]

Outremer has three sections, each of which reveals the same events of 1946–1964 from the individual viewpoint of three *pied-noir* sisters—Zon, Malène, and Gritte. The director chose to bring information to light or elide details in each section, thereby pointing to the performative nature of remembering. Thus, from its beginning, the film adopts an ironic tone as regards storytelling about the colony. It also consciously reveals connections between colonialism and performances of gender by taking a satirical approach to its depiction of settler femininity and masculinity. In fact, despite urging their younger sister Gritte to marry like them, both Zon and Malène are deeply unhappy due to restrictive gender norms. Early on, for example, the older sister, Zon, arouses her naval officer husband's ire by allowing another man to touch her while dancing the Paso Doble. In an apparent reference to belly dancing, which conflicts with her actual movements, he accuses her of acting like a gypsy and protruding her belly in a vulgar manner. Zon, meanwhile, chastises herself for her behavior, deciding, "je suis anormale" [I'm abnormal],[103] thereby pointing to colonizing women's traditional role as guardians of morality in the face of hypersexed "natives." She becomes sad and tearful when she tells her children she is expecting another baby, which further outlines her disempowerment in the male-dominated society in which she lives. Zon's private experimentation in front of the mirror with an Orientalist costume suggests that her melancholia relates to an inaccessible Arabo-Berber identity. Furthermore, she relies on her husband for her sense of self. When he dies, she wastes away from cancer, putting on his uniform before she herself passes away. Through wearing the exoticized bikini outfit and later her husband's uniform, Zon seems aware of the constructed nature of gender but cannot conceive of nontraditional performances in this regard. This limited mindset equally destroys her husband. Having told Zon that he does not wish to serve in Japan and that he has "les nerfs de femme" [women's nerves], she tells him he has to leave as she needs to admire him and he must be "un chef" [a leader]. She consequently contributes to his death while conducting naval duties overseas.

The middle sister, Malène (played by Rouan), is also negatively affected by expectations surrounding gender roles in the territory. Due to her husband Gildas's lack of interest in agriculture, she runs the family farm and pays the workers, who voice their objections at not meeting her husband. Malène expresses shame at wearing the trousers ("la culotte") in the relationship and disdainfully compares her weather-beaten skin to that of their indigenous servant, who bears the generic name Zohra. Like Zon, Malène tells her husband that she needs to look up to him and she chastises him for reading books instead of acting as she believes a man should. Moreover, in a fit of anger at her husband's detachment from the farm, she sets fire to the harvest. As the workers line up on the ground with their hands behind their back, she fails to take responsibility for her actions, even when Lopez, her second-in-command, wrongly accuses and beats an innocent young worker, Lakhdar. Malène's violent act in setting the harvest on fire (possibly an allusion to the scorched earth policy espoused by the OAS) and her insistence on staying on the land when her husband suggests moving to Argentina demonstrate that she is attempting to perform a concept of virile *pied-noir* masculinity that her husband lacks. Elsewhere in the film, her father wistfully alludes to the possibility of a subversive performance of femininity when he tells her, "Tu aurait pu être mon fils" [You could have been my son]. However, she is unable to embody this identity and dies when pro-independence fighters shoot her while she is driving her husband's car.

Life in Algeria also proves restrictive for the youngest sister, Gritte. Her father does not allow her to study medicine and she must content herself with nursing, while her sisters insist that she must marry. Furthermore, she is a representative of her country for her fiancé, Maxime, who tells her: "Mon Algérie, c'est toi" [You are my Algeria]. Gritte rebels against her expected role as a symbol and as a wife by refusing to marry and by having a clandestine relationship with an Arab rebel, to whom she provides supplies. She also reveals her distaste for her family's and friends' racist remarks by getting sick at the dinner table during one of their discussions. Again, however, a subversive performance of femininity proves impossible. French soldiers shoot her lover dead when he tries to rendezvous with her in the middle of the night. As the film draws to a close, Gritte appears completely powerless and alone when a pro-OAS boy insults her as she leaves the country and throws water on her as she passively sits on the side of the road with her suitcase. In this way, she becomes a feminine symbol of the suffering French Algerian woman who chose the suitcase over the coffin. Yet, her subsequent exile in France seems as if it may be empowering. In the final scene, she wears a wedding gown. When asked by the priest if she will marry a new character, Nicolas, she hesitates and sees an image of her dead sisters, who appear to whisper to her. Although she does not reveal her final decision, she may choose not to marry and could lead the liberated life she wanted.

However, it is important to consider the visual aspect of the film as well as the narrative. An early scene set during Gritte's engagement party in

1949 depicts the three sisters flying a plane over the family villa, which clearly reveals some of the ways in which they are empowered by their position as settler women. They land to cries of "Bravo les sœurs!" [Well done sisters!], and the subsequent party, with music and dancing, white dresses and naval uniforms, green shrubs and pink bougainvillea, lends a decidedly nostalgic atmosphere to the film. Furthermore, an opening scene featuring the sisters cheerfully rowing a boat in choppy waters suggests a unique relationship with the sea. A beach scene featuring the sun shining on sparkling blue water, Zon in a swimsuit, and Gritte in a bikini provides an example of land and seascapes combined with images of female bodies, which offer the viewer the type of visual pleasure and identification with the male gaze theorized by Mulvey. Crucially, as Murray points out, this type of scene also "invites identification with the gaze of the colonizer."[104] In this case, the female settler body is the object of the gaze, which naturalizes colonial presence in the territory. Moreover, as Naomi Greene suggests, "Recurrent shots of the ocean that separates them [the sisters] from the mainland, and which renders them a colony that is 'overseas' or 'outremer,' serve to underscore their distance, at once emotional and geographical, from France."[105] Their distance and that of French Algeria from an Algerian hinterland occupied by indigenous communities is also apparent in such shots. Thus, visual cues construct an identity that is neither French nor Algerian and evoke the viewer's sympathy with regard to the uncertain fate that awaits the women.

It is also important to note that although the film appears to condemn racism, Gritte's Arab lover obtains very little screen time and they are only together in very brief, silent sequences. First, he appears as a hooded man who follows her, pushes her from behind, then puts his arms around her neck and draws one of them across her throat, before letting her go, in a scene in which Gritte is visibly frightened. Next, Gritte, who is now hooded, gives him supplies in the dark outside her house and finally, they appear together in a very short scene in which he lies outside, resting his head in her lap. These obscure allusions to the relationship cast it in a questionable light. Moreover, by Roüan's own admission, she could not make the film in Algeria as a censorship committee there considered her script to show Arabs who were "rapists, treacherous and lazy"—an accusation she refutes.[106] However, the lack of speaking roles for indigenous characters in the film connects it to many of the texts studied, including those of Camus, in which indigenous Algerian characters are noticeable by their absence or their anonymity.

Roüan dedicates the film to her mother, who, perhaps like *Algérie française*, "était si jolie [. . .] qui aurait pu être si belle" [was so pretty [. . .] who could have been so beautiful]. By dedicating the film to her settler mother and by focusing on three sisters who suffer from events that invade their lives, the situation in Algeria again appears as a family tragedy. Indeed, the plot evacuates men from any major role in the film, thereby feminizing the settlers and casting them as victims of events beyond their control. Women's lack of involvement in politics is confirmed when Gritte's nieces demonstrate the values they have learned by telling their brother it is their role to set the table for a family dinner, while at dinner he tells them: "la politique ne vous intéresse pas, vous n'êtes que des filles" [politics does not interest you, you are only girls]. In general, the film includes few references to politics, apart from Lopez's assertion that the nationalist Ferhat Abbas is a traitor, and the family's debates about "les événements" [the events], in which they decide that the indigenous population will not be able to survive without them.[107] There is also a scene in which de Gaulle's (in)famous 1958 speech (in which he said he understood the French of Algeria) is broadcast on the radio during a rendezvous between Gritte and Maxime. In a contradictory attitude that reveals she does not comprehend the conflict, Gritte, who has helped the liberation cause, is delighted. In a moment of dramatic irony, she takes the speech as proof that the future of her community is safe, despite Maxime's warning that de Gaulle is no Prince Charming. The spectator's knowledge of the impending exodus comes into play here, which serves to arouse the viewer's sympathy for the well-meaning Gritte. In general, however, the film's elliptical structure is not easy to follow and denies the uninitiated viewer a global sense of politics or history.[108] In fact, as Murray notes, the cyclical narrative fixes "the era of French Algeria with a timeless quality."[109] This structure also recalls depictions in Camus's *Le Premier Homme* of naturalized, cyclical violence going back as far as Cain. Similarly, through this story, Roüan constructs the memory of a disempowered community with which the audience is inclined to sympathize.

The linking of the three settler sisters' personal lives with the colony is problematic as it minimizes colonial history in favor of a story of romantic love. As the tagline for the American version of the film states, against the image of the sisters rowing a boat in bikinis, this is a story about "Three Women with Man Trouble."[110] Although the director intended a recurring triumphant chorus from Gluck's Orpheus and Eurydice, "L'amour [. . .] est préférable à la liberté" [Love [. . .] is better than liberty] to be ironic,[111] it still evokes the story of thwarted lovers who cannot live without each other.[112] In addition to this, occasional glimpses of children suggest what might have been, were it not for the interference of adults. Malène's son plays soldiers with an indigenous boy, for example, while Malène mentions that Zon's daughter, Guénolée, kissed the aforementioned farm worker, Lakhdar. The sound of youths singing French children's songs as the credits roll further evokes innocence. It also reminds the viewer that the French education system imposed its values on innocent settler children.

Thus, like Cardinal, the director is critical of the effect of colonial society on performances of gender, although both seem more concerned with the settler rather than indigenous community, as suggested by the following quote from the director:

> I wanted to show people hemmed in by inherited property and preconceived notions, occupying prearranged positions [. . .] the men of that time were not allowed to cry, they were placed on pedestals, forced to be virile and magnificent statues [. . .] The women were addicted to one man. Such an education creates neurotic women, of which I am one. I was brought up to be married, so of course I never married.[113]

Against this backdrop, the next section examines the memoir of a particularly influential woman whose sense of belonging to the French Algerian community is less clear-cut due to her Jewish heritage—Hélène Cixous.

Cixous's "écriture féminine" [feminine writing] has seen her compared to other well-known "French feminists" in commentary that fails to consider the context of her upbringing.[114] As with Cardinal, however, an examination of the writer's origins is important when considering her feminist outlook. Cixous experienced exclusion from the settler population due to her Jewish heritage, particularly under the Vichy regime. Thus, as a female, Jewish "Algerian colonial," she has described herself as "triply marginalised."[115] This section considers Cixous's feminist, anti-colonial stance in her contemporary autobiographical novel, *Les Rêveries de la femme sauvage* (2000) [Reveries of the Wild Woman], which deals specifically with Algeria.

Like Camus's *Le Premier Homme*, this novel engages with a fictionalized version of the author's childhood from the perspective of an adult who left her birthplace many years before; the first lines of the book come to the narrator in a dream forty years after her departure. The "rêveries" [reveries] in the novel's title cast doubt over what is real and what is imagined, a technique celebrated by fellow Jewish French Algerian Jacques Derrida.[116] Derrida developed his ideas on deconstruction, requiring the rereading of texts from within, from his "tortured political stance" as a Jewish French Algerian liberal,[117] and Cixous's background similarly influenced her thinking. Her title links the author to eighteenth-century Francophone writer and philosopher Jean-Jacques Rousseau's *Les Rêveries du promeneur solitaire* [Reveries of the Solitary Walker].[118] However, it equally connects her to the Arabo-Berber population and to the Algerian landscape, since the "Wild Woman" of Algerian writer Kateb Yacine's play, *La Femme Sauvage*, represents "la patrie" [the homeland].[119] For the narrator of the story, the "Ravin de la Femme Sauvage" [Wild Woman's Ravine] also forms part of the local terrain. It is a nearby gorge and the subject of a nightmare—she dreams her brother will fall over its edge as he rides his bicycle.[120]

Despite having an immediate connection with the colonizing and colonized populations as well as the landscape, both the narrator and her brother are outsiders. Furthermore, as Jennifer Yee points out, they are excluded from the practicing Jewish community, particularly Sephardic Jews, since their mother is a nonpracticing Ashkenazi, while the death of their father means that the family are further isolated "as the children of a widow in a culture working along strictly patriarchal lines."[121] Thus, Cixous is a member of one of the "Stranger groups" of colonial society outlined by David Prochaska. Such groups "occupy intermediate positions" in the social hierarchy and are "set off [. . .] from both natives and Europeans by a combination of ethnicity, race, religion, and culture."[122] The writer would therefore appear to occupy a liminal space from which she can highlight and critique the construction of identities in the colonial setting.

The author's playful wording in *Les Rêveries de la femme sauvage* underscores the performative nature of identity as the product of discourse. It also points to the slippage of language, which can potentially divest the colonizing population of power, to which Homi Bhabha refers in his discussion of the Third Space.[123] Neologisms in Cixous's text certainly subvert the French language, and thus point to pain on all sides associated with the construct of "French Algeria." These include "maladie algérie" (16) [Algeria nausea], "Désalgérie" (69) [Unalgeria], "force malgérienne" (111) [Malgerian force], and "l'Algériefrançaise" (144) [Frenchalgeria]—a portmanteau that itself draws attention to the subsumption of Algeria's identity by France. The text also contains words that underline her desire to be part of the indigenous population as well as divisions along hierarchical and ethnic lines that prevent this, for example, "petizarabes" (45, 72) [Little'rabs] and "inséparabe" (45, 89) [Inseparab].[124] Furthermore, she subverts idealized depictions of the former colony with descriptions such as the following:

> Aveugles sans yeux par fonte purulente de l'oeil syphilitique et aveugles par purulence de l'œil spirituel, culs-de-jatte mentaux, hommes sans nez et Français sans odorat, lépreux à conscience chancrée française et Arabes naufragés de l'être, boîtes de conserve rouillées, selles dans les escaliers et au milieu de ça, il y a des lieux paradisiaques. (106)

> [Blind people without eyes from the purulent liquification of the syphilitic eye and blind from the purulence of the spiritual eye, mentally disabled, men without noses and French people without a sense of smell, lepers with a conscience infected by French chancres and Arabs ruined from being so, rusty tins, feces on the stairs and in the middle of that, there are heavenly places.]

Images of a paradisiacal Algiers are revealed as constructed or even "une falisification et une tricherie qui a beaucoup de succès" [a falsification and a very successful trick], when, for the narrator, it is "l'Enfer" (40) [Hell]. Upon entering this world, "on ne peut pas faire un pas dans la rue ni entrer dans un magasin sans être instantanément victime complice coupable ou contaminé" (41) [You cannot take a step on the street or go into a shop without being instantly complicit victim, guilty or contaminated]. Thus, the text undermines many of the positive memories evoked in the works studied above. Although the narrator's brother asks her to remove an unsavory incident from the narrative, she chooses to include it and when he suggests she call it "le Paradis Perdu" [Paradise Lost] she retorts that "L'Enfer Perdu" (120–21) [Hell Lost] would be a more appropriate title. By evoking death, the narrator also cuts short the creation of a "berceau" [cradle] of nostalgic memories that she and her brother were creating (85).

The narrator of this text alludes to harsh colonial realities, including a deep-rooted racism against the indigenous population inculcated by the French authorities, in addition to anti-Semitism: "En plus du racisme fondateur français [. . .] en plus du classicisme français, en plus de cette morbidité considérée comme une belle santé, bon appétit, il faut ajouter les antisémitismes" (43) [As well as the founding French racism [. . .], plus French Classicism—as well as this morbidity that is considered to signify good health, hearty appetite, anti-Semitism must be added]. Whereas many of the works studied emphasize fraternity or sorority and hospitality, the narrator points out that neither she nor her mother or brother were ever invited into Arab or Berber homes, nor was she, as a Jew, ever invited into her French friend Françoise's home. Perhaps in an allusion to Camus's ambiguous short story, "L'Hôte," the narrator questions whether one can claim as one's country a place where you are not an invited guest: "Un pays où l'on n'est jamais invitée est-ce un pays?" (99) [Is a country in which one is never invited a country?]. Unlike Daru in "L'Hôte," the narrator here acknowledges that her role as host cannot be justified. This is evident when she hands bread through the bars of her garden gate to a hungry little girl; she recognizes that she would have stolen bread if the situation were reversed, and suggests that as a member of the colonizing community, it is in fact she who has committed theft (113). Furthermore, as Fiona Barclay notes, in her descriptions of waiting for inspiration at the beginning of the text, Cixous appears "welcoming of otherness," while her use of language demands "readerly hospitality" or committed reading.[125] Cixous's text also appears as an example of one of the *scriptible* [writerly] texts theorized by Roland Barthes. The former make readers producers and act as an antidote to the treacherous simplicity of myths or *lisible* [readerly] texts, which the reader passively consumes.[126]

From her outsider perspective, the narrator can dissect colonial myths and emphasizes that she sees what the French cannot (111). As one of very few Jewish girls in her school, she highlights the effect of French education on her schoolmates, who unthinkingly perform their identities as settler girls, and who efface the colonized population in a building that resembles (or perhaps once was) a Moorish palace:

> Il n'y avait pas de femmes algériennes, pas de mauresque [*sic*], pas de palais, puisque c'était un palais-changé, dont les occupantes dites jeunes filles avec leur cortège de grandes secrétaires petites secrétaires grande Directrice grands et petits professeurs, répétaient tous les jours sans en être informées donc sans doute avec une efficacité pure de trouble et de pensée le programme initial secret: un plan d'effacement de l'être algérien. (124)

> [There were no Algerian women, not a single Moorish woman; there was no palace since it was a changed palace whose female occupiers, said to be young ladies, with their procession of big secretaries, little secretaries, big female principal, big and little teachers, practiced the initial secret program every day, without being informed about it therefore probably with a pure efficacy free from emotion and thought: a plan to erase the Algerian being.]

They are "acteurs, actrices" [actors and actresses] whose role is to propagate a concept of French Algeria that includes the "désinfection physique et mentale" (124) [physical and mental disinfection] of the colonized population. The narrator, who is herself complicit "au camouflage, au déguisement, au semblant, à la feinte, au masque" (149) [in the camouflage, the disguise, appearances, the pretense, the mask], makes a conscious effort to subvert the colonial gaze by deliberately using a broken camera in order to take pictures of her teachers and school friends that will never exist. She thereby seeks to "inexist" them: "je les inexistais. [. . .] Je les regardais du point de vue de l'absence de regard" (149) [I was inexisting them [. . .] I was watching them from the point of view of the absence of the gaze], although her plan fails when her classmates beg to see the photos.

The narrator, as a female who feels excluded from both the colonizing and colonized populations, shows melancholic tendencies and mentions suicide several times in the novel, stating: "Je regrettai que le suicide ne soit pas ma religion. En fin de journée je décidais de quitter l'Algériefrançaise faute d'Algérie" (144) [I was sorry that suicide was not my religion. At the end of the day, I decided to leave Frenchalgeria in the absence of Algeria]. Strict gender divisions in the colonial setting are also responsible for her unhappiness. This split is evident from her brother's outraged reaction when his mother gives him a woman's bicycle for his thirteenth birthday. He compares her gift to a crime, to a definitive act of amputation, and to death, as well as complaining that "les Arabes vont bien rigoler" (35) [The Arabs will have a good laugh]. Once he uses it, however, the bike comes to symbolize his effortless hypermasculinity, as it is "plus viril à la fin qu'il était féminin au commencement" (51) [more virile at the end than it was feminine at the beginning]. The narrator's movements, in contrast, are restricted. After an initial moment of freedom when she rides the bicycle, she crashes, to the amusement of the neighborhood children, and never uses it again. Instead, she retreats into the interior world of her reveries (52). The narrator's rejection of the bicycle—a symbol of Frenchness and freedom[127]—appears a means of avoiding punishment by the local children. Her refusal to ride it is therefore an unsuccessful attempt to perform "Algerian" femininity. In this light, her later decision to leave Algeria seems empowering.

In contrast, the children's mother is indifferent to the strict ways in which gender must be performed: "Toute sa vie elle n'a même pas perçu l'homme, ni le fils, ni la femme, ni la mère" (37) [Her whole life she was never even aware of man or son, woman or mother]. By remaining a widow who does not remarry, the narrator claims her mother faces "l'antiveuvisme, dont nous vîmes surgir les manifestations, une fois mon père disparu" (43) [anti-widowism, the signs of which suddenly materialized once my father died]. This particular mother comes from a line of German women who show a "discrète virilité" (91) [discreet virility] and her "manque de rouge à lèvres" (102) [lack of lipstick] invokes a lack of pretense and hypocrisy (102). In this way, the mother rejects any concept of femininity as kitsch. She also refuses to care about race and is thereby viewed as a "danger moral" (108) [moral danger], for which she is eventually punished; the postindependence administration imprison her and close down her midwifery clinic, thus she moves to France. However, in spite of Cixous's overt subversion of themes typically discussed in literature by the *pieds-noirs*, descriptions of the mother's virility, honesty, and hard work in her midwifery clinic recall the rhetoric of pioneering settlers and colonizing women's role in bringing healthcare advances to the indigenous population. In the manner of some of the Christian imagery evoked in other texts including Camus's, her mother is idealized as unblemished or "constamment vierge" (110) [ever virgin]. Moreover, a dishonest, greedy, indigenous Algerian woman, whom they call Maria or Farida, thwarts her work following independence. Maria/Farida, a cleaning woman who was invited by the mother to occupy a vacant apartment in her clinic, effectively takes over the building by denouncing other occupants, including the narrator's mother and brother, to the police. Thus, the narrator's family emerge as innocent victims of Maria/Farida's thirst for wreaking revenge on the French of Algeria. Maria/Farida's behavior seems symbolic of an ungrateful, inhospitable, and feminized country, particularly in light of the narrator's statement that both she, having left in 1955, and her mother, who leaves after independence, were aborted fetuses of Algeria (96, 16).

The narrator also exoticizes a feminized Algeria throughout the novel. Thus, she claims that the only way she was able to touch her homeland was through the family servant, Aïcha, who was her surrogate mother and wet nurse:

> c'est la seule Algérie que j'aie jamais pu toucher frotter retoucher tâter palper arquer mon dos à son mollet fourrer ma bouche entre ses seins ramper sur ses pentes épicées. Je me niche contre Aïcha. [. . .] Je la regarde enlever le voile qui la berce et la barque parmi les barques blanches et dessous c'est une femme qui est-la-femme. (90)

> [it is the only Algeria I was ever able to touch, rub, touch again, feel, palpate, arch my back against her calf, stick my lips between her breasts, crawl along her spiced slopes. I nestle into Aïcha. [. . .] I watch her take off the veil that cradles her and the vessel among all the white [sailing] vessels and underneath is the woman who is THE woman.]

The narrator discovers years later that Aïcha's real name was Messaouda and therefore realizes that her image of the woman was "une histoire" (94) [a story] or construct. Nevertheless, the above description invites Edward Said's critique of Orientalism.[128] In line with Orientalist discourse, the story equally depicts the territory as a land willing to be conquered by virile men. While the narrator cannot quite grasp Algeria, her father and brother conquer it through their car and bicycle—evoking previous generations of colonizers whose superior position on horseback was immortalized in equestrian statues—and are thus able to "prendre l'Algérie par la terre" (20) [take Algeria by the land]. Moreover, the narrator's description of her desire, aged nine, for a Moorish doll reiterates romanticized conceptions of a feminized Orient. When her father refuses to buy her the doll, it becomes a symbol of an exotic and inaccessible Algeria. It also symbolizes a colonial view of indigenous femininity that is excluded from her own identity:

> je veux tout et je veux chaque partie je veux le fin voile de visage, je veux le haïk de lin et de soie, je veux l'agrafe d'argent, je veux les anneaux des chevilles je veux le visage caché je veux les chevilles cachées je veux être l'agrafe et les anneaux je veux le saroual bouffant je veux les jambes cachées je veux être le saroual je veux l'Algérie. (135)

> [I want everything and I want every part: I want the fine face veil, I want the linen and silk haik, I want the silver hook, I want the anklets, I want the hidden

face, I want the hidden ankles, I want to be the hook and the anklets, I want the baggy harem pants, I want hidden legs, I want to be the harem pants, I want Algeria.]

The doll episode and the entire book, which begins with the narrator's attempts to recover words written about her motherland after a nighttime dream, which she cannot find in the morning, leave the reader with a sense of loss that is associated with Algeria. Indeed, the narrator's statement, "j'ai la nostalgie de ce qui n'existera jamais" (112) [I am nostalgic for something that will never exist] evokes the tactical discourse of "missed opportunities" that recurs in texts by many of the *pieds-noirs*, as discussed earlier. An episode in which the narrator's father gives a lift to two Arab men in his Citröen car shortly before his death equally underlines missed opportunities for fraternity. These men become "compagnons bibliques" [biblical companions] in the narrator's memory, as they call her father "frère" (47) [brother]. The exchange, in which the Arab men speak French and her father speaks Arabic, provides an insight into a situation in which all sides of the colonial divide might have been members of an Algerian family. Furthermore, although the narrator criticizes colonialism and acknowledges her complicity in it, her story still appears as a timeless family drama involving two innocent children, the narrator, and her brother, who suffer through no fault of their own. Indeed, her brother's assertion that "Tout préexiste [. . .] Sans ascendance ni descendance" (140) [Everything pre-exists [. . .] without ancestry or descendance] recalls the denial of a colonial past in Camus's *Le Premier Homme*. Instead of delving into the political reasons for her own and her family's eventual departure from Algeria (apart from criticisms of the French educational system's reification of "l'Algérie française"), the novel presents a narrative that Yee describes as a "doomed love story" in which the children "experience Punishment without having committed a Crime."[129] As so often, and all the more surprisingly in view of the critical eminence of the author, it is the narrator and her family, more than the underdeveloped Arabo-Berber characters such as Aïcha, who ultimately appear as victims of the colonial system. As a Jewish girl, the narrator's victimhood is complete, since, unlike her father and brother, she never possessed the land she must leave. Furthermore, while the exotic, motherly Aïcha is dead, the bitter Maria/Farida stands in for a new, independent Algeria. Thus, although the novel appears as a personal work in which the narrator concludes that writing has helped her to feel a sense of being at home in Algeria both retrospectively and presently (166), she also (whether consciously or unconsciously) constructs a positive memory of Jewish *Français d'Algérie*. Like the other stories analyzed, this novel depicts a situation born of tragedy, in which the female protagonist is a victim of circumstances. It also serves to position French Algerian men as uniquely masculine conquerors. Consequently, the next chapter will examine constructions of *pied-noir* masculinity.

NOTES

1. Valuable studies in this regard include Anne McClintock, *Imperial Leather: Race, Gender, and Sexuality in the Colonial Conquest* (New York: Routledge, 1995); Julia Clancy-Smith and Frances Gouda, eds., *Domesticating the Empire: Race, Gender, and Family Life in French and Dutch Colonialism* (Charlottesville, VA: University of Virginia Press, 1998); Ann L. Stoler, *Carnal Knowledge and Imperial Power: Race and the Intimate in Colonial Rule* (Berkeley, CA: University of California Press, 2002).

2. Useful scholarship on this subject includes Malek Alloula, *Le Harem Colonial (Images d'un sous-érotisme)* (Geneva: Slatkine, 1981); and Marnia Lazreg, *The Eloquence of Silence: Algerian Women in Question* (London: Routledge, 1994).

3. Janet R. Horne, "In Pursuit of Greater France: Visions of Empire among Musée Social Reformers, 1984–1931," in Clancy-Smith and Gouda, *Domesticating the Empire*, 21–42.

4. Patricia M. E. Lorcin, *Historicizing Colonial Nostalgia: European Women's Narratives of Algeria and Kenya 1900-Present* (Basingstoke: Palgrave Macmillan, 2012).

5. Ibid., 179.

6. Benjamin Stora, "Mémoires comparées: femmes françaises, femmes algériennes: Les écrits de femmes, la guerre d'Algérie et l'exil," in *L'Ère des décolonisations: Sélection de textes du colloque «Décolonisations comparées», Aix-en-Provence, 30 septembre–3 octobre 1993*, ed. Charles-Robert Ageron and Marc Michel (Paris: Karthala, 1995), 186. Philip Dine suggests that this term originated in Henry de Montherlant's *La Rose de Sable*, written between 1930 and 1932 and published in 1967. De la Hogue further traces usage of the term to a 1971 clinical study of the *pieds-noirs* by that title by a Dr. Guigon. Most notably, Jacques Derrida refers to his "nostalgérie" in his philosophical exploration of language and identity, *Le Monolinguisme de l'autre ou la prothèse d'origine*. See Philip Dine, *Images of the Algerian War: French Fiction and Film, 1954-1992* (Oxford: Oxford University Press, 1994), 150; Janine de la Hogue, "Les Livres comme patrie," in *Les Pieds-Noirs*, ed. Emmanuel Roblès (Paris: Philippe Lebaud, 1982), 121; Jacques Derrida, *Le Monolinguisme de l'autre ou la prothèse d'origine* (Paris: Galilée, 1996), 86.

7. Todd Shepard, *The Invention of Decolonization: The Algerian War and the Remaking of France* (Ithaca, NY: Cornell University Press, 2008), 201–2.

8. Ibid., 201.

9. Pierre Nora, *Les Français d'Algérie* (Paris: Julliard, 1961), 175.

10. Stora, "Mémoires comparées," 187, 176. Metropolitan French women were the most prolific writers during the war, during which time very few women in Algeria appear to have been writing or publishing. *Pied-noir* women, however, became the more prolific group from 1963. Of 137 women writers publishing in

French mentioned by Stora, 57 are *pieds-noirs*, 15 are Algerian Muslims, 11 are Jewish, and 54 are metropolitan French.

11. Ibid., 177–78.
12. Ibid., 172–73.
13. Glenda Riley, *Taking Land, Breaking Land: Women Colonizing the American West and Kenya, 1840-1940* (Albuquerque: University of New Mexico Press, 2003), 13. Cited in Lorcin, *Historicizing Colonial Nostalgia*, 11.
14. Francine Dessaigne, *Journal d'une mère de famille pied-noir* (Paris: France-Empire, 1972), 15. Dessaigne was born in metropolitan France, spent her childhood in Tunisia, and arrived in Algeria in 1946 with her husband. Furthermore, she noted in private correspondence to Martini in 1993, "Je ne suis pas Pied-Noir, au sens propre du terme" [I am not a *pied-noir* in the literal sense of the word]. Martini argues that this gives her an objective perspective, although the current chapter disproves this view. See Lucienne Martini, *Racines de papier: Essai sur l'expression littéraire de l'identité Pieds-Noirs* (Paris: Publisud, 1997), 255.
15. The perpetuation of this theme may be seen in a letter on the Centre de documentation historique sur l'Algérie (CDHA) [Center for historic documents on Algeria] website fifty years after Algerian independence, which states that "La recherche de compromis, ici avec les factions extrêmes de l'anticolonialisme, de l'autre côté de la mer avec les maitres [sic] d'un pouvoir autocrate, nous fait régresser dans la construction d'une histoire sereine et objective" [The search for compromise, in this case with extreme anti-colonial factions from across the water along with the masters of an autocratic power, is making us regress in our construction of a dispassionate and objective history]. See Joseph Perez, "Lettre d'Information du CDHA, Novembre 2012, numéro 19: L'édito," Centre de Documentation Historique sur l'Algérie, http://cdha.fr/sites/default/files/kcfinder/files/ Lettre%20n%C2%B019.pdf. Date accessed: March 22, 2013.
16. See Dine, *Images of the Algerian War*, 158; and Philip Dine, "The French Colonial Myth of a Pan-Mediterranean Civilization," in *Transnational Spaces and Identities in the Francophone World*, ed. Hafid Gafaiti, Patricia M. E. Lorcin, and David G. Troyansky (Lincoln, NE: University of Nebraska Press, 2009), 5.
17. See, for example, Clarisse Buono, *Pieds-noirs de père en fils* (Paris: Balland, 2004), 8.
18. Dine, *Images of the Algerian War*, 152.
19. Éric Savarèse, *L'Invention des pieds-noirs* (Paris: Séguier, 2002). See Chapter 4, 147–82.
20. Ibid. Savarèse also notes that this pioneering discourse holds the French of Algeria responsible for the benefits of colonialism but often blames the French administration for inequalities in the colonial system.
21. Dessaigne's description of the killing of Europeans in Oran by Muslims in December 1960 (10) appears in an entirely different light in a description of the repression and massacre of Muslims at this time by Algerian film director and writer Mohamed Bensalah. See Mohamed Bensalah, "11 Décembre 1960: Du devoir de mémoire au devoir d'histoire," Vinyculture, http://www.vinyculture.com/11-decembre-1960-du-devoir-de-memoire-au-devoir-dhistoire-par-mohamed-bensalah/. Date

accessed: March 26, 2013. Dessaigne also discusses the massacre of Europeans in Philippeville on August 20, 1955 (46), in what was an anti-colonial insurrection followed by repression, as described by Claire Mauss-Copeaux, *Algérie, 20 août 1955: Insurrection, Répression, Massacres* (Paris: Payot, 2011).

22. Verdès-Leroux, for example, suggests that the engagement of some of the *pieds-noirs* with or in the OAS was a result of "amour fou" [mad love]. *Pied-Noir* author Alain Vircondelet's autobiographical text, *Maman la Blanche* [Mama the White (City)], similarly positions decolonization as a result of too much love: "il fallait bien que cela finisse [. . .] nous avions vécu l'exaltation des sens avec trop d'impudeur, nous avions aimé la mer et la pierre chaude avec trop d'effronterie, il fallait partir" (84, 127) [it had to end [. . .] we had experienced the exaltation of our senses with too much indecency, we had loved the sea and the hot stone with too much effrontery, we had to leave]. See Jeannine Verdès-Leroux, *Les Français d'Algérie de 1830 à aujourd'hui* (Paris: Fayard, 2001), 344; and Alain Vircondelet, *Maman la Blanche* (Paris: Albin Michel, 1981), 127).

23. Minister André Malraux was the target of the OAS at the time. For more on Delphine Renard's story, see her memoir, *Tu Choisiras la vie* (Paris: Grasset, 2013).

24. Renard's suffering is also minimized compared to that of *pied-noir* girls in Anne Loesch's *La Valise et le cercueil* (Paris: Plon, 1963), 195.

25. Savarèse, *L'Invention des pieds-noirs*, 126.

26. Ibid., 125.

27. Desssaigne's use of the verb "nettoyer" [to clean] appears as an emotive evocation of a type of ethnic cleansing. This choice of verb is striking since Kristin Ross has pointed out that as France began to lose its empire, the colonies were increasingly presented as dirty and backward, while efforts were made to ensure that France was the antithesis of this—clean and modern with homes looked after by efficient housewives. See Kristin Ross, *Fast Cars, Clean Bodies: Decolonization and the Reordering of French Culture* (Cambridge, MA: MIT Press, 1999), Chapter 2, 71–122.

28. Blanchard and Lemaire estimate the number of dead at between 6,000 and 8,000 as a result of the suppression of riots at Sétif and elsewhere at this time. See Pascal Blanchard and Sandrine Lemaire, *Culture impériale: Les colonies au coeur de la République, 1931-1961* (Paris: Autrement, 2004), 22.

29. Judith Butler, *Gender Trouble: Feminism and the Subversion of Identity* (London: Routledge, 1999), 178. Here, Butler specifically refers to the narrative of gender norms, which is perpetuated through performance, although such norms are "cultural fictions" in reality.

30. Micheline Susini, *De Soleil et de larmes* (Paris: Robert Laffont, 1982), 208.

31. Loesch, *La Valise et le cercueil*, 11.

32. Benedict Anderson, *Imagined Communities: Reflections on the Origin and Spread of Nationalism* (London: Verso, 1991).

33. Dine, *Images of the Algerian War*, 149.

34. The theme of France as a *marâtre* who abandoned her children surfaces regularly in interviews, according to Verdès-Leroux in her *Les Français d'Algérie*, 377.

35. The author republished the novel for the thirtieth anniversary of the end of the Algerian War as *À l'heure de notre mort* [At the hour of our death—from the last lines of a Catholic prayer, the Hail Mary]. According to Elbe, cited by Martini, the slight change in title was a printing error. Martini notes that among the differences between both editions of the novel are less emotive images and blurbs on the front and back covers of the later edition, along with the suppression of some of the more "violent" descriptions of Arabs (e.g., "cons de fells" [bloody bandits] is replaced by "FLN"). She also notes the addition of some more references to the distant past of colonization, all of which, in Martini's view, lends a more serene tone to the novel. See Martini, *Racines de papier*, Chapter 2, 227–52.

36. Marie Elbe, *À l'heure de notre mort* (Paris: Albin Michel, 1992). Back cover.

37. Martini, *Racines de papier*, 229.

38. Elbe's references to Roman ruins, the arrival of the settlers in Algeria as Republicans in 1848 and patriots from Alsace in 1879, or later as victims of phylloxera-infected vineyards, as well as references to their pioneering instincts in Affreville and their blood sacrifice for France in both World Wars, stand out as some examples of the reiteration of familiar myths (38, 31, 36–37, 30).

39. Martini, *Racines de papier*, 232–33.

40. Jeanne, the most actively engaged female character in *À l'heure de notre mort*, states she acts as the agonies of her friend Gripfix: "m'importaient davantage que les synthèses politiques" (280) [mattered more to me than political reasoning], while Anne's motivation in *La Valise et le cercueil* is to help Jean. By comparing her role to that of Madelon (78), Anne further emphasizes her role as helpmate. Charles Rearick notes that the character of Madelon became famous due to a song that "celebrated woman in a traditional servant role." See Charles Rearick, "Madelon and the Men—In War and Memory," *French Historical Studies* 17, no. 4 (Autumn 1992): 1016.

41. Benjamin Stora, "Women's Writing between Two Algerian Wars," *Research in African Literatures* 30, no. 3 (Autumn 1999): 84.

42. James W. Pennebaker and Janel D. Seagal, "Forming a Story: The Health Benefits of Narrative," *Journal of Clinical Psychology* 55, no. 10 (1999): 1243. The authors note that the positive effects of writing about emotions "are not related to the presumed audience," 1246.

43. Ibid., 1249.

44. See Andrea L. Smith, *Colonial Memory and Postcolonial Europe: Maltese Settlers in Algeria and France* (Bloomington, IN: Indiana University Press, 2006), 157–58; and Anne Roche, "La perte et la parole: témoignages oraux de pieds-noirs," in *La Guerre d'Algérie et les Français*, ed. Jean-Pierre Rioux (Paris: Fayard, 1990), 526–37. Smith notes that, conversely, men recited details from the war in an apparently emotionless fashion, which suggested to the author that they were trying to avoid personal memories of it.

45. Moya Lloyd, "Performativity, Parody, Politics," in *Performativity & Belonging*, ed. Vikki Bell (London: Sage, 1999), 204.

46. Judith Butler, *Trouble dans le genre (Gender Trouble): Le féminisme et la subversion de l'identité*, trans. Cynthia Kraus (Paris: La Découverte, 2005), 17.

47. Shepard notes that a broadcast by metropolitan radio station Europe 1 suggested that "one thousand [European] men, but only men" were visible on the streets of Bab-el-Oued the day after the March 19, 1962, signing of the Evian Accords that officially ended the war. However, counter-representations of the subsequent Bab-el-Oued siege alluded to here (March 23–29), in which French soldiers sought to eradicate the OAS, reference femininity and youth. For example, Dessaigne's 1962 account of this siege is rich in descriptions of women and children, some of whom die in the gunfire, and who are left behind when the majority of men are taken for questioning by the French army. See Todd Shepard, "Pieds-Noirs, Bêtes Noires: Anti-'European of Algeria' Racism and the Close of the French Empire," in *Algeria & France 1800-2000: Identity, Memory, Nostalgia*, ed. Patricia M.E. Lorcin (New York: Syracuse University Press, 2006), 154; and Dessaigne, *Journal d'une mère de famille pied-noir*, 172–77.

48. Judith Butler, *Bodies That Matter: On the Discursive Limits of "Sex"* (New York: Routledge, 1993), 231. Butler's emphasis.

49. Stephanie Brown, "On Kitsch, Nostalgia, and Nineties Femininity," *Popular Culture Association in the South* 22, no. 3 (April 2000): 43–45.

50. Ibid., 44–45.

51. Ibid., 50.

52. Ibid.

53. Anne-Marie Fortier, "Re-Membering Places and the Performance of Belonging(s)," in Bell, *Performativity & Belonging*, 58.

54. Ibid., 57.

55. Martini, *Racines de papier*, 234.

56. Yacef produced the film and plays himself under the name "Djafar."

57. Ross, *Fast Cars, Clean Bodies*, 124–25.

58. Marie Cardinal, *Les Pieds-Noirs* (Paris: Belfond, 1988), 31.

59. Brown, "On Kitsch, Nostalgia, and Nineties Femininity," 43.

60. Gilles Perez, *Les Pieds-Noirs, histoires d'une blessure* (France: France 3, 2006).

61. Marie Gil, *De l'autre côté de la mer . . . Oran et l'Oranie* (Empury: Association Réalités du Morvan, 2001), 85.

62. Danielle Michel-Chich, *Déracinés: les pieds-noirs aujourd'hui* (Paris: Plume, 1990), 64.

63. Stora, "Mémoires comparées," 182.

64. Assia Djebar, *Femmes d'Alger dans leur appartement* (Paris: Albin Michel, 2002), 226.

65. Stora, "Mémoires comparées," 184, 183.

66. Pontecorvo released his 1966 film three years after the publication of Loesch's book in 1963 but Frantz Fanon's *L'An V de la révolution algérienne* (1959) inspired his production.

67. Susini perhaps erroneously uses the Arabic phrase *Inch'Allah*, meaning God willing.

68. Maurice Benassayag, "Familles, je vous aime," in Roblès, *Les Pieds-Noirs*, 172. See also Irène Karsenty's guide to *pied-noir* cooking in the same volume,

"C'était quoi, déjà, les oubliés?," 140–50. The Muslim, Jewish, and Christian communities of colonial Algeria again appear as a family here, as Karsenty suggests, 146, that during the various religious holidays, each community would offer cakes or sweets to their neighbors, who would return the favor, a custom she calls "L'assiette des trois religions" [The three-religion dish].

69. Susan Weiner, "Two Modernities: from Elle to Mademoiselle. Women's Magazines in Postwar France," *Contemporary European History* 8, no. 3 (November 1999): 396–97.

70. Ibid., 396, 402.

71. Ross, *Fast Cars, Clean Bodies*, 89.

72. See, for example, Marie-Thérèse Letablier, "Fertility and Family Policies in France," *Journal of Population and Social Security* 1, no. 1 (2003): 242–58.

73. Lorcin, *Historicizing Colonial Nostalgia*, 81.

74. Ibid., 67–68, 78.

75. Ibid., 81.

76. Albert Camus, *Le Premier Homme* (Paris: Gallimard, 1994), 199.

77. The politically loaded term "fraternization" implies the support of the colonized population for French Algeria and is especially associated with the participation of indigenous men and women in the events of May 1958. This includes celebrations at de Gaulle's return to power and the public unveiling of Muslim women to the cries of "Vive l'Algérie française" [Long live French Algeria], as described by Fanon in *L'An V de la révolution algérienne* (Paris: La Découverte, 2001), 46. The Muslim women described above thus appear loyal to the colony, despite their sons' fight for freedom.

78. This scene echoes Marie Cardinal's psychosomatic bleeding in *Les Mots pour le dire* (1975).

79. Benassayag, "Familles, je vous aime," 163, 168.

80. Cited by Michel-Chich, *Déracinés*, 64.

81. Perez, *Les Pieds-Noirs*.

82. Cardinal, *Les Pieds-Noirs*, 20.

83. A review by Lynda W. Schmidt, for example, comments on the book by "Frenchwoman Marie Cardinal." See Lynda W. Schmidt, "Review: The Words to Say It by Marie Cardinal," *The San Francisco Jung Institute Library Journal* 4, no. 4 (Summer 1984): 55.

84. Of the early texts studied here, only Elbe's is still in print.

85. As Alison Rice notes, the novel is not entirely faithful to real-life events. Cardinal's actual therapy was more concerned with her mother's physical abuse while the text focuses on her mother's attempt to abort her, suggesting that the author "is aware that remaining entirely faithful to lived experience does not necessarily make for compelling works of literature." See Alison Rice, *Polygraphies: Francophone Women Writing Algeria* (Charlottesville, VA: University of Virginia Press, 2012), 80. In his introduction to a 1993 edition, Phil Powrie also comments on the ambiguous status of the novel, noting that it was clearly marked "roman" [novel] on the cover page of the original edition, although not on later publications, while the back cover of the original and subsequent editions refer to "un cas vécu" [a lived

event]. See Marie Cardinal, *Les Mots pour le dire* (London: Bristol Classical Press, 1993), xx.

86. See Frantz Fanon, *Les Damnés de la terre* (Paris: Gallimard, 1991) and Bernard Sigg, *Le Silence et la honte: Névroses de la guerre d'Algérie* (Paris: Messidor, 1989).

87. Cardinal, *Les Mots pour le dire*, 80.

88. Vikki Bell, "Mimesis as Cultural Survival: Judith Butler and Anti-Semitism," in Bell, *Performativity and Belonging*, 138. Bell's emphasis.

89. Vikki Bell, "On Speech, Race and Melancholia: An Interview with Judith Butler," in Bell, *Performativity & Belonging*, 170.

90. Micheline in *De Soleil et de larmes* offers an extreme example of such grief as she mentions she tried to commit suicide when she thought that Jean-Jacques did not love her and also alludes to a suicide pact she made with Jean-Jacques toward the end of the war (235, 256).

91. Savarèse, *L'Invention des pieds-noirs*. See Chapter 5, 183–226. The French used the pejorative term *fellagha* to describe those fighting for Algerian independence.

92. The narrator's reference to thirty-seven years of submission ("soumission") recalls the 1960 petition signed by 121 intellectuals in France on the "droit à l'insoumission" [right to insubordination] of those supporting Algerian independence.

93. Marie Cardinal, *The Words to Say It*, trans. Pat Goodheart (London: Picador, 1984), 217–18.

94. Cardinal was born in 1929, which suggests her bleeding began around 1956.

95. Patricia M.E. Lorcin, "Teaching Women and Gender in France d'Outre-Mer: Problems and Strategies," *French Historical Studies* 27, no. 2 (Spring 2004): 303.

96. Cardinal, *Les Pieds-Noirs*, 80.

97. In an interview, Rouan states that when working on the script, she talked "non-stop" to her co-screenwriter Philippe LeGuay about her French Algerian family and education. She also notes that she left Algeria aged four but based her story on "a general impression" and some "very precise sensations" of her birth country. See Liza Béar, "Brigitte Rouan," *Bomb Magazine*, January 1, 1992, https://bombmagazine.org/articles/brigitte-rouan/. Date accessed: July 9, 2019.

98. Dominique Licops praises Roüan's "feminist, postcolonial" stance, while Carolyn Durham views the film as subversive of colonial discourse. See Dominique Licops, "Re-scripting History and Fairy Tales in Brigitte Roüan's 'Outremer,'" *Women's Studies Quarterly* 30, no. 1 (Spring/Summer 2002): 103 and Carolyn A. Durham, "Strategies of subversion in colonial nostalgia film: militarism and marriage in Brigitte Roüan's *Outremer*," *Studies in French Cinema* 1, no. 2 (2001): 89–97.

99. Alison Murray, "Review: Women, Nostalgia, Memory: 'Chocolat,' 'Outremer,' and 'Indochine,'" *Research in African Literatures* 33, no. 2 (Summer 2002): 235.

100. Vikki Bell, "Performativity and Belonging: An Introduction," in Bell, *Performativity and Belonging*, 6–7. Bell points out that Butler's theories of performativity encompass the visual as well as the textual context.

101. Bell, "On Speech, Race and Melancholia," 168.

102. Laura Mulvey, *Visual and Other Pleasures* (London: Macmillan, 1993). See in particular chapter 3, 14–26.

103. Brigitte Roüan, *Outremer* (France: Paradise Productions, 1990).

104. Murray, "Review: Women, Nostalgia, Memory," 237.

105. Naomi Greene, *Landscapes of Loss: The National Past in Postwar French Cinema* (Princeton, NJ: Princeton University Press, 1999), 146.

106. Liza Béar, "Brigitte Rouan."

107. Ferhat Abbas initially favored assimilation of the indigenous population but later called for self-determination.

108. For more on this, see Greene, *Landscapes of Loss*, 147.

109. Murray, "Review: Women, Nostalgia, Memory," 239.

110. Brigitte Roüan, "Overseas" (France: Aries Film Release, 1992).

111. Liza Béar, "Brigitte Rouan."

112. The opera tells the story of Orfeo who descends to the underworld to reclaim his dead wife, who eventually returns to the upper world with him thanks to the power of love.

113. *Press Notes, Overseas: Interviews with Brigitte Roüan* (New York: Dennis Davidson, 1991), 3. Cited in Licops, "Re-scripting History and Fairy Tales," 104.

114. See, for example, Ann Rosalind Jones, "Writing the Body: Toward an Understanding of 'L'Écriture Feminine,'" *Feminist Studies* 7, no. 2 (Summer 1981): 247–63.

115. Lynn Penrod, "Algeriance, Exile, and Hélène Cixous 1," *College Literature* 30, no. 1 (Winter 2003): 137.

116. Rice explains that Derrida identifies Cixous's neologism, "rêvexiste" [dream-real], which highlights the significance of reveries, as a crucial aspect of her writing. See Rice, *Polygraphies*, 78.

117. Edward Baring, "Liberalism and the Algerian War: The Case of Jacques Derrida," *Critical Inquiry* 36, no. 2 (Winter 2010): 241.

118. Rice points to the first words of Rousseau's text, which make an appearance in Cixous's *Les Rêveries de la femme sauvage* (77): "Me voici donc seul sur la terre" [So here I am alone on the earth]. See Rice, *Polygraphies*, 76–77. Rice also notes, 203–4, that Leïla Sebbar, who lived near the ravine in question, wrote a collection of short stories called *Le Ravin de la femme sauvage* [Ravine of the Wild Woman] after the publication of Cixous's novel.

119. Interview with Kateb Yacine on the eve of a staging of *La Femme Sauvage* [The Wild Woman] in Paris (2003). See Gabrielle Rolin, "Kateb Yacine à pied d'oeuvre," Jeune Afrique, http://www.jeuneafrique.com/Articleimp_LIN19013kat ebervueo0_kateb-yacine-a-pie. Date accessed: May 17, 2013. According to Richard Howard, this play was performed in Paris in December 1962 and January 1963. See Kateb Yacine, *Nedjma*, trans. Richard Howard (Charlottesville: University Press of Virginia, 1991), xxiii.

120. Hélène Cixous, *Les Rêveries de la femme sauvage: Scènes primitives* (Paris: Galilée, 2000), 31.

121. Jennifer Yee, "The Colonial Outsider: 'Malgérie' in Hélène Cixous's *Les rêveries de la femme sauvage,*" *Tulsa Studies in Women's Literature* 20, no. 2 (Autumn 2001): 195.

122. David Prochaska, *Making Algeria French: Colonialism in Bône, 1870-1920* (Cambridge: Cambridge University Press, 1990), 18.

123. For Bhabha, the "interstitial passage between fixed identifications opens up the possibility of a cultural hybridity that entertains difference without an assumed or imposed hierarchy." Homi K. Bhabha, *The Location of Culture* (London: Routledge, 1994), 4.

124. The language in Cixous's novel recalls Georges Perec's neologisms such as "Algéropètes" [Algerofarts] and "Algéroclastes" [Algeroclasts] (referring to French soldiers) in his anti-war novella on the subject. Georges Perec, *Quel petit vélo à guidon chromé au fond de la cour?* (Paris: Denoël, 1966), 47, 105.

125. Fiona Barclay, "Postcolonial France? The problematisation of Frenchness through North African immigration: A literary study of metropolitan novels, 1980-2000" (unpublished PhD dissertation, University of Glasgow, 2006), 247–50.

126. Roland Barthes, *S/Z* (Paris: Seuil, 1970), 10, 14–15.

127. The symbolic importance attached to the annual Tour de France from 1903 is evident from its placement of "French geography, society, and culture" in the public eye in Algeria. See Jonathan K. Gosnell, *The Politics of Frenchness in Colonial Algeria, 1930-1954* (New York: University of Rochester Press, 2002), 95. The significance of the bicycle as a symbol of freedom is evident in Haiffa Al Mansour's film, *Wadjda* (2012), which tells the story of a young Saudi Arabian girl's wish to ride a bicycle.

128. Said argues that highly romanticized images of indigenous femininity and of their "unlimited sensuality" work to subjugate the Orient. See Edward W. Said, *Orientalism* (London: Penguin, 2003), 207.

129. Yee, "The Colonial Outsider," 190.

Chapter 3

Performing *Pied-Noir* Masculinity

3.1 INTRODUCTION: (UNDER) STUDYING *PIED-NOIR* MASCULINITY

Critics have explored some of the problematic ways in which indigenous women became symbols of colonial territories, in addition to questionable representations of indigenous masculinity. Despite persisting stereotypes of *pied-noir* masculinity, however, the subject remains underexplored. The current chapter points to ways in which discourses from the colonial era influenced subsequent conceptions of *pied-noir* masculinity. It investigates the evolving identities of the *pieds-noirs* in metropolitan France post-1962 and, in so doing, complements Todd Shepard's assertion that understandings of masculinity were crucial to France's decolonization process.[1] It also unravels some of the ways in which narratives, more broadly, can influence migrants and ways in which migrants, in turn, can actively construct myths. This study goes beyond a focus on traditional traits of masculinity—protection of dependents showing heroism and bravery, providing for dependents, potency/virility, and political dominance/decision-making—to consider ideals of Islamic and Mediterranean models of masculinity, as discussed in chapter 1.[2] In this way, it uncovers idealized traits that came to form a postindependence "pied-noir" identity. By focusing on how men represent themselves, the current chapter builds on the previous section's concentration on women's narratives, in order to achieve an enhanced understanding of ways in which the former settlers seek to influence perceptions and performances of gender, including through fictionalized narratives. By comprehensively analyzing semi-fictional representations of masculinity by the settlers, it equally uncovers heretofore hidden discourses on homosexuality.

As with Albert Camus, *pied-noir* men's representations of relationships with women, particularly with their mothers, are especially significant. References to honor—a key concept in the Mediterranean context—are equally important.³ Alison Lever argues that the presentation of honor and shame as a typical system of values in complex and diverse Mediterranean societies is in fact misleading.⁴ However, discussions of honor played a role in conceptions of masculinity from the beginning of the conquest, as did constructions of both France and French Algeria as twin inheritors of an ancient Latin/Mediterranean civilization. France's official motivation for conquering Algeria was to regain masculine—and specifically Mediterranean—honor, which it had lost when the Dey of Algiers apparently struck the French consul with his fly swatter in 1827. The nation's victory in the Algerian War later became a means of "avenging" defeat in Indochina and reestablishing control over "an overseas empire profoundly affected by the Second World War."⁵ Furthermore, honor was at stake when the *pieds-noirs* started arriving in metropolitan France toward the end of the conflict. While some government officials claimed that those arriving were holidaymakers who would eventually return to Algeria, others suggested that they were "pretending to go on summer vacation in order 'to save face.'"⁶ Thus, given the significance of honor in the colonial context and in the aftermath of the war, it is perhaps not surprising that it bears a central place in depictions of *pied-noir* masculinity. As *pied-noir* Maurice Benassayag puts it in an essay on his community, the phrases "t'y es pas un homme" [you are not a man] and "la putain de ta mère" [your mother is a whore], as the ultimate attacks on honor, are "les insultes qu'un pied-noir supporte le moins" [the insults for which a *pied-noir* has the least tolerance].⁷

Despite settler men's role in creating France's empire, colonial psychiatry suggested an inadequate performance of masculinity compared with that of metropolitan French men. During World War I, for example, a study of the Maghreb by two psychiatrists considered not only the native population as "the most thwarted beings, the closest to nature," but also some poor white settlers as "the most defective products of civilization."⁸ This study established a racial hierarchy for military service with Muslim men portrayed as being prone to "violent episodes of angry mania."⁹ It described European settlers with Italian and Spanish roots, as well as Algerian Jews, as "more prone to breakdown," while it considered soldiers of "French stock" more robust.¹⁰ Muslim men therefore appear as violently hypermasculine while non-French European settlers appear weak or effeminate, in contrast to the model of masculinity apparently displayed by the *Français de souche* (those who were French-born).

Furthermore, anthropologist Andrea L. Smith recounts stories told to her by *pied-noir* interviewees that support the view that some regarded them as a separate "African" people, as early as the 1930s.[11] This ambiguous identity came to the fore toward the end of the war, when commentators in metropolitan France depicted the settlers as "not French."[12] Indeed, Shepard points to the gendering of the *pieds-noirs* at this time as irrational, deviant, racist, and violent males "who attacked helpless women and children," such as Delphine Renard, discussed in the present book in chapter 2, and actress Brigitte Bardot, who refused OAS demands for cash.[13] New left journalists such as Philippe Hernandez contributed to this narrative, as did Pierre Nora's personal, rather than historical, analysis, *Les Français d'Algérie* (1961) [The French of Algeria].[14] Toward the end of the war, left-wing writers presented the *pieds-noirs* as "Janus-headed, divided between those obsessed with proving their masculinity and *tapettes*" [queers].[15] Myths about settler men therefore bore the reflection of previous criticisms of the indigenous population. In this way, changing discourses shifted responsibility for colonization away from metropolitan France and onto the *pieds-noirs*. However, the authorities eventually required a change of tone in order to prepare the metropolitan French population for the reality of the settlers' mass migration. At this stage, "images of 'whole' families, men with women and children, were repeatedly produced to describe the people coming to France," while repatriates were now also posited as weak or child-like members of a Holy Family or as a metropolitan French family who were coming home.[16] The *pieds-noirs* were now "Europeans" of Algeria who formed part of a combined French-European family.[17] The former "outsiders" had therefore become "insiders," but depictions of them as weak children also recall paternalistic descriptions of the colonized population. Thus, throughout France's colonial history, observers cast *pied-noir* men as hypermasculine or homosexual, sometimes in line with an opposing rhetoric on colonized men as effeminate or hypersexed. Moreover, during the decolonization process, as Kristin Ross illustrates, Frantz Fanon depicted colonizing men as lacking (and therefore not to be imitated), in opposition to colonized men who became "whole" through revolution.[18]

In contrast to official post-1962 images of a French-European family, a specifically *pied-noir* family occupies a central place in the works of many of the former settlers. However, stereotypes of violent, macho men persist among the *pied-noirs* themselves and the wider community. For example, historian James McDougall, writing in 1995, stated that violence was "a crucial, constitutive reflex common among the European population" of Algeria.[19] Similarly, European studies scholar Rosemarie Jones, also writing in 1995, described the settler community as "a world of men, based on masculine, even macho, priorities, in which the greatest insult consists in questioning another's masculinity."[20] Benassayag's 1982 essay on his compatriots stresses the considerable significance of "les valeurs «viriles»" [virile values] for male *pieds-noirs*, as well as a profound attachment to the mother, which is not broken until death.²¹ Similarly, in a 2004 publication, Maurice, an interviewee of sociologist Clarisse Buono, presents hypermasculine qualities as a central, fixed aspect of his identity as a *pied-noir*:

> La femme pied-noir était très très fière. Par contre, le pied-noir, il était macho. Moi, par exemple, bon, c'est vrai que je suis pour l'égalité, la parité. Pour moi, la femme est égale à l'homme, mais le pied-noir [. . .] c'est mon côté latin qui ressort. [. . .] Pour moi, c'est quelque chose qui peut pas me quitter. [. . .] Personnellement, [. . .] chez moi, j'aide pas ma femme. C'est pas que je veux pas, c'est que je peux pas [. . .] Alors ma femme, qui est née à Marseille [. . .], elle me dit: "De toute façon, t'es un vrai pied-noir."²²

> [The *pied-noir* woman was very, very proud. However, the *pied-noir* [man], he was macho. With me, for example, well it's true that I am for equality, parity. For me, women are equal to men but for the *pied-noir* [man] [. . .] it's my Latin side which stands out. [. . .] As far as I'm concerned, it's something I can't escape. [. . .] Personally [. . .], in my house, I don't help my wife. It's not that I don't want to; it's that I can't. [. . .] So my wife who was born in Marseille [. . .], says to me: "In any case, you're a real *pied-noir*."]

The exaggerated ideal of masculinity above is worth considering in light of David Gilmore's assertion that when males feel oppressed or as if they are "losing," they try to prove themselves by developing a hypermasculinity.²³ Academics have already considered demonstrations of hypermasculinity by Arab populations in this regard.²⁴ However, it is pertinent to consider the identity threat posed to settlers, as a minority striving to maintain dominance in the colonial context and as a minority immigrant group following Algerian independence, as an important factor in constructions of identity. Against this backdrop, the current chapter examines depictions of *pied-noir* masculinity in narratives by men that appeared particularly from the 1970s—significantly, following the lead of the women authors previously discussed. It traces a surprising postindependence shift in focus as regards themes and memories privileged by some writers of the *École d'Alger*—Jules Roy, Emmanuel Roblès, and Jean Pélégri. It also analyzes divergent constructions of masculinity in the works of Gabriel Conesa, Roblès, and Daniel Saint-Hamont. Moreover, it studies the especially neglected area of representations of and by homosexual *pieds-noirs*. An examination of works by critically acclaimed poet Jean Sénac and the noncanonical memoir of Lucien Legrand are particularly significant in this regard.

3.2 FROM *L'ALGÉRIE DE PAPA* [DAD'S ALGERIA] TO *L'ALGÉRIE DE MAMAN* [MAMA'S ALGERIA]

Jules Roy, Emmanuel Roblès, and Jean Pélégri were contemporaries of Camus whose literature formed part of the *École d'Alger* movement. As politically conscious writers, their work following Algerian independence is of particular interest with regard to developing constructions of *pied-noir* memory and identity. Roy, a former air force colonel, provides a potentially subversive point of departure according to the following description of the writer in *Le Monde*: "Militaire antimilitariste, pied-noir anti-pieds-noirs, croyant anticlérical, héros antihéroïsme" [an anti-military soldier, an anti-*pied-noir pied-noir*, an anti-clerical believer, an anti-heroism hero].[25] Roy was also known for his friendship with the Kabyle pro-independence poet Jean Amrouche, whom he described as his "frère de sang" [blood brother].[26] While Roy credits Camus with opening his eyes to colonial inequalities, he credits Amrouche with opening his heart.[27] The *pied-noir* community, however, largely rejected the writer.[28] Catherine Savage Brosman outlines Roy's outsider status noting that, from 1960, and considered a traitor by French Algerians, he became "presque un homme sans patrie" [almost a man without a homeland], a status highlighted by the title of his memoirs, *Étranger pour mes frères* (1982) [Stranger to my brothers (a line from the Book of Psalms)].[29] Furthermore, a 1994 statement by Roy discloses a political slant at variance with the indifferent outsider of Camus's famous novel *L'Étranger*: "Nous étions les étrangers, nous avions volé leurs terres. Eux étaient chez eux. Et nous vivions entre nous. Dès que la nuit était tombée, on bouclait tout. Et on tirait" [We were the outsiders; we had stolen their land. They were in their homes and we lived among ourselves. As soon as night fell, we locked away everything and we fired].[30]

Roy cemented his outsider status when he published his best-selling anti-colonial essay *La Guerre d'Algérie* [The Algerian War], published in 1960.[31] As Philip Dine notes, this text made a significant contribution toward "the shift in metropolitan attitudes away from the previous colonial orthodoxy."[32] Roy presents *La Guerre d'Algérie*, written between July and August 1960, as taking up where his friend Camus, who had died the previous January, left off. Not only is it dedicated to Camus's memory, but the author explains that with the latter's death, he feels a responsibility to return to and write about Algeria (5, 28). This is something he is confident his friend and spiritual "frère" [brother] would have done on seeing the suffering caused by the war, despite Camus's previously declared silence on the issue (217–18, 223). Significantly, however, Roy, in reference to Camus's stated preference for his mother over justice, notes that he feels closer to the indigenous population than to his own brother (218). Having witnessed the dehumanizing effects of the war on the Arabo-Berber population, he concludes that "Il ne s'agit pas de préférer sa mère à la justice. Il s'agit d'aimer sa [sic] justice autant que sa propre mère" (226) [It is not about preferring your mother to justice. It is about loving your justice as much as your mother].

In his essay, Roy draws attention to the plight of the colonized population, to their deaths by the thousand during the war, and to the French army's use of torture. He also undermines Mediterranean myths of harmonious cultural intermingling (70). Nevertheless, on closer inspection, colonization is still a family affair in this narrative. The author depicts the war as a quarrel between two lovers bound by land—France and Algeria (201). However, in the case of an eventual "Algérie algérienne" [Algerian Algeria], built by both the French Algerian and Arabo-Berber populations, France becomes a feminized "vieille tante à héritage" [wealthy aunt] who will keep her distance from her pioneering nephews (226). Consequently, the conflict again appears as part of a fraternal feud (209–10). The text equally alludes to women's sorority on both sides (202, 212). Furthermore, a feminized landscape or "womb" becomes a binding force for both the indigenous population and a settler community that is honest, generous, prone to violence, passionate, courageous, and whose actions appear as a reaction to propaganda that demonized the FLN:

> Si mes compatriotes d'Algérie ont des défauts, ils possèdent au moins cette qualité: touchés par le langage direct qu'ils aiment, ils sont capables de générosité dans la violence comme dans la bonté, exactement comme les ratons, puisque c'est du ventre de la même terre qu'ils sont sortis et c'est là qu'ils retourneront. [. . .] Si la passion les aveugle parfois comme moi, du moins connaissent-ils la passion. [. . .] Nés de l'esprit d'aventure et de révolte, ils réagissent sous l'insulte. [. . .] On leur fait sans doute peur en décrivant les gens du F.L.N. comme assoiffés de vengeance et de haine à leur égard. (225–26)

> [Although my compatriots from Algeria have flaws, they at least have this quality: affected by the direct language that they love, they are capable of generosity in violence as in kindness, exactly like the *ratons* [young rat; racist term for North Africans], because they have come from the womb of the same land and to there they will return. [. . .] Although passion may sometimes blind them, as it does me, at least they know passion. [. . .] Born from the spirit of adventure and revolt, they react to insult. [. . .] Descriptions of those in the FLN as thirsting for vengeance and full of hatred towards them undoubtedly make them fearful.]

Thus, allusions to the masculinity of the *Français d'Algérie* recall both the macho ideals of courage and virility as well as Islamic world virtues—generosity, honesty, and showing passionate emotion in the correct context. These descriptions, when considered alongside the family trope, suggest the emergence of a Camusian narrative. Yet the essay is an appeal to end the war and to negotiate with the FLN, with the author definitively choosing the side of Algerian independence. In taking this stance, Roy knew he risked rejection by his compatriots (187, 223). He further risked rejection by the wider French community in his tract that took aim at one of the French army leaders' own justificatory account of his actions during the Battle of Algiers—Jacques Massu's *La Vraie Bataille d'Alger* (1971) [The Real Battle of Algiers]. *J'accuse le général Massu* (1972) [I accuse General Massu], the title of which recalls Émile Zola's famous 1898 defense of Alfred Dreyfus, took a stance against the use of torture during the Algerian War while the subject was still very much taboo. Indeed, the topic, brought to attention in Henri Alleg's *La Question* (1958) [*The Question*], which was banned shortly after publication, did not become a matter of national debate until 2000.[33] At that stage, Louisette Ighilahriz publicized, first in the press and the following year in an autobiography, her experience of being brutalized by the French army during the conflict.[34] This prompted Massu to express remorse for his use of torture, some thirty years after Roy's treatise and one week after the writer's death in June 2000.[35] Given the author's politically engaged position, an increased emphasis on colonization as a family saga in personal texts written in the aftermath of the war is therefore surprising and appears as an attempt to gain admittance to an imagined *pied-noir* community.

Les Chevaux du soleil [Horses of the Sun] is the title under which Roy grouped six of his novels published between 1967 and 1975, as well as the title of his 1980 twelve-part television adaptation of the novels.[36] Both the novels and their screen adaptation are structured as a family saga, which encourages increasing attachment to characters—from the illiterate Antoine Bouychou who first arrives at Sidi Ferruch as a soldier in 1830 and returns as a settler, through his descendants, to the various generations of the Paris family. The narrative was not popular among many of Roy's compatriots. One of Jeannine Verdès-Leroux's interviewees summed up her community's rejection of Roy by stating that he had shown a society based on injustice.[37] Another interviewee specifically criticized *Les Chevaux du soleil*, while praising Camus's *Le Premier homme*.[38] Following a reference to Roy's *Les Chevaux du soleil* saga, Janine de la Hogue similarly suggests that the *pieds-noirs* refuse to recognize some of their compatriots as brothers because of their political tendencies.[39] Conversely, this is the book that a progressive *pied-noir* teacher in Lyon gives the narrator of Algerian writer Azouz Begag's semiautobiographical novel, *Le Gone du Chaâba* (1986) [The Kid from the Slum].[40] Yet, although Roy does allude to colonial injustices in the series, it is also a work of nostalgia. This is all the more obvious in the series he adapted for a wide-reaching television audience. First broadcast on France's oldest

TV channel, TF1, in the early 1980s, the channel La Cinquème (now France 5) rebroadcast the series in 1996.[41]

In addition to its rendering of Roy's narrative of the colonial history of Algeria from 1830 to 1962, the series is of interest for its visual appeal. While episode 4 shows a *razzia* (violent raid) by the French army that destroys a village, most of the violence committed against the colonized population, including torture, takes place off-screen. Furthermore, the series minimizes the brutal OAS shooting of one man when an FLN shooting of a group of several men immediately follows (episode twelve). The novel version offers more political context, including an insight into de Gaulle's viewpoint.[42] However, visually pleasurable scenes dominate the television series, from the bright red and navy costumes of the soldiers of the conquest to the opulence of the balls held by the honorable character General de Roailles and his wife, who feature in early episodes. The frequent framing of characters against a backdrop of sunlight further facilitates the idealization of a bygone era. Shots of the bay of Algiers in the final episodes equally reinforce this effect; its palm trees and skyscrapers give a striking sense of progress when contrasted with the barren landscape of earlier episodes.

The series is semiautobiographical in its depiction of Roy's ancestors, the Paris family, and in its evocation of Hector, nicknamed Zizi as a child, who represents Roy. The depiction of Hector/Zizi bears similarities to the prototypical *pied-noir* masculinity that, as argued in Chapter 1, Camus also constructed. Zizi's performance of this identity is effortless in his youth. Born at the end of episode seven (1901), he is, by episode nine (June 1914), a twelve-year-old who lives by the sea with his mother and her second husband, primary school teacher Henri Dematons (who, unbeknown to Zizi, is his biological father). Zizi's affinity with the Mediterranean landscape is especially evident in a scene in which he swims in a sparkling blue sea with his Muslim best friend, Hassan. A close-up lingers on the boys' bronzed bodies, as they sunbathe and talk of Zizi's love for his cousin Marguerite. In this scene, both the settler and indigenous body become objects of the gaze, which normalizes the presence of both as equally subjugated inhabitants of the country. This idyllic scene from Zizi's childhood also positions him as a hybrid character who is equally at home with the settler and indigenous communities. Yet, a later scene subsequently differentiates Hector's identity as a distinct member of the settler clan. By episode ten (1930), Zizi is now an adult—Hector— and a courageous sublieutenant in the French army. A crucifix adorns his bedroom in his family home, while his wardrobe is full of soutanes (episode ten). This imagery references Hector's past in a seminary and highlights his identification with his Catholic mother as opposed to his metropolitan French father Henri's secular teachings.

By 1956 (episode eleven), however, Hector's performance of his identity becomes problematic. He arouses the suspicion of his family by showing sympathy toward the rebels and he refuses to stay in the army during the independence struggle as he objects to the mistreatment of prisoners. His immediate family criticize this decision, as does General Griès—another relation—who accuses Hector of wishing to divorce the army. In the final episode, set in April 1961 and significantly titled "Le paradis perdu" [Paradise Lost], Hector arrives in Algeria as a journalist who now works for a left-wing French newspaper. When he tells his relatives that he has returned because he was born there, his cousin Daniel's wife, Carmen, replies that being born in Algeria does not make him a *pied-noir* but that "Il faut vivre ici" [You must reside here]. Having distanced himself from his family and the French army, Hector then refuses the invitation of a farm worker to join the revolution. This worker's nickname, "Meftah quatre" [Meftah Four], underscores Hector's family's complicity in the racist structures of colonialism.

Arguably, the most significant and visually dramatic scene of the series takes place at this point. Hector visits the Catholic cemetery, which vandals have destroyed by uprooting crucifixes and damaging tombstones. As he sets eyes on the Paris family tomb, which looters have raided, he is fatally shot several times in the back. Having provoked the disapproval of both sides in the conflict, the identity of Hector's killer remains a mystery. What is clear, however, is that, as he lies dying on his mother's grave while his hands grasp the Algerian soil, complete with flashbacks of his childhood, Hector, through his suffering, becomes a symbol of *pied-noir* identity.[43] Not only will he remain with his mother, but his death on his family's tombstone as the majority of the *pieds-noirs*, including his own family, prepare for exile, means that his body will remain in Algeria. This makes him, according to his own family's definition, an authentic *pied-noir*. Moreover, the unprovoked attack on Hector, along with the honorable ideals that provoke his departure from the army, leaves the audience with an abiding sympathy for him that effaces his culpability in the perpetuation of the colonial system, including the racist attitude he displays when his friend Hassan marries his cousin Marguerite.[44] In a later text, *Adieu ma mère, adieu mon coeur* (1996) [Farewell My Mother, Farewell My Heart], Roy explains that he based Hector's return to Algeria and visit to his family's tomb on his own experience, and that he wrote of being fatally shot there "comme pour rendre justice aux miens" [as if to do justice to my people].[45] By fantasizing about dying in his homeland, which he does again in this memoir detailing his return visit there in the 1990s (156–57), Roy appears to be striving to fulfil a tragic destiny and thereby become an accepted member of the *pied-noir* family.

An abiding grievance of many of the *pieds-noirs* is the abandonment of family tombs after 1962.[46] *Adieu ma mère, adieu mon coeur* is worth discussing in this regard, as Roy recounts risking his life to visit Algeria during its *décennie noire* [dark decade] in order to put flowers on his mother's tomb, which was raided on Algerian independence (144). As Roy stands at his mother's grave, he addresses her directly at times, reflecting on her fear of Arabs and wondering how she would view an independent Algeria in which Arab bodyguards protect him. Although he states that his mother and all settlers were wrong in their racism, he claims that their attitude was the result of a life that they lived quickly, with no time to understand their actions until it was too late (75, 125). This description bears a striking resemblance to Camusian evocations of accelerated time. Roy also idealizes his mother, insisting that, as an illegitimate child, he was her only sin (115). Moreover, he invokes his position as a "bâtard" [bastard], which grants him an affinity with the indigenous population, who are "bâtards" [bastards] in the eyes of the *pieds-noirs* (134–35). In this regard, he assures his dead mother that neither he nor Algerians are illegitimate as they are almost brothers after a century spent together, or half brothers born of the same land (116, 133). By depicting himself as a half brother to Algerians in this way, he becomes one of the land's unrecognized heirs. Moreover, independent Algeria is putrefying in this text (192). Thus, his French Algerian mother, to whom he bids farewell, embodies the real Algeria for him (141, 155). Standing at his mother's tomb, he also evokes his guilt for having chosen justice over his mother, who, unlike Camus's mother, was dead before the Algerian War had started (141). Roy's personal expression of love for family and country here, as well as his conflicting political ideals, echo an earlier statement made during an interview in 1994: "L'indépendance, j'en avais fait une affaire de coeur. Peut-être que je me suis trompé. Il faut que je réfléchisse. Je ne raisonnais pas alors. Je me suis déjà reproché le tort que j'ai fait aux miens" [I made independence an affair of the heart. Perhaps I was mistaken. I need to think about it. I was not thinking rationally at the time. I have already reproached myself for the wrong I did to my people].[47]

Although Roy broached the injustices of colonialism during the war and in subsequent texts, Hector's death on his mother's grave forever cements his devotion to both his mother and his motherland, and thus positions him as a tragic victim. Moreover, although the writer chose justice over his mother in his anti-colonial text, he indisputably confirms his personal devotion to his mother and motherland in his published description of his postindependence return to Algeria. While he still refuses to condone colonialism in this later text, he declares his love for his family and for the *pieds-noirs* (173). A similar postindependence move toward the mother is evident in the writing of another politically engaged writer, Emmanuel Roblès.

Seth Graebner has usefully documented Roblès's close relations with the indigenous population from the 1930s and his status as the first, or perhaps only, European writer in Algeria to have a fully developed indigenous protagonist, Smail ben Lakhdar of *Les Hauteurs de la ville* [The Heights of the City], which was first published in serial form in 1947.[48] Graebner further argues that Roblès's writing is uniquely productive as he constructs a Mediterranean identity which had origins in Arab Andalusia rather than in a universalist France, thus facilitating (at least temporarily, in literature) the creation of an inclusive, united identity for both the colonized and colonizing populations.[49] An examination of Roblès's fictionalized novel on childhood, *Saison violente* (1974) [Violent Season], which focuses on the summer of 1927, reveals that the narrator certainly shows solidarity with the indigenous population and the narrative draws attention to anti-Semitism. Yet the narrator shares his nostalgia for "quelque chose qui n'existait pas" [something that did not exist].[50] Whereas Graebner argues that Roblès's nostalgia is productively reflective in the novel, it reveals a problematic focus on a French Algerian model of identity that the narrator associates with the settler mother. It is worth mentioning at this point that Roblès himself juxtaposed a type of nostalgia for their youth that he and his literary friends experienced as immigrants to France after World War II with the acute nostalgia of the *pieds-noirs* who are now distant exiles all over the world.[51] The author wrote *Saison violente* in the context of this second form of exile.

In this narrative, the narrator's hard-working and barely literate mother, who raised him on her own when his father died three months before his birth, becomes symbolic of idealized French Algerian motherhood. As in texts by Camus, the maternal figure is inaccessible and chaste. Both mother and son find it difficult to communicate their feelings to each other and, in an echo of Jacques Cormery's distant relationship with his mother in *Le Premier Homme*, the narrator declares that they never talked freely (15). Despite the narrator's own loss of faith, the maternal figure in *Saison violente* provides a link to a Christian heritage; her cousin is a priest and she intended to be a nun before a family tragedy interrupted her studies at the convent (16). However, the narrator's and his mother's Oriental/Arab heritage due to his grandmother's Andalusian identity is also mentioned several times (37, 152, 161).[52] His mother thus appears as an example of the Oriental European femininity analyzed in chapter 2. The narrator fears he is losing this idealized figure when she suggests she may remarry: "je croyais discerner dans sa tendresse pour moi une sorte d'usure, d'érosion. Elle m'apparaissait plus lointaine, moins attentive à mon égard" (76) [I thought I discerned a sort of weakening, an erosion of her tenderness for me. She seemed more distant, less attentive toward me]. He becomes agitated when he realizes that she is not just his mother but also a woman, particularly when she begins performing her femininity by wearing lipstick, blusher, and earrings (57). Having constructed her identity as a virginal, "pure" woman who is loyal to the memory of his dead father, he must confront the reality that "ma mère était une créature différente de ce que j'imaginais" (17–18) [my mother was a different creature to what I imagined]. Not only does she fail to live up to her exalted image, but he may also have to share her with another man. Thus, the narrator realizes that his vision of his mother, who appears symbolic of French Algeria, was an illusion. Yet, by the end of the story, through his love for his friend Véronique, the narrator comes to understand his mother's femininity. He finally comprehends her wish to remarry and, in a move that implies a renewed, more mature rapport with his mother, he gives his approval for the match.

Significantly, the narrator's coming-of-age simultaneously marks a break from his father's settler history. He initially associates himself with his dead father's "passion aveugle pour la vie" (28) [blind passion for life]. Later, however, he declares: "je n'éprouvais plus le même besoin de me relier à lui [mon père] pour me sentir exister, et [. . .] je découvrais mon appartenance à la terre avec l'autonomie et la vigueur d'un arbre" (165) [I no longer felt the same need to link myself to him [my father] to feel my existence, and [. . .] I was discovering my belonging to the land with the autonomy and vigor of a tree]. A distancing from his father consequently corresponds to the formation of a unique identity and a new understanding of the Algerian land, to which he is rooted. This new identity also involves leaving childhood behind and becoming a man, which the narrator does at the end of the novel. However, his coming-of-age is associated with entry into an eternity of unhappiness and with death, possibly that of French Algeria. In what may be an allusion to Roy's *Les Chevaux du soleil*, horses symbolize his entry into manhood, revealing nostalgia for a doomed childhood kingdom of sunlight: "je savais que je devrais un jour mourir et, certaines nuits, j'entendais ce galop de chevaux qui saccageaient mon royaume de soleil" (175) [I knew that I would have to die one day and, some nights, I heard the gallop of horses which wrecked my kingdom of sun]. Once again, therefore, although the narrator of this story recognizes the unjust nature of colonialism, his *pied-noir* identity suggests a movement away from his father's settler past and an identification with his mother that cements his affinity with his motherland.

The narrator's progression in *Saison violente*, from a need to root himself in his dead father's memory to an understanding of his and his mother's separate identities but nevertheless strong bond, makes an examination of Jean Pélégri's memoir, *Les Oliviers de la justice* (1959, adapted as a film in 1962) [The Olive Trees of Justice], which focuses on his father's death in Algeria, particularly pertinent. The text is dedicated to Pélégri's father Michel and to the author's son (also Michel), which immediately evokes continuity with regard to generations of French Algerian men. On reading further, the family's attachment to the Algerian landscape is clear, beginning with the narrator's *colon* (settler) grandfather.[53] This is the type of Algeria, then, which de

Gaulle declared was over the same year that Pélégri published his memoir. The then president's pejorative evocation of the colony, "L'Algérie de papa est morte" [Dad's Algeria is dead], is known as one of the defining comments of France's Fifth Republic.[54] Pélégri's text depicts the loss of "l'Algérie de papa" using a decidedly more sympathetic tone than de Gaulle, as the narrator evokes his vine-growing father's death against the backdrop of an Algeria that, in the midst of the anti-colonial struggle, also appears to be sick. The narrator criticizes colonialism in the book, yet his father appears as a "goodwilled colonizer" who treats his workers well and amazes them with various technological inventions (such as a radio and a movie camera) that he brings home to his farm after each visit to metropolitan France (51–57).[55] Thus, his father acts as a symbol of a type of paternal, benevolent, and progressive colonialism. Indeed, according to the narrator, his father and his staff on the farm formed "une grande famille" (124) [a big family].

The author indisputably makes a sincere effort to highlight the injustices of colonialism in the above text. However, in the wake of independence, Pélégri associates the Algerian landscape less with colonial men than with the mother in his significantly titled 1989 essay, *Ma Mère, l'Algérie* [My mother, Algeria]. In his foreword, the author states that, in what may be his last work, he cannot remain neutral during this "période décisive" [decisive period] in Algeria's history—the increasing violence there during the late 1980s.[56] As with his earlier publication, *Les Oliviers de la justice*, he criticizes injustices committed by the colonial authorities, from the horrific massacre of thousands at Sétif in 1945 (69–70) to the everyday lack of education for the Arabo-Berber population (46–47, 122). Camus is noticeably absent from the French Algerian writers Pélégri lists as kindred spirits in *Ma Mère, l'Algérie*—Roy, Roblès, and Jean Sénac—as well as indigenous Algerian writers—Mohammed Dib, Kateb Yacine, Mouloud Feraoun, and Mouloud Mammeri (105, 76–77).[57] Furthermore, in what appears as an intriguingly regendered allusion to Camus's inability to choose sides, he notes that his father died speaking Arabic, "Comme s'il m'enjoignait, lui mon père, de ne pas choisir entre lui et la justice" (88) [as if he, my father, was ordering me not to choose between him and justice].

Despite Pélégri's ostensible choice of justice, however, his descriptions of writing in Arabic from right to left in order to think in the other direction and become the "other" suggest an ulterior motive:

> Celle de reconquérir, par l'écriture, un territoire et un pays dont avec les miens je me sentais injustement exclu. Une motivation qui se retrouve, en sens inverse, dans la génération des écrivains algériens précédant l'indépendance, qui, par recours au français dans toute sa magnificence récupéraient à leur manière, par l'écriture et la langue de l'autre, un territoire et des terres volés. (95–98)

[That of reconquering, through writing, a territory and a country from which, along with my people, I felt unfairly excluded. This is a motive that existed the other way around for the generation of Algerian writers prior to independence who, by resorting to French in all its splendor, reclaimed a territory of stolen lands their way, through writing and the other's language.]

Thus, the author problematically alludes to the recolonization of Algeria through language and casts the *pied-noir* and indigenous populations as equally, even cyclically, disinherited from their own land. He also draws attention to his feeling, from 1961, that "les Pieds-Noirs seraient pris pour boucs émissaires et rendus responsables de tout" (107) [the *pieds-noirs* would be used as scapegoats and blamed for everything]. The colonizers thus appear to have become the colonized and he states that he wishes to bear witness "pour ces autres frères qui risquaient d'être à leur tour les victimes du colonialisme et des humiliés de l'histoire" (109) [for these other brothers who in turn ran the risk of being the victims of colonialism and part of history's humiliated].

Moreover, Pélégri's presentation of lessons learned from a feminized Algerian landscape focuses on the *pieds-noirs* rather than on the indigenous Algerians, despite his claim that his text will serve as a mirror to the Algerian people (8). One of the lessons apparently learned from Algeria—his mother—is his masculinity, which is a characteristically hybrid identity. The writer stresses that his boyhood friends were from all backgrounds and he evokes the now familiar concept of timelessness, which effaces history, as well as idealized honor, virility, fraternity, and a passion for life:

> nous étions complices, dans un temps immobile et suspendu comme le soleil éclatant de l'été. Et le temps passait, insaisissable, uniforme, dans une communion parfaite avec l'espace de la plaine et la chaleur de l'été [. . .], nous jouions aux dames et au morpion. Avec passion. Comme si l'honneur de chacun était en jeu. Et souvent avec des injures en l'une ou l'autre langue. Après quoi [. . .] nous parlions [. . .] de sexe et de virilité, de champions cyclistes, de chevaux, des femmes toujours cachées et toujours invisibles. (15–16)

> [we were thick as thieves, in a time that stood still and was suspended like the dazzling summer sun. And time passed, elusive, unchanging, in perfect communion with the space of the plains and the summer heat [. . .], we would play checkers and tic-tac-toe with passion, as if the honor of each person was at stake. And there were often insults in either language, after which [. . .] we would talk of [. . .] sex and virility, of champion cyclists, of horses and of women, who were still hidden and still invisible.]

He also devotes the final pages of the book to criticisms of independent Algeria (discussing, for example, the subjects of corruption, censorship, and a lack of women's rights) and to allusions to missed opportunities for multiculturalism. Instead of associating Algeria with his father and, by extension, a virile race, he now personifies it as "Comme une mère" [Like a mother]—but a mother who is no longer herself (125).

Pélégri's choice of title for his later text, coupled with his switch in emphasis from associating Algeria with the father to the mother, overtly fuses archetypes of the mother and motherland. This recalls Simone de Beauvoir's discussion of the myth of the "éternel féminin" [eternal feminine], which traps women in idealized, socially constructed roles associated with, for example, nature (including the sea), motherhood, or the motherland, at the expense of the individual's experience.[58] By echoing this myth, Pélégri depicts settler men as legitimate sons of a country that, presumably, needs her sons just as much as the author claims he needs her (125). In this light, reorienting Camus's choice between his mother and justice as a choice between the father and justice reinforces the mother's unquestioned place of belonging. Moreover, as the offspring of Algeria, the presence of the settlers in other countries, including particularly France, which in this narrative is an inferior "marâtre, une mère dénaturée" [stepmother, an unnatural mother] (70), becomes abnormal. It is also worth noting that Verdès-Leroux cites Pélégri's *Ma Mère, l'Algérie* in addition to works by Camus and Gabriel Conesa—all of whom emphasize the mother—to show what life was like for the *pieds-noirs*, thereby revealing the significance of these writers in constructing a collective memory.[59] Furthermore, although the authors/narrators of the above works by Roy, Roblès, and Pélégri' focus on Algeria as mother, they remember *l'Algérie de papa* fondly. Despite their progressive views, all three authors' post-1962 emphasis on the feminine and on the family lends authority to their stories and, despite apparent differences, aligns with Camusian constructions of a *pied-noir* identity. The next section examines constructions of masculinity after the Algerian War, many of which also bear remarkable resemblances to Camus's earlier texts.

3.3 THE MAKING AND UNMAKING OF MACHO MEN

Journalist Gabriel Conesa's memoir, *Bab-el-Oued: notre paradis perdu* (1970) [Bab-el-Oued: our paradise lost], is another conduit of collective memory. The back cover of the book underlines the author's intent to rehabilitate the settlers' time in the colony: "S'il s'adresse d'abord aux Pieds-noirs, son ambition est de toucher tout le monde et que chacun se dise: «Ces Pieds-noirs, j'aurais aimé les connaître quand ils étaient encore vivants»" [Although he addresses the *pieds-noirs* first and foremost, his ambition is to touch everyone so each person will think: "I would have liked to get to know those *pieds-noirs* when they were still alive"].[60] Self-conscious references to writers from the French Algerian tradition such as Louis Bertrand, Musette, Gabriel Audisio, and Camus position the author within a familiar literary group (101, 110, 120, 119, 7, 73).[61] In a similar manner, references to the Rue d'Isly tragedy and to a family of brothers who were the children of Bab-el-Oued (205, 37, 23) evoke a unique community formed by a shared traumatic history. The author also constructs a narrative that emphasizes distinctly different gender roles. This text is thus worth considering as one in which the author consciously strives to shape perceptions of *pied-noir* identity.

While the novel largely effaces the colonized population, it idealizes colonial Algeria and *pied-noir* masculinity.[62] The following description is especially noteworthy for its echoes of Meursault in Camus's *L'Étranger*—specifically his acts of violence, passion for leisure activities, and refusal to pause to mourn his mother's passing:

Peuple jeune, faussement sommaire, épris de distractions saines, rapide à s'enflammer et aussi à dégonfler par le rire ou le commentaire les passions d'un sang généreux parce que méditerranéen et mêlé. C'était aussi l'allure décidée de ceux qui ayant rendez-vous avec le temps ne peuvent s'arrêter pour contempler le chemin parcouru, un peu comme ces coureurs qui partis en tête ne doivent plus se retourner pour ne pas se désunir. (177)

[A young people, deceptively straightforward, with a great love of healthy pursuits, quick to become inflamed but the passions of a blood that is generous, because it is Mediterranean and mixed, are also quickly quenched through laughter or discussion. They also had the resolute pace of those who must answer to time, who cannot stop to reflect on how far they have come, a bit like those runners who start off in the lead and must not turn around so as not to lose their stride.]

The author explains the glory of being a man in this environment and underlines the virility of men as heads of families in which women, unlike men, remained chaste until marriage (84–85). Moreover, although Bab-el-Oued was a European quarter, its inhabitants feature as hybrid men born from behavior learned on both sides of the Mediterranean, with, for example, an energetic use of gesture learned from both "les Arabes" [the Arabs] and the Italians (85). Both boys and men participate in activities such as cards, soccer, dog fighting, *corridas* [bullfights], and, due to the "réactions capricieuses" [temperamental reactions] (102) of bulls in Algeria, *charlotades* (parodic, exaggerated performances of *corridas*).[63] In this way, they perform their masculinity appropriately, demonstrating pioneering sports skills, as the following description of soccer illustrates:

> Il ne suffit pas d'être robuste, rapide et courageux pour jouer au football. Il faut quelque chose de plus: une adresse diabolique, une subtilité de renard et un don qui ne s'explique pas, celui de sentir, d'agir, de s'exprimer avec ses pieds comme un danseur. (65)

> [It is not enough to be robust, fast and brave to play soccer. You need something more: a devilish dexterity, the subtlety of a fox and an inexplicable gift—to be able to feel, act and express yourself with your feet like a dancer.]

Against representations of them as perverse or violent, particularly during the siege discussed in chapter 2, the inhabitants of Bab-el-Oued emerge as a *peuple jeune* [youthful people] who engage in healthy distractions. By way of contrast, the author suggests that the *coup* of May 13, 1958, ends a French regime that could not decide if it was a boy or a girl (188)—a problem *pied-noir* men do not appear to have.

Furthermore, the maternal figure is once again a key trope. Conesa's overt association of his mother's birth and death with colonial Algeria is worth citing here:

> Ma mère et l'Algérie ne sont qu'une seule et même personne. L'une et l'autre ont commencé à vivre vers 1885. Ensemble elles ont grandi et ont servi la France; ensemble elles sont passées du néant à l'épanouissement. Aujourd'hui à quatre-vingt-quatre ans, elles retournent ensemble au néant. (9)

> [My mother and Algeria are one and the same person. Both of them began their lives around 1885. Together, they grew up and served France; together, they blossomed out of oblivion. Today at 84 years of age, they are returning to oblivion together.]

The familiar lack of communication between mother and son recurs and the narrator describes his mother's lack of tenderness. However, Conesa credits his mother (and French Algeria) with having inculcated in him his masculinity as a member of a nascent race: "C'est elle qui, sans un mot, m'a appris à préférer le courage à la mollesse, la lutte à la discussion, la pudeur virile aux effusions, toutes ces vertus indispensables aux peuples à peine esquissés, aux races encore contestées" (14) [She is the one who wordlessly taught me to favor courage over weakness, struggle over discussion, virile reserve over demonstrations of emotion—all those virtues that were indispensable to an emergent people, to races that were still contested].

References to Conesa's mother do not immediately evoke traits associated with femininity, which is almost entirely absent from Conesa's representation of Bab-el-Oued. There is no description of his wife (despite a brief reference to his wedding and the birth of his son) and he states that cafés were meeting places for men, which "les femmes ne pénétraient qu'accompagnées" (156) [women only entered if accompanied]. Indeed, paradoxically, although Algeria is associated with his mother, he decides that when it comes to Bab-el-Oued, "en dépit de son étymologie qui le voudrait du féminin, je n'ai pu jamais en parler qu'au masculin" (221) [despite its etymology which would make it feminine, I could only ever talk about it in the masculine].[64] Nevertheless, women from the colonized population feature in this memoir. As suggested regarding Camus's works, such women appear more as symbols of a feminized colonial "other," although in Conesa's narrative they happily consent to a union with the colonizer as "les putains de la Casbah" (63) [whores of the Casbah]. The narrator of the latter work describes the prostitutes' habit of chatting among themselves between clients, thereby creating "une ambiance détendue, familière et presque familiale" (64) [a relaxed, familiar and almost familial atmosphere]. In this way, the text effaces the exploitation and subjugation of these women, although military imagery evokes the men's "conquest" in this regard:

> Beaucoup d'entre nous ont fait là [dans les maisons closes] [. . .] leurs premières armes, grâce à cette prostitution bon enfant et qui osait dire son nom. D'ailleurs, à leur manière les maisons étaient un des lieux où soufflait l'esprit. Les jeunes gens y allaient en bande, avec la ferme intention de rire, et en repartaient rarement déçus. (65)

> [It is there [in brothels] [. . .] that many of us earned their first stripes, thanks to that good-natured prostitution which was not taboo. Moreover, in their own way, these establishments were one of the places where you found spirit. Young people used to go to them in groups, fully resolved to have a laugh, and they rarely left disappointed.]

Regarding the naturalization of indigenous women's role in prostitution, the observations of Emmanuel Sivan, in his study of popular culture among the settlers from 1890 to 1920, are worth noting:

> The Casbah was made into a *quartier réservé* [red-light district] for the commercial and hygienic convenience of the Europeans [. . .] girls were driven into this profession [. . .] by the impoverishment resulting from *l'oeuvre colonisatrice* [the colonizing mission].[65]

In Conesa's text, however, colonized women willingly occupy brothels while colonizing women raise children at a simpler time when, in the author's nostalgic (re)construction of events, they did not even dream of demanding equal rights (85). Colonial Algeria consequently emerges as a place where people, including the colonized population, knew their roles. Contrary to suggestions, discussed in chapter 2, that settler society lacked a feminine presence, women's few appearances indicate Conesa's view that they are simply occupying their rightful place.

The author's evocation of a postindependence identity stands in stark opposition to a straightforward way of life in Algeria. Suffering now intertwines with this naturally joyous population's identity:

> Il y a quelques années, nous ne connaissions même pas cette expression [pied-noir] et si on nous avait dit que nous étions des Pieds-Noirs, nous aurions haussé les épaules et songé aux Indiens d'Amérique du Nord. Mais au fil des années de désespérance, elle s'est, en s'imprégnant de larmes et de sang, chargée de signification. Au fur et à mesure que nous gravissions notre chemin de croix, que les coups pleuvaient sur nos reins et nos têtes et que les calomnies et les insultes nous marquaient comme au fer rouge, nous prenions conscience de devenir quelque chose de différent, différent des autres Français et différent de nous-mêmes. (200–201)

> [A few years ago, we did not even know this expression [*pied-noir*] and if we had been told that we were *pieds-noirs*, we would have shrugged and thought of North American Indians. But over years of despair, the expression, by becoming steeped in tears and blood, became loaded with meaning. As we struggled up our Way of the Cross, as blows rained down on our backs and our heads and as we were branded with slander and insults, we became aware that we were becoming something different, different from the other French and different from ourselves.]

In addition to the Christian motif foregrounded here, suffering appears to result from fratricide, a divorce from France (189–90), and thwarted love (190). The author positions the *pieds-noirs* as children who are very different from their metropolitan French brothers, as a separated mother and father has raised each group (78). Conesa infuses masculinity with extra significance for the colonizing brothers of this feuding family, as he describes his gender as both a mark of distinction and a straitjacket "[qui] pèse sur tous les actes, les pensées et les moments de la vie" (84–85) [which weighs on all acts, thoughts and moments in life]. He nevertheless contends that the world belongs to those who perform an exaggerated masculinity or who "brandissent leur orgueil de mâle comme un drapeau" (121) [brandish their male pride like a flag]. On publishing this memoir eight years after Algerian independence, the author consequently appears to wave the flag for French Algerian masculinity, which he can idealize thanks to the "death" of the colony.[66]

Other postindependence (re)constructions of *pied-noir* masculinity are similarly Camusian and Roblès's *Saison violente* is worth briefly returning to as another example in this regard. The narrator's preoccupation with honor and revenge, including through supernatural means learned from his Andalusian grandmother, situates him within an Arabo-Mediterranean world (23–24, 149–50). Here, we are told, "la séparation des sexes s'opérait tôt" (53) [the separation of the sexes took place early], as part of an Iberian tradition that prevented boys and girls from mixing (100). Furthermore, the Spanish-dominated city of his birth, Oran, is the preserve of men at night, as women are rarely seen out but are present in love songs and therefore remain "invisibles-mais-présentes" (116) [invisible but present]. As with Conesa's text therefore, women and men appear to have had clearly defined roles, while descriptions of the narrator's and his childhood friends' efforts to catch a glimpse of the prostitutes of "les rues chaudes" [the red-light district] (68) underline their attempts, from a young age, to perform as macho men for whom women are objectified. There are also familiar references to his and his friends' sporting prowess as they play soccer and practice wrestling, boxing, jujitsu, and weightlifting (79–80, 132).

Of particular interest here is that a Frenchwoman, Madame Quinson, rejects the narrator as being only half-French, attempts to civilize his manners, and advises him to Frenchify his surname (93–94, 111). The narrator describes this rejection in Camusian terms as exile from the kingdom: "«cinquante-pour-cent» m'atteignait au vif tant, à mes yeux, cette expression marquait la volonté de me laisser à la porte, de m'empêcher d'entrer dans le royaume" (111) ["fifty per cent" hurt me to the core, so much did this expression, in my eyes, signal the will to leave me at the door, to prevent me from entering the [French] kingdom]. For Graebner, this failure to recognize the narrator as fully French is especially productive as "Emmanuel finds himself in a position analogous to that of a French-educated Arab or Amazigh faced with the impossible demand to assimilate."[67] Yet, unlike most indigenous Algerians, he is a French citizen and has the opportunity of receiving an education, which enables him to claim an affinity with French culture and knowledge of "Louis XIV et Robespierre, Racine et Michelet, la Loire et la Beauce, Molière, Balzac, Hugo!" (112) [Louis XIV and Robespierre, Racine and Michelet, the Loire and the Beauce [region], Molière, Balzac, Hugo]. Indeed, the narrative dwells on Christian and Jewish French Algerians, rather than the Arabo-Berber populations. In this way, the narrator and his friends evoke a *pied-noir* masculinity that differs from the many texts that focus solely on settlers with a Christian background. Nevertheless, casual displays of violence associated with the weather (the story takes place in the heat of summer) echo Meursault's act of violence in *L'Étranger*. The narrator's friend Marco further embodies violent, unpredictable masculinity (55–56), which again evokes a pioneering destiny. Moreover, the narrator's entry into adulthood occurs through a violent act—police beat him and a young man repeatedly slaps him during a demonstration that aims to show solidarity with the Jewish population and protest against racism (170–71). In consequence, constructions of *pied-noir* masculinity once again invite identification with innocent suffering and unhappiness.

French Algerian author and screenwriter Daniel Saint-Hamont's *Le Macho* (1979) [The Macho Man] dates from a similar period to the works of Conesa and Roblès but appears to be a radical departure from them. This story is part of a series that recounts the adventures of a young *pied-noir* man and his family.[68] Its title suggests an ironic allusion to depictions of the *pieds-noirs* as a hypermasculine race and the text comically undermines traits typically associated with *pied-noir* masculinity. Thus, instead of the glorification of bronzed, youthful, virile Mediterranean bodies, the narrator tells us that he is a thirty-two-year-old whose youth is fading, that he has difficulty speaking to girls, and that his looks are nothing to speak of, as he has greasy skin and wishes he were tall, blonde, and blue-eyed.[69] The narrator undermines conventional narratives; instead of joyfully engaging in life's pleasures, he is an antisocial pessimist who cannot remember a single happy event in his life (65, 22). As an exile in France, he associates his former home, Algeria, not with *nostalgérie* but with stunting his development. The novel further subverts Camusian constructs as the narrator does not idealize his parents. Early in the novel, he informs the reader that he learned cowardice from his mother and mediocrity from his father (21). Like the narrator of *Saison violente*, he also comes to realize that his mother is not "la Femme des Femmes, la Sainte des Saintes" [The woman of all women, the saint of all saints], and that she is a woman as much as she is a mother (251).

Moreover, the whole novel appears as a pantomime-like performance, as the narrator addresses his audience in an attempt to draw them into the narrative and encourage them to sympathize with his frequently outrageous points of view (214, 147–48). It is also worth noting that when the doorbell interrupts a speech to his love interest Marie-France, whose name symbolically evokes her metropolitan French identity, he states: "Au théâtre, tellement c'est banal comme interruption qu'un auteur il oserait plus la mettre dans sa pièce" (269) [In the theatre, this is such a banal interruption that a writer would no longer dare to put it in a play]. By drawing attention to the fictional nature of the novel in this way and to the narrator's attempts to prove his "macho" identity, the author points to performativity. The narrator himself commits to a theatrical performance as a typical *pied-noir* son by bringing his mother his dirty laundry from Paris. When she complains, he informs the reader: "C'est une petite comédie entre nous. Si je l'y [*sic*] avais rien donné à laver, elle aurait rien dit, mais elle aurait eu de la peine" (182) [It's a little act for us both. If I had given her nothing to wash, she would have said nothing but she would have been upset]. Similarly, every time he leaves home, he participates in his mother's performance of "L'ambiance-départ" (233) [the atmosphere that accompanies leaving], which consists of codified behavior, including "le troisième acte" [the third act] in which his mother shares some moments alone with him (237). Following the tenderness that Marie-France has shown him, however, he seems willing to abandon his macho performance, at least temporarily, noting: "De temps en temps, un homme a le droit de craquer, non? Il a le droit de laisser tomber le masque!" (165) [Sometimes a man has the right to crack does he not? He has the right to let the mask drop!].

The text also comically undermines familiar representations of casual violence. When, for example, a woman on the street insults the narrator, he claims he would have hit her except he took pity on her when she told him she knew karate (81–82). Similarly, he says nothing to Marie-France when she insults his sexual performance. His failure to react conflicts with his confession that "assassiné j'étais! Sauf que la blessure elle était intérieure" (59) [I was destroyed! Except the injury was internal]. When he feels he is losing face in front of Marie-France as he converses with her friends, he describes himself as a "sanglier prêt à charger" [wild boar waiting to charge], but again takes no action (106). Instead, he ends up running away when Marie-France throws a glass ashtray at him because of his sexist comments (117–18). His problematic plan to sleep with Marie-France again "envers et contre tout" [in the face of all opposition], if necessary taking his colleague Sex Machine's advice to use force, fails as Marie-France laughs at his fumbling confessions of love and openly questions his macho status (158, 160). In addition to avoiding violence, he is afraid of being alone in his apartment after dark, as illustrated by his "tic" of checking under his bed (64). Hence, in this novel, the narrator's attempts to convince us of his hypermasculinity prove unsuccessful. His conception of idealized French Algerian masculinity, illustrated in the following quotation, therefore seems derisory: "L'homme il doit courir les djebels, il doit transpirer, se cacher, tuer des animaux pour manger, tuer des autres hommes pour le plaisir (ou pour leur prendre leur femme)" (18) [Men should roam the jebels [mountains], they should sweat, hide, kill animals for food, kill other men for pleasure (or to take their woman from them)].

Unlike many of the novels studied, conventional *pied-noir* masculinity appears in this novel as something that should not be emulated. Having left

Marie-France's guests at a fondue party horrified due to his sexism (106), the narrator later blames his upbringing for such restrictive conceptions of gender norms. Although he is not necessarily reliable, his impression that values learned in Algeria had a negative impact on his development is borne out by later discussions with his *pied-noir* friends Paulo and Simon (a similarly macho character who is also, paradoxically, gay), who are equally unlucky in love due to what they all eventually recognize as selfish behavior. Furthermore, the narrator maintains that he and all *pied-noir* men have a complicated attitude to sex, which is associated with their mothers and the colonial context:

> Nous autres, le sexe le plus compliqué du monde on a. [. . .] Pour savoir les raisons, c'est difficile. Mais je crois que tous, ou presque, on a eu une mère comme ma mère, et qu'on s'est jamais remis du traumatisme. En France, évidemment on a compris qu'on n'était pas tout à fait normaux, mais c'était trop tard [. . .] Vous mettez [. . .] cinq types [pieds-noirs] ensemble, vous leur servez l'anisette et la kémia, vous installez un magnétophone, et vous leur demandez de parler des femmes. Une heure après, sur la bande, vous entendrez un vrai catalogue de perversités. Pas de grandes perversités, bien sûr, mais des petites choses qui compliquent la vie. [. . .] Le troisième, il a jamais oublié la première femme qu'il a niquée: la petite Mauresque qui faisait le ménage à la maison, alors il enroule sa femme dans un drap pour faire comme si c'était un voile. (35–36)

> [We have the most complicated sex in the world. [. . .] It's difficult to know the reasons why. But I think that everyone, or nearly everyone, had a mother like my mother and we never got over the trauma. Obviously in France people understood that we weren't quite normal, but it was too late. [. . .] Put [. . .] five [*pied-noir*] guys together, serve them [the traditional *pied-noir*] anisette and *hors-d'oeuvres*, set up a tape recorder and ask them to talk about women. An hour later, you will hear a real catalogue of perversities on the tape. Not big perversities, of course, but little things that complicate matters. [. . .] The third guy has never forgotten the first woman he screwed: the little Moorish woman who did the housework at home, so he wraps his wife up in a sheet to pretend it's a veil.]

The narrator of *Le Macho* therefore reiterates depictions of French Algerian men as perverse or abnormal. He admits that he contemplates sexual violence against women, although he would never act on such thoughts (88). His encounters with a *pied-noir* woman, Ginette, nonetheless link sexuality to consensual violence.

It is only following a conversation with Ginette, a married mother with whom he is having an affair, that the narrator claims to understand that women and mothers are people. His sudden, comical renunciation of *machismo* at this point again underlines his performance of masculinity as a mere charade. However, a symbolic association of the domestically oriented Ginette with colonial Algeria and of the liberated Marie-France with the metropole echoes the now familiar concept that the *milieu* in which they lived and the colonized population influenced the settlers' behavior. Nonetheless, as discussed in the previous chapter, women in metropolitan France during the period in question were also associated with domesticity and legally subject to their husbands' authority.[70] Consequently, the narrator's suggestion that Ginette's submissive role differentiates her from French women may not be accurate but it naturalizes the subjugation of the colonized population, a subject that, significantly, the novel fails to address.

The narrator's projection of a hypermasculine identity onto his work colleague, Sex Machine, whose country of origin he does not bother to determine, believing him to be from "la Martinique ou La Réunion" (144) [Martinique or Reunion], is equally problematic. His descriptions of Sex Machine echo racist descriptions of the "puissance sexuelle" [sexual power] of Black men in colonialist rhetoric.[71] He further implies that Sex Machine is morally lacking by alluding to his supposed use of black magic (142). The author may seek to undermine the narrator's views here, just as he undermines the narrator's sexist views on gender roles throughout the novel. Yet Sex Machine's performance of masculinity appears to confirm such stereotypes, as he boasts of having slept with at least a thousand women and says he hits them if they give him trouble (144–45). Thus, despite an apparent subversion of stereotypes of *pied-noir* masculinity, this narrative once again differentiates *pied-noir* identity from that of colonized populations, although it paradoxically aligns with them in the case of femininity.

Furthermore, while the novel effaces the situation of the colonized population, the settler community appears in a sympathetic light in one of the narrator's few references to Algeria's violent past, involving a childhood memory of a bomb exploding in the cinema during a screening of *Moby-Dick* (185). This shocking memory is followed by the evocation of a uniquely *pied-noir* experience of time(lessness), which once again obviates the need to discuss colonial violence, for which, judging by his performance of masculinity, the narrator is not guilty: "J'ai l'impression que tous les gens de chez nous, en leur enlevant la Terre, on leur a aussi enlevé le Temps, et que leur horloge intérieure ne s'est jamais vraiment réparée" (185–86) [I think that for people from home, by taking their Land from them, Time was also taken from them and their inner clock never really recovered]. His personal repression of trauma also appears as a national repression, as inferred by Marie-France's disinterest in his life in Algeria (101). Marie-France's one reference to the

Algerian War additionally signals generalized prejudice against the *piedsnoirs*; it draws on negative images of exploitative *colons* whose main aim is to "faire suer le burnous" [slave-drive the indigenous population]: "De toute manière, les Algériens sont beaucoup plus heureux aujourd'hui. Vous les avez trop fait souffrir" (100–101) [In any case, the Algerians are a lot happier today. You made them suffer too much]. Despite this type of prejudice, the narrator is desperate to win (Marie-) France's approval and to fit in, or as he puts it, evoking the type of humor later used by Bruce Feirstein in his satirical analysis of masculinity, *Real Men Don't Eat Quiche* (1982): "autour d'une fondue, je passerai inaperçu" (273) [I will go unnoticed around a fondue].

Through his efforts to navigate life in France, the narrator of *Le Macho* emerges as a picaresque character, following in the footsteps of Musette's extremely popular French Algerian rogue Cagayous, the hero of a series of tales originally published between 1891 and 1920. As suggested by William Granara, picaresque characters equally played a significant role in Arab fiction, from the classical Arabic *maqama*, which had overlaps with the picaresque novel and reemerged in the nineteenth century before writers gave it a modern reworking from the 1930s.[72] Granara notes that picaresque characters, including the character Si Mokhtar in Kateb Yacine's *Nedjma* (1956) provided "an appropriate literary landscape for Arab nationalism(s) on the rise," as the "picaresque ethos encapsulates the political and psychological displacement of the modern North African."[73] Moreover, the picaresque genre increased in popularity during the 1960s, with one critic identifying characters in novels by Camus as "picaresque saints."[74] In the case of *Le Macho*, the narrator, as in most of the texts studied so far, is a marginalized character from a humble background. He also comments satirically on society in a fictional story using an autobiographical format.[75] Furthermore, his use of *pied-noir* slang in the novel recalls the *pataouète* dialect favored by the character Cagayous.[76] His colloquial speech patterns equally echo the type of speeded-up "French Algerian time" discussed in chapter 1. Indeed, Joëlle Hureau has commented on the rapidity of speech of the *pieds-noirs*, including using shortcuts and beginning each sentence with its most important word or phrase.[77] More importantly, however, like the picaresque hero, the narrator of *Le Macho* appears as a likeable rogue. Just as picaresque characters created by indigenous Algerian writers served to evoke the displacement of colonized populations, the narrator here evokes a particular kind of exile. As an outsider who struggles to adapt in order to perform his masculinity correctly in metropolitan France, he elicits sympathy for the *pieds-noirs*. Moreover, while this novel appears to unmake the models of idealized masculinity seen in texts by Conesa and Roblès, it still reinforces *pied-noir* difference with regard to the performance of gender.

3.4 *PIED-NOIR* PRIDE: PIONEERING SEXUALITY

Le Macho features one of the few representations so far of *pied-noir* homosexuality—the narrator's no less macho friend Simon, whose hint that the *pieds-noirs* who hate him have repressed their own homosexuality (128) echoes Butler's theorizing on repressed homosexuality as a forbidden object that leads to melancholic identities. The narrator's shock at discovering that a *pied-noir* could be gay and his comment that "L'air plus viril que lui on pouvait pas avoir!" (128) [You couldn't appear more virile than him!] together underline a desire to stress normative heterosexuality. Representations of homosexual *pied-noir* men by the former settlers are rare, although critics have suggested a latent homosexuality with regard to the protagonists of *L'Étranger* and "L'Hôte."[78] It is worth pointing out that homosexual or otherwise "deviant" indigenous characters feature in some of the works studied thus far. For example, the narrator of Cixous's *Les Rêveries de la femme sauvage* recounts an unsettling incident as a young girl with a door-to-door cheese seller she calls "Yadibonformage" [*sic*] [Yadigoodchease]. When the salesman finds her alone, he asks if she is bleeding yet and rubs his finger suggestively along his basket, telling her that this is what people in his community or "Chez lui" [where he is from] do.[79] His offer to do this to the child, which she declines, naturally confuses and upsets her, leaving her with "une tache sur la pensée" [a stain on her mind].

A transgender settler features in Roblès's *Saison violente*, as a woman who cannot have children but who later adopts an orphan with her husband (31, 177). The discovery that this "woman" actually has underdeveloped male genitalia suggests the performative nature of gender, but this character reidealizes gender norms as her quarry-worker husband is unfaithful and abuses her while she remains a devoted, faithful housewife, accomplishing "tous les devoirs d'une véritable femme" (31) [all the duties of a real woman]. There is also a brief mention of homosexuality in Elbe's *À l'heure de notre mort*, which is worth discussing here. When talking about how girls stay close to their mothers for life, some characters suggest that this is also true of gay men and invoke the example of a local fortune-teller who was happy to have a gay son: "Mme Estrella, la cartomancienne, elle avait un fils coulo, elle était bien contente.[80] Celui-là, à l'OAS, y l'avaient mis dans l'action psychologique sur les CRS" [The fortune-teller, Madame Estrella, had a queer son and she was really happy about it. In the OAS, they used him for psychological warfare against the riot police].[81] This settler character's close relationship with his mother suggests he is performing his masculinity in an acceptable manner. His sorry end—he is bled to death by the FLN and his body is thrown on a rubbish heap—also casts him as a suffering *pied-noir* outsider. Moreover, referencing the deployment of a homosexual by the OAS against the state's police force simultaneously serves to reidealize the normative heterosexual masculinity of *pied-noir* men and to cast metropolitan French men as deviant. Against the backdrop of these rare examples of nonnormative sexuality that in fact reidealize distinctive gender roles, it is useful to analyze works by two homosexual writers, starting with the French Algerian poet Jean Sénac.

Sénac's position as an anti-colonial, homosexual poet clearly demarcates him from traditional representations of the *pieds-noirs*. Thinking from outside the settler *milieu* undoubtedly influenced his writing. The poet himself envisioned his works "within the tradition of gay authors from Walt Whitman to Garcia Lorca to Jean Genet."[82] Sénac also maintained a decade-long friendship with Camus until 1958. Both came from similarly humble backgrounds and keenly felt the absence of their respective fathers. In fact, Camus acted as a paternal figure to the younger Sénac, whom the former referred to as his son.[83] However, the friendship ended due to their differing stances on the Algerian War, with Sénac choosing justice over his metaphorical parent, Camus, by claiming: "Camus a été mon père. Ayant à choisir entre mon père et la justice, j'ai choisi la justice" [Camus was my father. Faced with a choice between my father and justice, I have chosen justice].[84] The poet also differentiated himself from many of his fellow *Français d'Algérie* through his stance in favor of an independent Algeria from the early days of the Algerian War. A scathing attack on colonial society from his *Carnets* [Notebooks] dated July 7, 1954, before the onset of the conflict, gives a flavor of his position:

> L'orgueil, l'aveuglement des Européens d'ici est insensé. Il n'y a rien à attendre d'eux, rien. Il faut les placer devant le fait établi et leur donner à choisir: l'Algérie ou le départ. Je ne crois pas à une autre solution. Ils sont trop assurés de leur supériorité raciale.[85]

> [The pride, the blindness of Europeans from here is insane. You can expect nothing from them, nothing. They should be presented with the fact of the matter and given a choice: Algeria or leave. I do not think there is any other solution. They are too sure of their racial superiority.]

The writer, who had settled in France during the Algerian War, moved back to Algeria (specifically Algiers) after independence. He thus corresponds to the definition of a *pied-vert* [green-foot], defined by Éric Savarèse as a *pied-noir* who lived in Algeria post-1962.[86] In this light, his works, particularly his representations of masculinity, provide a possible counterpoint to the more conventional narratives studied.

Sénac constructed a new identity as a male outsider by openly discussing his homosexuality in his 1968 collection, *Avant-corps*.[87] This provides a valuable perspective that calls into question the heterosexual hypermasculinity upon which many narratives by the *pieds-noirs* insist. The writer had struggled with his sexual orientation. Despite his desire to lay bare his identity in his 1962 autobiographical novel *Ébauche du père*, which he envisaged as a "strip-tease," Sénac simultaneously evokes his use of "travestis" [drag] and admits to inventing "un tas de vérités" [a jumble of truths].[88] Thus, by publicly admitting his homosexuality, Katia Sainson suggests that "Sénac emerged from his own period of self-determination no longer masking his true self, no longer performing verbal drag, by producing poetry in which he shied away from acknowledging the complexities of his identity."[89] As noted in the introduction to the current book, "In imitating gender, drag implicitly reveals the imitative structure of gender itself—as well as its contingency."[90] Verbal drag (which Sénac eventually resists) therefore highlights the imitative nature of the lived and literary performance of normative heterosexual *pied-noir* hypermasculinity. Significantly, Sénac's vision of masculinity further differs from that of other settlers as it includes cultural and physical intermingling between all populations in the territory. The usual rhetoric, as quoted by Jean-Jacques Jordi in an interview, is worth referencing in contrast: "En Algérie on est tous frères mais on sera pas beaux-frères" [In Algeria we were all brothers but would never be brothers-in-law].[91]

In *Lettre à un jeune Français d'Algérie* (1956) [Letter to a young French Algerian], Sénac criticizes colonial injustices harshly and insists that settlers will have to give up their privileges.[92] He also puts forward his idea of a future independent Algeria that is fully inclusive of both the former colonizing and colonized populations: "Avant toute chose, il faut que tu saches, et cela de façon irrévocable, que si je n'ai jamais conçu l'Algérie sans eux [la population indigène], je ne peux désormais non plus la concevoir sans toi" [Firstly, you must know, without a shadow of a doubt, that although I never conceived of Algeria without them [the indigenous population], I cannot henceforth conceive of it without you either].[93] It is through this type of narrative, therefore, that he reveals what Hervé Sanson calls his intention to "performer la société métissé que les textes et déclarations du FLN reconnaissent" [perform the blended society recognized by FLN texts and declarations].[94]

The below extract from the letter reveals the poet's construction of an original variety of masculinity that includes both Arabo-Berber and French Algerian men living and working together to build a new community:

> L'Algérie se fera avec nous ou sans nous. Mais, si elle devait se faire sans nous, je sens qu'il manquerait à la pâte qui lève une mesure de son levain. [. . .] Mais si l'Algérie reste attachée à l'Orient, elle a néanmoins choisi un ensemble de

structures qui relèvent de l'Occident, et c'est pourquoi je reste persuadé que, vieux Occidentaux, cette révolution nous concerne, que nous avons un rôle à jouer dans cette nation et que nous avons, nous aussi, un certain nombre de briques à apporter à l'édifice commun. Ainsi, tout en participant à la vie de la nation, nous recevrons à notre tour un sang jeune et une vigueur réveillée. [. . .] Je crois que l'Orient et l'Occident ont besoin de se rajeunir et d'incarner ensemble une idée neuve de l'homme. L'Algérie devrait être le creuset de cette culture et de ce message pacifique.[95]

[Algeria will be formed with or without us. But, if it had to be formed without us, I feel that the rising dough would be missing a measure of its yeast. [. . .] But although Algeria remains attached to the Orient, it has nevertheless chosen a set of structures that draw from the Occident, and that is why I remain convinced that this revolution involves us, old Westerners, that we have a role to play in this nation and that we also have some bricks to bring to the communal building. Thus, by participating in the nation's life, we will in turn receive young blood and renewed vigor. [. . .] I believe that the Orient and Occident need to modernize and together embody a new concept of man. Algeria should be the melting pot for this culture and this peaceful message.]

However, the above quotation also elaborates on the pioneering tradition to evoke the construction of a new Algeria. It implies that the *Français d'Algérie* could serve to unite the Orient and Occident in an alliance that the Orient appears to have chosen. Such imagery recalls the union of East and West envisaged by the Saint Simonian movement in Algeria in the nineteenth century, although the school still based its model of association rather than assimilation on the belief that the Occident was superior.[96] Furthermore, the writer's increasing disillusionment with his country is evident in works written after the war.

Postindependence, the Algerian authorities refused citizenship to Sénac. This coincided with a new emphasis on his *gaouri* (non-Muslim or foreigner) status, which again positions him as a more familiar kind of outsider. His engagement with the concept of fraternity between the two populations, a theme he spoke about in correspondence with, among others, Roblès and Pélégri, using a shining sun as his autograph, is also familiar.[97] His preoccupation with the mother in the absence of the father, particularly in *Ébauche du père: pour en finir avec l'enfance* (completed in October 1962; published posthumously in 1989) [Sketch of the Father: To Put an End to Childhood] further aligns his works with conventional narratives by the *pieds-noirs*. Indeed, the narrator of this autobiographical novel suggests that it becomes a letter to his mother, who again relates to the French homophone "mer" [sea], which is a true home to both mother and son (36). The following extract from the novel highlights the significance of the mother (and perhaps the motherland) in Sénac's concept of a hybridized Algerian cultural identity:

> Maman, je vous aime, maman, vous étiez païenne! Que n'avez-vous pas été, sans le savoir et le sachant! Catholique, israélite, adventiste, musulmane et guèbre, adoratrice du soleil. Et parfois hindoue et libre-penseuse. Et tout cela sans le chercher, sans le savoir, du bout de l'âme, et chaque fois profondément. [. . .] La liberté, c'est vous qui me l'avez apprise![98]

> [Mama, I love you, Mama you were pagan. What were you not, without knowing it and knowing it! Catholic, Israelite, Adventist, Muslim and Guebre, sun-worshipper. And sometimes Hindu and free-thinker. And all that without seeking it, without knowing it, from the depths of your soul, and always deeply. [. . .] You are the one who taught me freedom!][99]

While this evocation of hybridity implies the potential empowerment of the indigenous population, the narrator's contention that he, as an illegitimate son, and "l'Arabe" [the Arab] are "frères de sang" [blood brothers] who occupy "bâtard" [bastard] status in society, connects him with a similar use of this trope by Jules Roy.[100] Moreover, his suggestion that his mother, who dislikes priests, returns to Catholicism following a flirtation with Adventism as the latter lacks "cérémonie" [ritual] (175) aligns her with a unique settler Christianity. An evocation of a young European's death and the lynching of an Arab boy by youths in Oran laments the "Ville maudite!" [Damned city] and "Races affrontées" [Clash of races] (156–57) while evoking sun, blood, and sand in a manner that naturalizes the violence. The novel's subtitle, which implies a search for a father figure in order to move beyond childhood, underscores the theme of a *peuple jeune*. Furthermore, the narrator states that he is reluctant to use the novel form but lacks the patience to write a poem as "J'ai trop de choses à dire" (17) [I have too many things to say]. In this, he evokes a sense of urgency that recalls the speeded-up time alluded to earlier. Surprisingly then, considering the poet's political stance before the war, many of the themes evoked in Sénac's *oeuvre* are suggestive of works by more conventional *pied-noir* writers.

Later celebrations of the beauty of Algerian youth and references to sex recall previously seen idealized, and even Orientalized, constructions of a youthful Algeria, although this time with an emphasis on homosexuality. His *Avant-corps* collection (1968), for example, evokes "Adolescents dont la seule mémoire provoque un orgasme farouche" [Adolescents, just the memory of whom provokes a fierce orgasm].[101] A quotation from "La Course" [The rush], contained within *Le Mythe du sperme-Méditerranée*

(1967) [The myth of the Mediterranean Sperm]—a title that evokes Algeria as part of a sexualized Mediterranean territory—suggests the poet's desire for sexual unions with indigenous Algerians rather than with "civilized" men:

> Tu parles de cheveux blonds, de poitrines / Civilisées. Je ne comprends / que le sexe qui vrombit à vide sur les rocs. [. . .] Et des noms: Ahmed! Mahrez! Kamel! Antar! / Oh, encule-moi! O Youcef, j'ai sucé jusqu'au Coran / Ta course. [. . .] Je ne comprends / Que le ciel et la mer accouplés, jumeaux.[102]

> [You speak of blond hair, of Civilized chests. I only understand sex that throbs emptily / aimlessly on the rocks. [. . .] And names. Ahmed! Mahrez! Kamel! Antar! Oh, bugger me! Oh Youcef, I have sucked off your rush as far as the Koran, [. . .]. I only understand the sky and the sea coupled, twins.]

The type of union alluded to here may signify a literary attempt to "perform" a type of idealized "société métissée" [blended society], to use Sanson's phrase. This said, the poet projects collective, rather than individual identities onto indigenous Algerian men while depicting physical and, with regard to Islam, verbal violence. The above descriptions of a union between sky and sea are also Camusian in tone. Moreover, Robert Aldrich notes that in Sénac's personal life, his "'tricks' were often teenagers who lacked access to women."[103] This recalls the sexual activities of nineteenth-century writers such as André Gide and Oscar Wilde in Algeria, who ignored the imbalance of power between young people and adults and between the colonized and colonizing populations. Yet in Aldrich's analysis of Sénac's representations of homosexuality, the sexual climate of colonial and early postindependence Algeria appears healthy, allowing contact between "ebullient *pieds-noirs* and sociable Arabs" compared with the "moralistic regime" of the Algerian government of the 1970s.[104] Indeed, Sénac relates his increasing disillusionment with postindependence Algeria to a decline in sexual prowess, as the following line from "Des vierges vont se donner" (1967) [Virgins are going to give of themselves], published in *Le Mythe du sperme-Méditerranée*, illustrates: "Tout est foutu—les comités de gestion, le rire, nos érections?" [Everything is fucked—the management committees, laughter, our erections?].[105] In light of such disenchantment, French Algerian journalist Jean Daniel's opinion is worth considering: "As a European and a Christian, Sénac chose to ignore that the Arabo-Muslim dimension of the Algerian independence movement was irreconcilable with Sénac's universalism."[106]

As with Camus, and perhaps because of his universal vision that never materialized, some Algerian intellectuals writing in the wake of the violent *décennie noire* have reclaimed Sénac as Algerian, precisely the identity that eluded him when he was alive.[107] As discussed above, Jean Pélégri also aligned himself with the poet in his *Ma Mère, l'Algérie*, following Sénac's death at the hands of a murderer in 1973.[108] Perhaps ironically, given Sénac's long-held political views, his contested identity, alienation, and premature, tragic death also position him alongside many of the constructions of suffering *pied-noir* masculinity already studied. Yet Sénac's open descriptions of homosexual sex, which advance concepts of hybridity, are particularly significant due to the general absence of such representations by the former settlers. This may result from the conservative context of the settlers' arrival in France, before the gay rights movement took off in the 1970s. An examination of a more recent representation of homosexuality in colonial Algeria is therefore valuable at this point.

The production of picture postcards of indigenous Algerian women by French photographers in the early 1900s illustrates the demand for sexualized or even fetishized images from the colony.[109] Descriptions of homosexuality in the colonies by writers such as Gide also illustrate the fetishization of such experiences for readers in the metropole, who could reimagine the Orient as a place of permissiveness inhabited by promiscuous natives. Lucien Legrand's 2011 *Autobiographie d'un pied noir gay* [Autobiography of a gay *pied-noir*] retrospectively, even nostalgically, appeals to constructions of North Africa as a site of licentious behavior, as the jacket blurb informs us that "Très tôt, Lucien a su qu'il était homosexel. Très tôt aussi, il a attiré les hommes et s'est donné à eux. Simplement, sans culpabilité, au hasard des rencontres et de ses désirs" [Lucien knew he was homosexual from an early age. He also attracted men and gave himself to them from a very early age. This happened simply and without a sense of guilt, through chance meetings and according to his desires].[110] This explanation immediately naturalizes homosexual encounters in colonial Algeria, but not when it comes to colonizing men, as the back cover goes on to inform us: "la société coloniale de l'après-guerre n'était pas spécialement ouverte, et le machisme régnait dans le monde pied noir. [. . .] Mais Lucien ne s'est jamais refusé le droit d'être lui-même" [colonial society in the post-war period was not particularly open, and machismo reigned in the *pied-noir* world [. . .] but Lucien never denied himself the right to be himself]. The book's promotional material thus reiterates normative *pied-noir* masculinity, despite a further reference to the text as "iconoclaste" [iconoclastic] and to its breaking with clichés (back cover).

According to Legrand, his own family and wider colonial society marginalized him from a young age. Born in 1938 in Algiers, he states that he only became legitimate when his parents married, following his father's first wife's suicide, in 1943 (10, 20). His relationship with his father was fraught as he failed to perform his masculinity in accordance with his father's expectations.

His father beat him and forced him, as a child, to fight another boy who called him a "pédé" [queer] (29–30). This difficult relationship prompted him to run away on two occasions and, according to the author, provoked a mental disorder and suicidal thoughts (33). He also describes rejection by his extended family and schoolmates in Algeria (48, 20). Despite the author's emphasis on a unique outsider status, however, some familiar tropes recur. Thus, although he claims he did not enjoy soccer, which set him apart from other boys, he describes his manner of dodging the ball (in his role as goalkeeper) as a "passe de corrida" [*corrida* pass] (25)—a technique that implies the skill associated with Mediterranean bullfighters. This still positions him within the type of normative masculinity performed by many of the *pied-noir* characters studied above. He also underlines his position as the head of his family for most of his adult life and his close relationship with the maternal figure. Legrand consequently describes his desire to protect his mother from his violent father, who forced her to have up to ten backstreet abortions (27–28, 56). The author's reverence for his mother coexists with the traditional view regarding women's place in the home. He notes, for example, that his sisters accused him of trying to "imiter le paternel" [imitate the paternal figure] as he used to order them inside when he saw them chatting to friends (39). He also criticizes a sister, who is a student with a new baby, for her failure to cook and shop for her husband (156–57). Indeed, the reader must question his claim that he is not "misogyne" [misogynistic], particularly as he continues "mais il faut reconnaître que ce sont les femmes les plus virulentes" (182) [but one must admit that it is women that are the most virulent].

Legrand's descriptions of his personality also echo the rhetoric of *pied-noir* men as audacious and passionate: "j'étais aventureux, spontané, enthousiaste, extrêmement impatient, gai, passionné, et doté d'un esprit vif—tellement vif que mes paroles allaient plus vite que mes pensées. [. . .] Je disais tout haut ce que les autres pensaient tout bas" (131) [I was adventurous, spontaneous, enthusiastic, extremely impatient, cheerful, passionate and endowed with a quick wit—so quick that my words were faster than my thoughts. [. . .] I used to say aloud what others were thinking]. His pioneering spirit in France is also implied by descriptions of his many different jobs and businesses, as he works his way up from serving as his father's painting apprentice, following military service during the Algerian War, to become joint owner of a restaurant/hotel/bar in France. Furthermore, descriptions of his many different homosexual liaisons from a young age in Algeria, but also in France and on his other travels, at a time when homosexuality was taboo, position him as a type of sexual pioneer. Interestingly, publicity for a documentary by director Sébastien Lifshitz, *Bambi* (2013), reveals a similar emphasis on settler innovation. This features a transgender settler, born Jean-Pierre Pruvot, who, having left Algeria in the 1950s, became an iconic cabaret star in Paris called

Marie-Pierre or Bambi. Bambi is justifiably described as "l'une des pionnières sur le chemin des hormones et de la chirurgie"[111] [one of the pioneers with regard to hormones and surgery] and as "une pionnière" [a pioneer] at a time when the word transsexual "n'existait même pas encore" [did not even exist yet].[112] Here again, descriptions of Bambi's journey from her small village of Les Issers in colonial Algeria to her discovery of "nouveaux territoires" [new territories], and references to her tenacity and determination, evoke the pioneering spirit of the *pieds-noirs*.[113] Furthermore, since Paris becomes the site of "une liberté énorme" [immense freedom], *pied-noir* identity again stands apart from a more liberal metropolitan French identity.[114]

Similarly, in Legrand's story, homosexuality, which the male members of his family—his father and uncle—can never accept, is particularly taboo because of his identity as a *pied-noir*. Yet, the metropolitan French also frowned upon homosexuality at the time. Sainson notes that a law voted by the National Assembly in France in July 1960 "identified homosexuality as a 'social plague' and "clamped down on those public acts described as 'being against nature with an individual of the same sex.'"[115] Although Saint-Germain-des-Prés was "a center for European gay culture" during this period, a journal called *Arcadie*, founded in 1954 with the aim of gaining acceptance for hidden homosexuality, still referred to the mistreatment of homosexuals, noting: "In the eyes of the representatives of the law too often even today, the homosexual is treated as an animal to be slaughtered."[116] Legrand himself refers to prejudice against homosexuals in France. For example, he mentions lesbian government officials who marry men as a cover (99, 205). Furthermore, he feels compelled to resign from a job in Paris in the early 1980s when colleagues discover that he is homosexual, particularly in light of publicity about AIDS at the time (189). He further experiences prejudice when he and his partner open a restaurant in Arville in the Loire Valley (202–3).

Despite encountering such prejudices in France, however, the author emphasizes the particular difficulties of being a "pied noir gay" [gay *pied-noir*] and evokes a uniquely hypermasculine culture, epitomized by his father, "le parfait *macho*" [the perfect macho] (45). His efforts to avoid detection by acting like a heterosexual man at a friend's wedding or on a work night out, and his comment, "je jouai le jeu" (114) [I played the game], suggest Legrand's awareness of gender identity as a construct. Indeed, his many performances in drag with his homosexual friends show the imitation involved in the performance of gender. One such performance includes a "wedding" to his partner Gillot in October 1969 near Fontainebleau, at which he wears full bridal dress and signs an imitation "livret de famille" [official family record book] in front of wedding guests, who all adopt a role for the day (144–48). The performance of such a ceremony almost forty-five years ahead of France's first gay marriage on May 29, 2013, following the adoption of the Taubira law on "mariage pour tous" [same-sex marriage], could initiate resistance to ideals of gender.[117] However, the narrator's choice of enacting femininity by wearing a wedding gown, tiara, wig, and makeup again suggests a camp performance of femininity reminiscent of kitsch, as opposed to the true "art" of masculinity.

Given the author's conscious construction of gender identities, this text is a conduit of collective memory in the manner of many of those studied so far—with the elaboration of a positive image of Legrand coming to represent the *pieds-noirs* in general. Significantly, the indigenous population is largely absent from this text.[118] Despite the author's personally difficult childhood, he claims that life was pleasant before the Algerian War, in a description that fails to acknowledge the suffering of the colonized population, and instead emphasizes his disapproval of the conflict:

> La guerre d'Algérie a été une désolation pour les pieds-noirs et les Arabes, car on vivait dans une harmonie parfaite; les Français avec leur gaieté, leur acharnement, leurs conseils; des rapports de bon voisinage, des amitiés nouées entre les hommes, sous un ciel qui n'épargnait ni les un ni les autres; dans la voix, dans les gestes, dans les attitudes des pieds-noirs, il y avait l'Orient. Nous étions des gens de toute sorte avant qu'un malheur commun nous modifie au long de ces huit années de tumulte. (57)

> [The Algerian War was a disaster for the *pieds-noirs* and the Arabs as we were living in perfect harmony: the French with their cheerfulness, their tenacity, their advice; [there were] neighborly relationships, friendships formed among men, under a sky which spared neither one side nor the other. The Orient was to be found in the speech, gestures and attitudes of the *pieds-noirs*. We were all sorts of people before a common misfortune changed us throughout those eight tumultuous years.]

The author's decision not to go into detail about the horrific atrocities committed on both sides during the Algerian War here is significant. He links his half brother's mental breakdown after six months of military service, from which he never recovered, to his brother's family history rather than to the violent history of Algeria's past, which he does not discuss in the book. Moreover, an explanation of the *pied-noir* term for a metropolitan French person—"pathos"—(spelt "patos" in other texts) and of the Rue Michelet in Algiers as the equivalent of the Champs-Elysées in Paris (63, 47) suggest a non-*pied-noir* target readership. A reminder that the author of this autobiography is an ordinary man "qui pourrait être vous, avec cette simple différence que ses préférences ont pu ou peuvent déranger certains" (back cover) [who could be you, with this simple difference: that his predilections have upset or may upset some] also suggests an attempt to win sympathy.

There are, however, figures who are not bound by codes of normative masculinity (or femininity), namely child and adolescent narrators. The final chapter examines constructions of identity that feature such characters.

NOTES

1. Todd Shepard, *The Invention of Decolonization: The Algerian War and the Remaking of France* (Ithaca, NY: Cornell University Press, 2008), 192.

2. David Gilmore, "Cultures of Masculinity," in Armengol and Carabí, *Debating Masculinity*, ed. Josep M. Armengol and Àngels Carabí (Harriman, TN: Men's Studies Press, 2009), 31–32.

3. For a study of the concept of honor in Algeria, see Pierre Bourdieu, "The Sentiment of Honour in Kabyle Society" in J. G. Peristiany, ed. *Honour and Shame: The Values of Mediterranean Society* (Chicago: University of Chicago Press, 1974), 191–241.

4. Alison Lever, "Honour as a Red Herring," *Critique of Anthropology* 6, no. 3 (December 1986): 104.

5. Philip Dine, *Images of the Algerian War: French Fiction and Film, 1954-1992* (Oxford: Oxford University Press, 1994), 109.

6. Shepard, *The Invention of Decolonization*, 214.

7. Maurice Benassayag, "Familles, je vous aime," in *Les Pieds-Noirs*, ed. Emmanuel Roblès (Paris: Philippe Lebaud, 1982), 171.

8. Richard C. Keller, *Colonial Madness: Psychiatry in French North Africa* (Chicago: University of Chicago Press, 2007), 129. Keller demonstrates that this psychiatry formed part of colonial structures that tried to dominate colonized populations in North Africa.

9. Ibid., 130.

10. Ibid., 131.

11. Andrea L. Smith, *Colonial Memory and Postcolonial Europe: Maltese Settlers in Algeria and France* (Bloomington, IN: Indiana University Press, 2006), 182–83.

12. Todd Shepard, "Pieds-Noirs, Bêtes Noires: Anti-'European of Algeria' Racism and the Close of the French Empire," in *Algeria & France 1800-2000: Identity, Memory, Nostalgia*, ed. Patricia M. E. Lorcin (New York: Syracuse University Press, 2006), 152.

13. Shepard, *The Invention of Decolonization*, 185–86.

14. Ibid., 200–202. Nora, for example, claims that the settlers suffer from a type of racist delirium: "Le délire est tel que la contradiction n'embarrasse personne. La pire haine pour les Arabes peut se transformer en une déclaration d'amour" [The delirium is such that no one is embarrassed by contradiction. The worst hatred for Arabs transforms into a declaration of love]. He also claims: "La réalité algérienne est fruste et violente. De la conquête, les colons ont gardé des habitudes militaires" [Algerian life is unsophisticated and violent. The colonists have kept military habits from the conquest]. See Pierre Nora, *Les Français d'Algérie* (Paris: Julliard, 1961), 46, 58.

15. Shepard, *The Invention of Decolonization*, 199. Shepard's emphasis.
16. Ibid., 160–62.
17. Ibid., 224.
18. Kristin Ross, *Fast Cars, Clean Bodies: Decolonization and the Reordering of French Culture* (Cambridge, MA: MIT Press, 1999), 159.
19. James McDougall, "Savage Wars? Codes of Violence in Algeria, 1830s-1990s," *Third World Quarterly* 26, no. 1 (2005): 121.
20. Rosemarie Jones, "*Pied-Noir* Literature: The Writing of a Migratory Elite," in *Writing across Worlds: Literature and Migration*, ed. Russell King, John Connell, and Paul White (London: Routledge, 1995), 131.
21. Benassayag, "Familles, je vous aime."
22. Cited by Clarisse Buono, *Pieds-noirs de père en fils* (Paris: Balland, 2004), 94.
23. Gilmore, "Cultures of Masculinity," 39.
24. Linda Jones, for example, links demonstrations of hypermasculinity in the Arab world to "backlashes" against Western hegemony. See Linda Jones, "Islamic Masculinities," in Armengol and Carabí, *Debating Masculinity*, 107.
25. Anonymous, "1er Novembre 1954 : La Tousssaint algérienne. Les déchirures d'un juste," *Le Monde*, November 4, 1994.
26. Jean Amrouche and Jules Roy, *Correspondance Jean Amrouche, Jules Roy (1937-1962)* (Aix-en-Provence: Édisud, 1985), 11. This collection documents Roy's correspondence with Amrouche and their friendship, which sometimes came under strain due to their different backgrounds.
27. Anonymous, "1er Novembre 1954."
28. Jeannine Verdès-Leroux, *Les Français d'Algérie de 1830 à aujourd'hui* (Paris: Fayard, 2001), 263–64.
29. Catharine Savage Brosman, "Les Frères ennemis: Jules Roy et l'Algérie," *American Association of Teachers of French* 56, no. 4 (March 1983): 579.
30. Anonymous, "1er Novembre 1954."
31. Jules Roy, *La Guerre d'Algérie* (Paris: Julliard, 1960).
32. Dine, *Images of the Algerian War*, 83.
33. Henri Alleg, *La Question* (Paris: Minuit, 1961). Paratroopers arrested the pro-independence Henri Alleg during the Battle of Algiers and he described the torture he endured at their hands in this text. Jean Sénac, discussed later in this chapter, referred to Alleg's imprisonment in a 1957 poem, "Paix en Algérie," published in *Matinale de mon peuple* (1961). See Jean Sénac, *Oeuvres poétiques* (Arles: Actes sud, 1999), 335.
34. Florence Beaugé, "Torturée par l'armée française en Algérie, Lila recherche l'homme qui l'a sauvée," *Le Monde*, June 20, 2000. See also Louisette Ighilahriz, *Algérienne: récit recueilli par Anne Nivat* (Paris: Fayard, 2001).
35. Jean-Louis Roy, "Jules Roy contre la torture," *Le Monde*, July 22, 2000.
36. Roy wrote the screenplay for the television series with Pierre Cardinal and François Villiers. For Roy's revised edition of all six novels, see Jules Roy, *Les Chevaux du soleil: La saga de l'Algérie de 1830 à 1962* (Paris: Omnibus, 1995). For the screen version, see François Villiers, *Les Chevaux du soleil* (France: Koba Films, 1980).

37. Cited by Verdès-Leroux, *Les Français d'Algérie*, 263–64.
38. Ibid., 263.
39. Janine de la Hogue, "Les Livres comme patrie," in Roblès, *Les Pieds-Noirs*, 121.
40. Azouz Begag, *Le Gone du Châaba: roman* (Paris: Éditions du Seuil, 1986), 216.
41. Catherine Ahmed and Raphael Eulry, "Aventures et passion en Algérie française," *Le Monde*, August 25, 1996. *Le Monde* described the adaptation as "un beau succès" [a great success] when first broadcast and warmly praised it for its lack of sentimentality in advance of its rebroadcast.
42. De Gaulle features in Part 6, "Le Tonnerre et les Anges," 755–951. See Roy, *Les Chevaux du soleil*.
43. In the novel version, Hector does not make it as far as the tomb and dies grasping the soil at the entrance to the ransacked cemetery. See Roy, *Les Chevaux du soleil*, 931, 941–42. The scene from the television series is reminiscent of the fate of the character Pierre Nivel, a *pied-noir* journalist in the film *Là-bas mon pays* [My country over there]. Similarly, Pierre is the victim of a shooting in Algeria when he returns there in the 1990s. Flashbacks to Pierre swimming in the sea and images of the sun as he dies suggest his death in Algeria rights the wrongs of his original departure. See Alexandre Arcady, *Là-bas mon pays* (France: Alexandre Films, 2000).
44. After seeing Marguerite and Hassan together, Hector returns to his barracks and almost commits suicide with his gun, thereby suggesting a melancholia caused by his repudiation of Arabo-Berber identities.
45. Jules Roy, *Adieu ma mère, adieu mon coeur* (Paris: Albin Michel, 1996), 154.
46. See, for example, Françoise Condotta, "Cimetières d'Oranie: Une décennie de silence," *Midi Libre*, December 18, 2013.
47. Anonymous, "1er Novembre 1954."
48. Seth Graebner, *History's Place: Nostalgia and the City in French Algerian Literature* (Lanham, MD: Lexington, 2007), 236–37. Graebner points to the many differences between Roblès's novel and Camus's *L'Étranger*, not least the fact that the protagonist, Smail, kills a European character for political reasons.
49. Ibid., 235–44.
50. Emmanuel Roblès, *Saison violente* (Paris: Seuil, 1974), 182.
51. Emmanuel Roblès, "Préface," in Roblès, *Les Pieds-Noirs*, 11.
52. Andaulsia's historic links with North Africa date to its position as the center of Islamic rule in Spain for several centuries.
53. Jean Pélégri, *Les Oliviers de la justice* (Paris: Gallimard, 1959).
54. Emmanuel Hecht, "Petites phrases de la Ve," *L'Express*, July 6, 2011.
55. The expression "colonisateur de bonne volonté" [good-willed colonizer] is from Albert Memmi, *Portrait du colonisé précédé de Portrait du colonisateur* (Paris: Gallimard, 1985), 68.
56. Jean Pélégri, *Ma Mère l'Algérie* (Algiers: Laphomic, 1989), 8.
57. Kateb Yacine died of leukemia and Mouloud Mammeri died in a car crash in 1989, the year Pélégri published this essay. Mouloud Feraoun was assassinated by the OAS in March 1962.

58. Simone de Beauvoir, *Le Deuxième Sexe I: Les faits et les mythes* (Paris: Gallimard, 1976). See in particular Section three—"Mythes," 237–408. De Beauvoir comments, for example, on the association of femininity with passive land awaiting masculine seed or a passive sea that submits to the blazing rays of a masculine sun, 244.

59. Verdès-Leroux, *Les Français d'Algérie*, 57, 77, 265, 371, 392.

60. Gabriel Conesa, *Bab-el-Oued: Notre paradis perdu* (Paris: Robert Laffont, 1970).

61. Louis Bertrand founded settler literature in the late nineteenth century, Musette (Auguste Robinet) depicted his famous fictional settler protagonist Cagayous in the late nineteenth and early twentieth centuries, and Gabriel Audisio was one of the founders of the *École d'Alger* in the 1930s.

62. Significantly, the title of section two of the novel is "Souvenirs du paradis" [Memories of Paradise].

63. Despite Conesa's depiction of Algerian bulls as capricious and lacking nobility (102), Oran (along with Tangier, Casablanca, and Melilla-Ceuta) was one of four major centers of bullfighting in North Africa in the late nineteenth and early twentieth centuries. See Elisabeth Hardouin-Fugier, *Histoire de la corrida en Europe du XVIIe au XXie siècle* (Paris: Connaissances et Savoirs, 2005), 202; cited in Cathal Kilcline, "Constructions of Identity in Mediterranean France: A Study of Sport and other Popular Cultural Forms" (unpublished PhD dissertation, National University of Ireland, Galway, 2009), 236.

64. The *pieds-noirs* frequently translate Bab-el-Oued as "la porte de la rivière" [gateway to the river]. Although both "bab" (door or entrance) and "el oued" (valley or transitory riverbed) are masculine, Bab-el-Oued, as the name of a district, is feminine in Arabic.

65. Emmanuel Sivan, "Colonialism and Popular Culture in Algeria," *Journal of Contemporary History* 14, no. 1 (January 1979): 37.

66. The title of the memoir's third section, "Le coup de grâce" [deathblow], alludes to this ultimate death.

67. Graebner, *History's Place*, 240.

68. The series starts with *Le Bourricot* (1974) [The Donkey] and *Le Coup de Sirocco* (1978) [The Sirocco's Blow] and concludes with *La Valise à l'eau* (1981) [The Suitcase in the Water] and *Et le Sirocco emportera nos larmes* (2012) [And the Sirocco Will Sweep Away Our Tears].

69. Daniel Saint-Hamont, *Le Macho* (Paris: Fayard, 1979), 13, 26–29.

70. The iconic association of cars and men during the same period suggests their mobility. See Ross, *Fast Cars, Clean Bodies*, 97.

71. Frantz Fanon, *Peau noire, masques blancs* (Paris: Seuil, 1952), 128.

72. William Granara, "Picaresque Narratives and Cultural Dissimulation in Colonial North African Literature," *The Arab Studies Journal* 11, no. 2 (Autumn 2003/Spring 2004): 41–56.

73. Ibid., 54.

74. Cited by W. M. Frohock, "The Failing Center: Recent Fiction and the Picaresque Tradition," *Novel: A Forum on Fiction* 3, no. 1 (Autumn 1969): 63–64.

75. The narrator makes sarcastic observations about the inner workings of the post office where he works and the low salaries of its employees, for example.

76. This form of French spoken by the settlers included borrowings from Arabic, Spanish, Italian, and Maltese.

77. Joëlle Hureau, *La Mémoire des pieds-noirs: de 1830 à nos jours* (Paris: Perrin, 2010), 272–73. Hureau gives the example: "Honte j'ai de sortir" [Ashamed, I am, to go out].

78. Dunwoodie discerns a "sexual charge" in the scene in which Daru goes to bed with his prisoner and with regard to Meursault's homosexual urges cites J. L. Stamm's article, "Camus's *Stranger*: His Act of Violence," *American Imago* 26, no. 3 (1969): 281–90. See Peter Dunwoodie, *Writing French Algeria* (Oxford: Oxford University Press, 1998), 233–34.

79. Hélène Cixous, *Les Rêveries de la femme sauvage: Scènes primitives* (Paris: Galilée, 2000), 114–15.

80. The fortune-teller's name derives from the Spanish word "estrella," meaning star.

81. Marie Elbe, *À l'heure de notre mort* (Paris: Albin Michel, 1992). 191. The pejorative nature of the term used to denote homosexuality, "coulo," which comes from the French word "cul" (ass), speaks for itself. However, a dictionary of *pied-noir* expressions states that this term has now become "une insulte gratuite et relativement gentille" [a gratuitous and relatively kind insult]. See Léon Mazzella, *Le Parler pied-noir: mots et expressions de là-bas* (Paris: Rivages, 1989), 39.

82. Nadia Louar, "At the intersection of queer and postcolonial discourses. Rerouting the queer with Jean Sénac and Jean Genet," in *Rerouting the Postcolonial: New Directions for the New Millennium*, ed. Janet Wilson, Cristina Sandru, and Sarah Welsh Lawson (London: Routledge, 2010), 233.

83. Hamid Nacer-Khodja, *Albert Camus, Jean Sénac ou Le fils rebelle* (Paris: Éditions Paris-Mediterranée, 2004), 63.

84. Ibid., 101.

85. Jean Sénac, "Jean Sénac: Carnets inédits (extraits)," in *Algérie: Un rêve de fraternité*, ed. Guy Dugas (Paris: Omnibus, 1997), 847.

86. Éric Savarèse, *L'Invention des pieds-noirs* (Paris: Séguier, 2002), 227. *Pieds-rouges* (red-feet)—left-wing Europeans, particularly French citizens, who went to live in the newly independent country with the intention of contributing to the construction of a Marxist state—also joined the *pieds-verts*.

87. The architectural term "avant-corps" refers to part of a building that protrudes from the main edifice and translates as "forepart" or more literally as "fore-body."

88. Jean Sénac, *Ébauche du père: pour en finir avec l'enfance: roman* (Paris: Gallimard, 1989), 18, 55, 23.

89. Katia Sainson, "'Entre deux feux': Jean Sénac's Struggle for Self-determination," *Research in African Literatures* 42, no. 1 (Spring 2011): 46, 41–42.

90. Judith Butler, *Gender Trouble: Feminism and the Subversion of Identity* (London: Routledge, 1999), 175.

91. Jordi is interviewed in Gilles Perez, *Les Pieds-Noirs, histoires d'une blessure* (France: France 3, 2006).

92. Sénac, "Jean Sénac," 851.

93. Ibid., 849.

94. Sanson's phrase refers to Sénac's dedication of his volume *Matinale de mon peuple* (1961) [Early Rising of my People] to both European and Arabo-Muslim pro-independence revolutionaries such as Fernand Yveton and Mustapha Bouhired. See Hervé Sanson, "Jean Sénac, citoyen innommé de l'Ailleurs," *Insaniyat: Revue algérienne d'anthropologie et de sciences sociales*, no. 32–33 (2006), http://insaniyat.revues.org/3432#text. Date accessed: February 28, 2014.

95. Sénac, "Jean Sénac," 850–51.

96. Abdallah Zouache, "Socialism, Liberalism and Inequality: The Colonial Economics of the Saint-Simonians in 19th Century Algeria," *Review of Social Economy* 67, no. 4 (December 2009): 453.

97. Guy Dugas, "Les auteurs," in Dugas, *Algérie*, 991. Sénac's concept of fraternity (and sorority) corresponded with his vision of a socialist Algeria, as exemplified by a poem written in 1963, "Citoyens de beauté" [Citizens of Beauty], which extolled the Algerian revolution. See Sénac, *Oeuvres poétiques*, 399–404.

98. Sénac, *Ébauche du père*, 28.

99. Richard Losch explains that a Guebre is a follower of Zoroastrianism, a religion founded by the Persian prophet Zarathushtra Spitama. Of particular importance to followers of this faith is the worship of fire, which symbolizes light, and the god Ahura Mazda, who is associated with the sun. See Richard R. Losch, *The Many Faces of Faith: A Guide to World Religions and Christian Traditions* (Grand Rapids, MI: Eerdmans, 2002), 13–16.

100. Sénac, *Ébauche du père*, 69.

101. Jean Sénac, *Avant-corps précédé de Poèmes iliaques et suivi de Diwân du Noûn: poèmes* (Paris: Gallimard, 1968), 66.

102. Sénac, *Oeuvres poétiques*, 540–41.

103. Robert Aldrich, *Colonialism and Homosexuality* (London: Routledge, 2003), 389.

104. Ibid., 388–89.

105. Sénac, *Oeuvres poétiques*, 542.

106. Summarized and cited by Sainson, "Entre deux feux," 34.

107. Danielle Marx-Scouras, "The Specter of Jean Sénac," *L'Esprit Créateur* 43, no. 1 (Spring 2003): 45.

108. The circumstances of the poet's death from a fatal stabbing remain contested—theories for the killer's motives vary from robbery to an act of Islamic fundamentalism.

109. See Malek Alloula, *Le Harem Colonial (Images d'un sous-érotisme)* (Geneva: Slatkine, 1981).

110. Lucien Legrand, *Autobiographie d'un pied noir gay* (Paris: Publibook, 2011). The title of this autobiography and the jacket blurb use the spelling "pied noir," although the main text uses "pied-noir" throughout. Publibook specializes in self-publishing, which is an effective means by which minorities can bring their narratives into the public sphere.

111. Noémie Luciani, "Bambi à voir; Marie-Pierre, transsexuelle, ex-reine du Paris by night," *Le Monde*, June 19, 2013.

112. Anonymous, "'Bambi,' quand un petit garçon d'Algérie devient femme d'exception," AFP, June 14, 2013, LexisNexis. This quotation is from the director.
113. Ibid. Quotation from the director.
114. Ibid. Quotation from Bambi/Marie-Pierre Pruvot.
115. Sainson, "Entre deux feux," 39.
116. Ibid.
117. An opponent of this law, Dominique Venner, who committed suicide at Notre Dame Cathedral in Paris in protest against it, was a former OAS militant. See Anonymous, "Suicide d'un écrivain d'extrême droite à Notre-Dame, hommage de Le Pen," AFP, May 21, 2013, LexisNexis.
118. Despite the author's emphasis on the taboo nature of homosexuality among *pied-noir* men, all of his frequent homosexual encounters in Algeria (and afterwards) are with men who have European names.

Chapter 4

Performing Childhood and Adolescence through French Algerian Narrators

4.1 INTRODUCTION: CONSTRUCTING CHILDHOOD AND ADOLESCENCE IN LIFE AND LITERATURE

This chapter critically examines the significance of the many voices of child and adolescent narrators in works that continue to emerge within the now familiar framework of the *pied-noir* family. It uncovers a tendency of *pied-noir* authors to write of their youth from the late 1970s and with renewed vigor from the 1990s. This forms part of a long-established tradition in French writing that emphasizes youth in its engagement with processes of recollection, as exemplified by the childhood experiences narrated in Marcel Proust's renowned multivolume work, *À la recherche du temps perdu* (1913–1927) [In Search of Lost Time].[1] Thus, both the *récit d'enfance* [childhood memoir] and the novel of adolescence are important genres in French literary history.[2] The trend is also part of a general rise in what Rita Bouckaert-Ghesquiere calls "adult children's literature," which blurs the boundaries between autobiographical childhood memoirs aimed at children and those aimed at adults.[3] Bouckaert-Ghesquiere notes the growth of this genre after World War II and its surge in popularity since the 1970s.[4] Moreover, the four main thematic groupings of such autobiographical texts, as outlined by Bouckaert-Ghesquiere—those foregrounding a broken childhood due to war, a lost land, a wounded childhood due to personal or family circumstances, and childhood memories[5]—are all suitable lenses through which to examine personal and collective trauma resulting from the Algerian War. Against the backdrop of Bouckaert-Ghesquiere's assertion that such works have a therapeutic role for authors and can demonstrate a nuanced viewpoint in addition to avoiding "explicit judgments,"[6] this chapter considers the potential of young narrators to disrupt conventional discourses related to *pied-noir* memory and identity.

Discourses inform concepts of childhood and adolescence as well as their portrayal in works by adult authors. As Patricia Pace suggests, "As with anyone's body, there is no direct access to the child's body except through language."[7] Changing concepts of the duration of adolescence, as illustrated by psychologist Jeffrey Jensen Arnett's theorizing of "emerging adulthood" from the age of eighteen to twenty-five, equally underline its performative nature.[8] Elaborating on these social constructs through literature, however, is potentially productive. Julia Kristeva's view on the liberating "open psychic structure" facilitated by recreating adolescence through literary production is worth quoting here: "The writer, like the adolescent, is the one who will be able to betray his parents—to turn them against him and against themselves—in order to be free."[9] In this way, as Mary Hilton and Maria Nikolajeva's volume on the literature of adolescence points out, representations of youth in literature can act as "a very powerful ideological tool,"[10] which can potentially contribute to the "social and aesthetic transformation of culture by [. . .] encouraging readers to approach ideas, issues and objects from new perspectives and so prepare the way for change."[11]

This chapter investigates ways in which young narrators can facilitate a consideration of societal issues in a fresh light and with particular freedom and candor. In so doing, it builds on Anne Roche's observation, following interviews with the former settlers, that "de jeunes pieds-noirs, nés en Algérie mais l'ayant à peine connue, peuvent avoir une approche tout à fait différente" [young *pieds-noirs*, who were born in Algeria but were barely familiar with it, can have a completely different approach].[12] Roche's research indirectly points to a child's outlook as the most likely site for engagement with different memory communities from the war:

> Si les enfants jouent avec les petits Arabes, les relations chez les adultes, qui ne sont pas nulles, sont vectorisées de façon précise: il y a moins échange (du moins dans ce qui est verbalisé du témoignage) qu'apport, qui va généralement dans le même sens.

> [Although young children played with little Arabs, relations among adults, which were not inexistent, were vectorized in a precise manner: there was less exchange (at least according to what is verbalized in testimony) than supply, which generally went one way.][13]

In (re)creating a childhood that included contact between young members of the colonizing and colonized communities, writers can therefore strive to engage with all sides. Indeed, they could potentially open up Homi Bhabha's linguistic "Third Space" discussed in chapter 2 of the current book, and thereby disrupt the production of meaning in dominant colonial narratives.

Moreover, narratives of childhood experience signal not only a space between childhood and adulthood but also between past and present, as suggested by the famous opening line of L. P. Hartley's semiautobiographical classic, *The Go-Between* (1953): "The past is a foreign country: they do things differently there."[14] Evoking the past from this liminal viewpoint facilitates productive possibilities as, particularly during times of political tension, children can enunciate viewpoints that adults may be restrained from voicing. Resultant reviews of the past may permit what Nancy E. Virtue calls "critical witnessing," which facilitates the Freudian "working through" of trauma by actively engaging with the complexities of the past, as opposed to the obsessive reenactment of traumatic events.[15] Works featuring young narrators therefore seem well placed to reassess the legacy of colonialism without imposing a discourse of binary oppositions and colonial hierarchies, and have already proven a popular means of allowing writers from indigenous populations to "reflect on colonial society with a new, inquiring approach, as if with the naive gaze of the child."[16]

This said, performances of childhood and adolescence in literature can promote nostalgia, defined by Svetlana Boym as a yearning for "the time of our childhood" and "a romance with one's own fantasy."[17] Works featuring young narrators are therefore a particularly apt way of evoking nostalgia for the "paradise lost" of colonial Algeria in relation to the inevitable passing of childhood. Young narrators also facilitate fable in addition to fairy-tale imagery, which can potentially reiterate myths associated with colonial Algeria. Furthermore, a youthful theme corresponds to the notion of the *Français d'Algérie* as a *peuple jeune* [young population] prematurely forced from their homeland. This concept dates back to the writings of Louis Bertrand but particularly recalls the tropes of youth and Adamic innocence in Albert Camus's writing, as discussed in chapter 1.[18] Indeed, Camus's descriptions of young couples deciding to get married by exchanging engraved sweets in "L'Été à Alger" (*Noces*) paints a very memorable portrait of "le peuple enfant de ce pays" [the childish population of this country].[19]

Fictive representations of youth may also attempt to regulate readers' own performance of their identities and their perceptions of historical events. Jacqueline Rose's contention, in her seminal work on children's literature, that this genre constitutes the identity of both the adult and child through language that is "imposed and reimposed over time," is of particular significance here and for the current book as a whole.[20] As previous chapters reveal, works aimed solely at adults similarly inform the performance of identity. Rose's statement that "the child is constantly set up as the site of a lost truth and/or moment in history, which it can therefore be used to retrieve," also indicates that literature involving young narrators is an obvious choice for those wishing to retrieve a lost French Algeria, particularly an idealized one that never existed.²¹ Following Rose's analysis, this chapter suggests that adult children's literature can construct a "fantasy of childhood," as the language used becomes "a means to identity and self-recognition" for adults as much as for children.²² The current analysis therefore considers the contemporary preponderance of works featuring young narrators as central to the particular circumstances of continuing "memory wars" in France. In this way, some works seek to influence the attitudes of potential younger as well as older readers.²³ Just as many *pied-noir* women writers evoke marginalization and lack of power, so too do many adult authors speaking through child narrators, who cannot be held responsible for the actions of adults and who can appear on an equal footing with the colonized population of Algeria.

Thus, this chapter reveals processes by which tales featuring young narrators can come to represent the wider story of a community in exile. Yet, some of the texts studied also reveal the productive possibilities opened up by young narrators. This chapter uncovers texts that destabilize familiar narratives and are consequently part of a cathartic process. Indeed, the narrators of some stories subvert stereotypes of childhood and draw attention to colonial injustice and violence. Other narratives are especially valuable for their divergence from conventional representations of gender or their deconstruction of family and community myths. The chapter also exposes ways in which Camus's legacy continues to affect a younger generation of writers who grapple with their *pied-noir* heritage. Contemporary texts therefore continue to echo initial depictions of the *pieds-noirs*. The first section begins by considering the implications of a welcome humor and frank tone invoked by authors such as Daniel Saint-Hamont, Élie-Georges Berreby, and Hélène Gadal. An examination of the restrained, dispassionate style of novels by Virginie Buisson and Jean-Noël Pancrazi follows, while the chapter concludes with a consideration of works focusing on the theme of *pied-noir* identity as set forth by writers with little or no lived experience of colonial Algeria: Brigitte Benkemoun and Claire Messud.

4.2 À LA RECHERCHE D'UNE VÉRITÉ PERDUE [IN SEARCH OF LOST TRUTH]: SEEKING SINCERITY OR COLONIZING CONSCIOUSNESS?

This section examines perhaps one of the best-known representations of the *pieds-noirs* in France, Daniel Saint-Hamont's *Le Coup de Sirocco* (1978) [The Sirocco's Blow], which is part of the series of novels that includes *Le Macho*, discussed in the previous chapter. Film director Alexandre Arcady, with whom Saint-Hamont frequently collaborates, released an adaptation of *Le Coup de Sirocco* as a commercially successful film in 1979 with a young

Patrick Bruel, himself a *pied-noir* who went on to become a pop star, in the lead role.[24] Roger Hanin, also a *pied-noir*, starred as the protagonist's father. The film version was especially popular among the former settlers, who "applauded or wept" as they viewed it.[25] Furthermore, Raphaëlle Branche notes that during a general "apaisement des mémoires" [apeasment of memoires] at this time, the movie disseminated knowledge about the *pieds-noirs* to a wider audience who had previously regarded them as, "ces cousins d'Algérie encore mal connus" [those still quite unknown cousins from Algeria].[26] However, Branche contends that films such as this also encouraged the emergence of nostalgia, which minimized the inequalities of the colonial situation.[27] Similarly, Sophie Watt contends that the narrative produced by the film (as well as other films directed by Arcady) is "part of a gradual nostalgic rehabilitation of France's colonial past in French popular culture."[28] Significantly, Watt points to the overlapping of the personal history of the protagonists of the film with that of France's regretful colonial loss.[29] *Le Coup de Sirocco*, the personal tale of one *pied-noir* boy, therefore played a significant role in the (re)construction, not just of a *pied-noir* identity but also of France's broader colonial and postcolonial self-image.

Again, this story is a mixture of fiction and autobiography.[30] Yet, Jean-Jacques Jordi, who left Algeria himself as a child, cites the novel to illustrate the difficulties faced by the *pieds-noirs* on their arrival in France in 1962.[31] This section considers the novel, to which the film is largely faithful.[32] The same narrator from *Le Macho* features, although his adolescent voice dominates in this earlier book, which is set in the immediate aftermath of the Algerian War and follows his family's repatriation from Algeria to France. The narrator mentions toward the end of the novel that he is telling his story almost twenty years after the events in question.[33] Yet his youthful viewpoint relays events with immediacy, often in the present tense. Moreover, the protagonist appears, in his adult incarnation, as an eternal adolescent or emerging adult, as he still balks at the thought of a committed adult relationship, claiming he is now in love with a married woman, although he does not love her four children (148). This adolescent voice suggests the narrator's physical and emotional liminality, not just between childhood and adulthood but also between his past in colonial Algeria and his present in metropolitan France, although there is no engagement here with indigenous Algerians, who are largely absent from the story. Indeed, this *pied-noir* family's association with couscous, which they hope to introduce to a French clientele, is significant as there is no mention of the product's origins among the Arabo-Berber population and it instead appears as a marker of *pied-noir* identity.[34]

The narrator's behavior suggests an exaggerated performance of the egocentrism cited by psychologists as a trait of adolescence.[35] This allows for several of the many comic moments in the novel. Two "prototypical representations of social cognitive processes during adolescence," according to the theory of adolescent egocentrism, are: "the imaginary audience," which refers to "adolescents' tendency to believe that others are always watching and evaluating them," and "the personal fable," which refers to adolescents' belief that they are "unique" and "special."[36] Interestingly, psychologist Lesa Rae Vartanian describes both the imaginary audience and personal fable labels as "twin constructs" that have appeared in psychological studies for over thirty years and categorize adolescent thinking as "faulty, biased, and/or fantastical" but which have "not been substantiated with empirical data."[37] However, the narrator's performance conforms to these constructs. Indeed, he exemplifies a self-involved adolescent who is conscious of an audience that is, at least partly, in his imagination. This is evident from his interior monologue as he walks the streets of Paris, imagining he is in a race: "Je faisais le reporter, je décrivais comment j'étais le premier, comment j'avais laissé tous les autres concurrents derrière" (49) [I played the reporter, I described how I was first, how I had left all the other competitors trailing behind].

Performing his "personal fable" enables the narrator to ignore societal conventions and to comment frankly on the taboo subject of the war in a humorous, often disarming manner. For example, he casually likens his girlfriend Monique's initial rejection of his sexual advances to the imposition of "des zones interdites, comme l'armée en Algérie" (67) [no-go zones, like the army in Algeria]. He also draws comparisons between his fear of marrying her and his fear of a bomb blast in Algeria (182–83). Later, he claims that "la perte de l'Algérie" [the loss of Algeria] was only a minor sin compared to his refusal to sleep with Monique (185). Moreover, the narrator draws attention to the French army's more problematic practices, absurdly linking their "counterterrorism" strategy to personal experience as regards his mother's ability to obtain answers:

> L'armée en Algérie elle a raté une grande chance: c'est de ne pas avoir utilisé ma mère dans les interrogatoires. Avec elle, les parachutistes jamais ils auraient eu besoin de faire des tortures, ou des choses terribles comme ça, pour que les fellaghas parlent. Le plus grand chef fellagha, on l'aurait laissé une journée avec ma mère, seuls dans un bureau, à la fin il aurait griffé la porte pour appeler la sentinelle en pleurant, en sanglotant: «Je vais tout vous dire, je vais tout vous avouer, mais faites partir cette femme. Dites au général avec la moustache qu'il a gagné.» (201)

> [The army in Algeria missed a big opportunity: they did not use my mother in interrogations. With her, the paratroopers would never have had to use torture or awful things like that to make the Fellaghas [rebels] talk. You could have left the biggest Fellagha leader alone in an office for a whole day with my mother—in

the end he would have scratched on the door to call the sentry while crying, sobbing: "I'll tell you everything, I'll admit everything to you, but make this woman leave. Tell the general with the moustache that he has won."]³⁸

This reference to the repressed specter of France's troubling use of torture is significant in the context of the late 1970s, before national debates on the subject exploded in 2000, as discussed in chapter 3. Furthermore, as the narrator watches his father following conman Louis Bonheur through a wasteland that will supposedly house their new business, he humorously refers to another taboo subject, noting: "On marche dans la boue et les fondrières comme une patrouille de harkis" (159) [We are walking in the mud and the quagmires like a patrol of *harkis*]. Once again, this reference is noteworthy since the French state neglected the *harkis*'s role in fighting for France during the Algerian War. In fact, this community of indigenous Algerians was virtually unknown in France until their children, driven by frustration at their living conditions, engaged in riots in the Bias Camp east of Bordeaux in May 1975.³⁹

Thus, the narrator's youth and exaggerated performance of the adolescent egocentric "personal fable" allow him to draw preposterous parallels between his personal interactions with his girlfriend or parents and the still painful and, at the time, neglected subject of the Algerian War. These episodes point to his suppression of genuinely traumatic experiences from the conflict, while he admits that leaving Algeria is too painful a subject to discuss with his best friend Paulo (118). In this way, he reflects the unresolved trauma of the war at national level, which Jo McCormack labels the "Algerian Syndrome."⁴⁰ Thus, despite the novel's lack of engagement with the former colonized population, it inscribes some of the realities of uneasy colonial and postcolonial relations upon France's present. Additionally, the young narrator's comical undermining, through his cynical commentary, of idealized youth and Camusian Adamic innocence serves to distance the novel from conventional tropes.

The narrator hence appears as a site of truth but his frequently comical candor works to disguise the link that the reader is encouraged to draw between his personal story and that of the *pieds-noirs* in general. This *pied-noir* boy from a modest background is representative of a community that struggles to fit in following a distressing departure from its homeland. In this way, his adolescent angst sympathetically evokes the alienation and nostalgia of a population in exile, as is evident in the following extract:

Je suis seul maintenant, et j'ai froid dans le noir. [. . .] Pourquoi j'ai cette sensation d'être à la fois si proche et si lointain? D'être moi-même et un autre? Tout a basculé [. . .] On m'a volé les mots du soleil! Qu'il est long, ce voyage. Qu'elles seront longues à apprendre toutes ces habitudes de l'exil. Qui connaîtra jamais, dans la recherche aux souvenirs, la hauteur du mur immense qui nous sépare du vieux pays? Qui sentira le poids des morts abandonnés, la terrible filiation interrompue? (222–23)

[I am alone now and I am cold in the dark. [. . .] Why do I have this sensation of being both so near and so far, of being myself and another? Everything has changed radically. [. . .] The sun's words have been stolen from me. How long this journey is. How long it will take to learn all the customs of this exile. Who will ever know, in sifting through memories, the height of the immense wall that separates us from the old country? Who will feel the weight of the abandoned dead, the horror of discontinued lineage?]

Furthermore, the sources of his family's misfortunes stem from villainous characters who would not be out of place in a fairy tale—Charles de Gaulle, France, and French conman Louis Bonheur. The narrator's father, for example, states that "de Gaulle [. . .] c'est lui qui nous a mis dans le malheur" (29) [de Gaulle is the one who brought this misfortune on us]. Similarly, the narrator blames de Gaulle for the shooting dead of his compatriots on March 26, 1962, in Algiers: "Quand il s'ennuyait, il disait: «Je m'ennuie, tuez-moi quelques dizaines de Français d'Algérie . . .» Alors l'armée mitraillait les gens rue d'Isly" (108) [When he was bored, he would say, "I'm bored, kill a few dozen French Algerians for me . . ." So the army would gun down people on Rue d'Isly]. A personified France also poses problems. The family's arrival in the country causes the narrator's mother to become depressed, while their initial reception, when they are mistaken for beggars, is the ultimate rehearsal or "répétition" for "la fin du monde (33) [the end of the world]. The narrator's comment, "on était là comme des coulos à aimer la France, à lui donner notre coeur, et elle, un coup de pied au derrière elle nous donne comme récompense" (105) [we were there like queers loving France, giving her our hearts, and she gave us nothing but a kick in the behind in return], equally portrays the *pieds-noirs* as victims. By the same token, the ironically named Frenchman Louis Bonheur [Louis Fortune] tries to con the narrator's father Lucien, and insults him for failing to secure a loan by Bonheur's deadline. This final insult casts the former colonizers as colonized: "Les ordres c'est vous qui les recevez, vous êtes né pour ça, vous êtes un petit. Allez donc manger votre couscous dans votre douar" (218) [You are the one who takes orders, you were born for it, you are a nobody. So go and eat your couscous in your tent].[41]

Ultimately, the narrator's marginalized position evokes many of the literary representations of outsiders already studied, including that of Meursault in *L'Étranger*. Indeed, his affinity with the Camusian family is evident from his decision, in an echo of Camus's preference for his mother over justice, to choose both his mother and speech patterns that evoke a *pied-noir* identity:

> Dans notre langue, tout était si mélangé qu'on savait plus très bien où le français s'arrêtait et où l'arabe commençait. «C'est tellement vulgaire», disaient des Français. Si la vulgarité, c'est d'être obligé de plus parler comme ma mère, alors oui, je suis vulgaire: je choisis ma mère. (106)

> [In our language, everything was so jumbled together that we no longer really knew where French stopped and Arabic began. Some of the French used to say: "It is so vulgar." If vulgarity means being forced to talk more like my mother then yes, I am vulgar: I choose my mother.]

The narrator's parlance, together with his candid and often comical descriptions, invites a comparison with the equally informal and humorous observations of the young narrator of *L'Enfant pied-noir* (1994) [*The Pied-Noir Child*], written by Algiers-born author, painter, and sculptor, Élie-Georges Berreby. This later novel, published over thirty years after Algerian independence, again differentiates French identity, of which language is conventionally the primary constituent, from that of the settlers:

> Pour avoir une bonne note en rédaction, il ne faut jamais perdre de vue Victor Hugo. Si on écrit à l'école comme on parle entre nous, les maîtres, les pauvres, ils ne comprennent rien. Pas même le mot "mancaora," ils connaissent. Avec eux, il faut dire: "école buissonnière." Pareil que la marquise de Sévigné. A force à force [*sic*], les rédactions, je m'applique à les écrire en français de France. Mais en dehors de l'école, je parle normalement.[42]

> [In order to get a good grade in essay writing, you must never forget Victor Hugo. If we write in school the way we talk among ourselves, the poor teachers do not understand anything. They do not even know the word "mancaora" [to play hooky]. With them, you have to say "play truant," as if you were the Marquise de Sévigné. In the end, I take care to write my essays in French from France. But outside school, I talk normally.]

Lucienne Martini includes this novel and Jean-Noël Pancrazi's *Madame Arnoul* (1995), discussed below, as part of a new era in works by *pied-noir* authors, which go beyond the pain of the loss of Algeria and which are therefore more easily accepted and understood by a wider audience.[43] That *L'Enfant pied-noir* won the "12/17" literary award for authors of literature for adolescents is suggestive of its appeal.[44] The context of increasing Islamist violence during Algeria's *décennie noire* [dark decade] must also be considered, as must the author's intention that the work would be pedagogical and show his own adolescent son that despite his "manque de tout" [shortage of everything], he had a happy childhood.[45]

Like the previous novels studied, this work is best considered semiautobiographical. The front cover informs the reader that the text is a "roman" [novel]. However, the back cover insists that "ce savoureux récit d'une enfance à Bab-el-Oued se double d'une authentique témoignage sur une époque charnière des relations entre communautés pied-noir et algérienne" [this delectable tale of a Bab-el-Oued childhood also serves as an authentic testimony of a crucial period for relations between *pied-noir* and Algerian communities]. This implies that the text's fictionalized version of events is a type of "true history."[46] The author's website goes further, stating that "Élie-Georges Berreby a narré son enfance dans *L'ENFANT PIED-NOIR*" [*sic*] [Élie-Georges Berreby narrated his childhood in The *Pied-Noir* Child].[47] While the author was already working as a traveling salesman and freelance journalist at the outbreak of World War II, according to his website, the young narrator, Joé Bari, was born later; he begins his story just before his ninth birthday in the early 1950s and ends it with the departure of his mother, sister, and brother to Spain after the outbreak of the Algerian War, while he chooses to stay in Algeria with his grandmother.

Joé contrasts with the adults in the book who tend to avoid the truth (85). His sincerity points to adults' hypocrisy, including that of his aunt Gladys, whose patronizing attempts to "educate" Joé, by making him neglect his studies in order to complete chores (87, 95), recall Madame Quinson's attempts to "civilize" the narrator of Emmanuel Roblès's *Saison violente*. Young Joé is also wiser than the adults in his life. Hence, he asks questions where adults blindly follow, as illustrated by his comments on his grandmother's unfailing belief in the powers of an ancient holy rabbi:

> Ce saint rabbi bar Yohai, s'il guérit ma mère, fait revenir mon père et nous procure un appartement moins humide, obligé je serai de croire en lui. Mais ce saint rabbi, il a guéri Tata Annette pour la laisser dans de terribles difficultés alimentaires, avec un mari qui buvait son travail et dans un logement trop petit. Va comprendre. (58)

> [I will be obliged to believe in this holy Rabbi Bar Yohai if he cures my mother, makes my father come back and gets us a less damp apartment. But this holy rabbi cured Auntie Annete only to leave her with terrible dietary problems, a husband who drank his wages and housing that was too small. Go figure!]

The narrator's liminal position, symbolized here by his status as the son of an Italian-Catholic father and Jewish mother, as well as by his position between childhood and adulthood, is, to a certain extent, productive. It enables him, thanks to his own developing sexuality, to broach the subject of homosexuality among the settler population, which, as discussed in chapter 3, is an uncommon topic in literature featuring adult *pied-noir* narrators. Joé implies that homosexuality within his community is acceptable if it is discreet (and consensual) and hints at sexual experimentation by his older friend Salviat, who later dates Joé's sister Françoise:

> Dans le quartier, les enculeries sont discrètes. J'en connais un qui se le fait mettre le soir dans l'ancienne gare. Il aime ça, mais il se ferait tuer plutôt que de l'avouer. C'est Salviat qui nous a confié le secret. J'en ai déduit qu'il y allait de temps en temps. (111)

> [In the neighborhood, buggery is discreet. I know someone who gets screwed in the evenings in the old train station. He likes it but he would get himself killed rather than admit it. Salviat is the one who let us in on the secret. I deduced from this that he used to go there from time to time.]

Moreover, Joé's beloved cousin Cécile is possibly in a homosexual relationship, as he notes that: "Elle vit et travaille avec une amie libraire. La vérité, ces deux femmes, elles s'entendent comme des amoureuses" (60) [She lives and works with a book-seller friend. The truth is that these two women get along like lovers]. However, during the Algerian War, a childhood acquaintance of the boys called Bouzid Belhouch shoots Salviat in the head as he plays a first division soccer match, in which he has scored three goals (198). The "Front révolutionnaire" [Revolutionary Front] then shoot Cécile in the head as she leaves her bookshop, in a case of mistaken identity (202–3). The unhappy fate of these two characters alludes to the intolerant climate of the future independent Algeria and to the fate of openly homosexual public figures such as Jean Sénac. Furthermore, Salviat's sporting success reinscribes him within conventional *pied-noir* masculinity. In describing a former young classmate from an impoverished background, Roland Koby, whose mother's partner forces him into prostituting himself to sailors (110–11), Joé further emphasizes normative heterosexuality. Indeed, the shame of Roland's situation causes him to commit suicide, and in a final note to his teacher, he explains: "Pour moi, il est plus facile de partir que de rester" (111) [For me, it is easier to leave than to stay]. This particular boy's tragic story again appears as an allegory for the *pieds-noirs* as a community.

In consequence, the novel simultaneously contradicts and confirms depictions of *pied-noir* men as homosexual and/or perverted during and in the immediate aftermath of the Algerian War in a way that reiterates normative gender roles while nevertheless implying a tolerance of discreet difference. There are two deviant settler adults who prey on children in the story: the partner of Roland's mother, a Cretan who, in addition to forcing the boy into prostitution, engages in sexual relations with both mother and son "sans se gêner" (111) [without hesitation]; and an old Maltese shopkeeper who unsuccessfully tries to lure Joé into his bedroom in exchange for cash (16). Joé also gets to know a cruel young bully, Pinto (whose sidekick is the aforementioned Bouzid Belhouch), who aims to run a brothel when he is older and who procures young boys and girls for pimps (79). However, these characters may be read as representative of an exploitative minority in a colonial world of innocent children such as Joé. The narrative also implies that the Casbah and its indigenous inhabitants negatively influence Pinto's behavior: "Pinto, il n'est pas comme nous. Il est de la rue Rovigo, la rue qui monte le long de la Casbah. [. . .] Tous les macs, toutes les putes, il les connaît" (79) [Pinto is not like us. He is from Rue Rogivo, the street that goes up by the Casbah. [. . .] He knows all the pimps and whores]. This sort of comment calls to mind Berreby's pedagogical aim. Indeed, the narrator's humorous, engaging commentary works to encourage sympathy with the *pieds-noirs* from a readership that is, in all likelihood, largely adolescent.

Furthermore, themes from previously discussed works recur in this novel. The first section, "La mer" (the sea), is Camusian in tone as Joé describes his joyful pursuits of swimming and playing soccer in Bab-el-Oued with his similarly impoverished friends.[48] Rival streets later join forces to form a soccer team that includes an indigenous Algerian, Ali Yaya, thereby suggesting the potential for fraternal harmony. Significantly, this is disrupted when the team's important "revenge match" against a rival team largely made up of indigenous Algerians is canceled on a symbolic date—November 1, 1954 (the outbreak of the war)—as the team's sponsor, Joé's friend Nono, dies. The absence of Joé's father also has Camusian echoes, as does his ambiguous relationship with his mother, who does not understand him. Thus, in an echo of Camus's famous statement, "J'ai mal à l'Algérie" [I have an Algeria ache] in "Lettre à un militant algérien" (1955) [Letter to an Algerian Militant], the narrator poignantly informs us that "J'ai mal à ma mère" [I have a mother ache].[49] Additionally, young Joé exhibits tenacious, resourceful qualities as he struggles to feed his family, an aspect of the story that contributes to pioneering imagery. He is poorer than some indigenous Algerian shoeshine boys (*yaouleds*), who threaten him when he sets up as a shoeshine boy himself, as do a group of delivery boys (*yaouleds porteurs de couffins*) when he follows their lead by carrying clients' shopping baskets to and from the market. He is therefore equal to or in a worse position than the indigenous population as, in an echo of works by Camus, Conesa, and Roblès, the novel foregrounds class issues, rather than racial tensions.

Conventional constructions of *pied-noir* masculinity also recur here through the narrator's emphasis on violence. Violent action seems like a requirement to ward off greater evil as the narrator explains that he had to beat up the boy who insulted his mother on the day of her operation: "Nous, on sait que pour éloigner le mal il faut faire pisser le sang. A savoir ce qui se serait passé à l'hôpital si Arnaud n'avait pas saigné" (106–7) [We know that to ward off evil, you need to make blood gush. Who knows what would have happened at the hospital if Arnaud had not bled]. This emphasis on violence as a necessity harks back to Camus's description of boxing in his essay "Le Minotaure ou la halte d'Oran" [The Minotaur or the Stop in Oran], in the collection *L'Été*.[50] Joé's reaction to an insult involving his mother—he goes "Maboul" (96) or mad and "rabia" (106) or rage overtakes him—signals the now familiar notion of the hot-headedness of *pied-noir* men as well as their profound attachment to the mother. His superstitious consideration of violence as a necessity also recalls the attitude of the narrator in Roblès's *Saison violente*, who catches ants in a tube in the hope that on the seventh day of their imprisonment, his mother's cruel former employer will double over in pain.[51] Joëlle Hureau, as a historian, suggests that the *pieds-noirs* are a superstitious people, influenced by different religions and by both saints and marabouts.[52] Joé's belief that a neighbor, Mme Mesguish, can use magic to ward off an envious "mauvais oeil" (44) [evil eye] and Nono's burial of a doll on the advice of a witch, in order to free Joé from the burden of his father's sins (151–52), similarly evoke the merging of European and African traditions. These incidents also suggest the necessity of symbolic acts of aggression where real ones are impossible. The novel therefore naturalizes the use of violence in the colonial setting. Indeed, as in the case of Camus's *Le Premier Homme*, it evokes violence alongside biblical references to Cain, who committed murder but who was also the first farmer. In this case, Joé, as the only sibling who is aware that his father killed his fascist brother in Italy, feels burdened by the family secret and lives in fear that he in turn will kill his brother, Dany "Comme Caïn a tué Abel" (73) [as Cain killed Abel]. For the reader, however, Joé is clearly not responsible for the sins of his father.

Moreover, fairy-tale elements of the novel point to a potential paradise that has gone wrong, thus perpetuating fantasies about Algeria's colonial past. His mother's hospitalization forces Joé to leave his home and friends in order to stay with his Uncle Etienne and his wife Gladys in the second section of the book, "Putain de sa mère!" [His mother is a whore]. The pupils at Joé's new school treat him like an outcast, as does Gladys, who behaves like an evil stepmother. The third section, "Le soleil dans les yeux" [Sun in his Eyes], sees the narrator's blossoming friendship with Gladys's wealthy young adolescent nephew, Nono, whom the narrator christens "Bouddha" [Buddha]. The latter possesses an almost mystical ability, helped by his privileged background, to solve Joé's problems: "avec deux doigts entre les dents, [il] pouvait siffler le destin et lui ordonner de réviser ses coups" (183–84) [putting two fingers into his mouth, he could summon destiny by whistling and order it to revise the blows it dealt].[53] Following Nono's death from typhus fever on the same day as the beginning of the war of independence, a downward spiral of death and destruction ensues. This includes the narrator's own attempt to drown himself on learning both of Nono's death and, through reports of the uprising, that Algeria is in reality a colony. However, Joé is not responsible for his childish belief in the tale of "la plus grande France" [greater France]. In this way, fairy-tale elements and a poignant tone reinforce the notion that acknowledging the reality of Algeria's colonial status sooner might have prevented its loss. In Joé's case, he learns that his mother's refusal to recognize Algeria as a colony led to the break-up of his parents' marriage. Furthermore, Joé's youth and inexperience explain his initial inability to see Algeria as a colonial territory. Once again, therefore, one boy's personal story serves as an allegory for a French Algerian family.

Hélène Gadal's novel, *Petite pied-noir deviendra grande* (2002) [Little *Pied-Noir* Girl will Grow Up], published during France's continuing "memory wars" of recent years, provides a useful point of comparison to both Saint-Hamont's and Berreby's earlier works discussed above, as a child's sincere and engaging voice again perpetuates models of communal identity that appear unchanging. An explanation on the back cover states that Gadal, who left Algeria at the age of eleven, wrote the story for her daughters:

> Lors d'un séjour dans la ville d'enfance de mon mari, alors qu'il nous montrait tous les lieux qui l'avaient vu grandir, j'ai réalisé que je ne pourrais jamais parcourir avec mes filles ces endroits qui ont tant compté pour moi. C'est pour elles que j'ai eu envie de raconter mon enfance.[54]

> [During a stay in the town where my husband spent his childhood, as he was showing us all the places that had seen him grow up, I realized that I would never be able to take my daughters around the places that meant so much to me. It is for them that I wanted to tell the story of my childhood.]

This text is therefore a personal *lieu de mémoire* [site of memory] for the author. However, the tale, narrated by a *pied-noir* protagonist called Jacqueline who tells her story from the day of her seventh birthday, through to her departure for France on her eleventh birthday and her initial experiences of exile, again serves as a conduit of collective memory.

Jacqueline's view facilitates humor and the development of conventional tropes as she conflates myth, imagination, and reality. For example, she regards the story of her grandparents' meeting, as told to her by them, as "mieux qu'un conte de fées" (29) [better than a fairy tale]. This family legend features her impoverished grandfather Hector who, she explains, was often barefoot, "ce qui même pour un Pied-noir est très douloureux" (29) [which even for a *pied-noir* is very painful]. Jacqueline recounts Hector's rise to success as a self-taught man who becomes manager of a large farm.

She also describes his difficulty finding a suitable wife or "chaussure à son pied" [the shoe that fits], an expression used by the adults that she believes "peut s'expliquer par le fait qu'il n'en avait pas porté pendant longtemps" (30) [can be explained by the fact that he had not worn any for a long time]. Her grandfather eventually marries the narrator's metropolitan French grandmother Marguerite, following his military service in World War I, and the story has a happy ending, as Marguerite grows to love Algeria and its inhabitants. However, while Jacqueline's comically literal understanding of her grandfather's search for a shoe that fits ironizes the notion of her grandfather's perpetually bare feet, the text still reinforces both the pioneering spirit of the *pieds-noirs* and their blood sacrifice for France—another key theme in narratives by the *pieds-noirs*. Furthermore, a reader not familiar with the history of the settlers would be inclined to believe this likable character when she states that the *pieds-noirs* got their name from indigenous Algerians because of the black shoes worn by the first "Français en Algérie" [French in Algeria]—a myth that distinguishes the colonists from a population that had apparently never seen footwear and from humble settlers like her barefoot grandfather (9).

The novel again foregrounds fairy tales. Jacqueline's allusion to Sleeping Beauty during her baby brother's christening both underlines a harmonious present and creates a sense of foreboding with regard to the future: "Me voilà transposée dans mon conte préféré: La Belle au bois dormant. Les bonnes fées font don à cet enfant de toutes les qualités. Un sentiment d'inquiétude m'envahit. L'affreuse fée va-t-elle se manifester elle aussi?" (18–19) [I am transported into my favorite tale: Sleeping Beauty. Good fairies give this child all the attributes. A worried feeling comes over me. Will the wicked fairy appear too?]. The *fellaghas* or rebels, in their struggle for independence, later intrude upon her generally happy world as they are the subject of adults' anxious conversation and become, for her, the embodiment of bad fairies. Charles de Gaulle is also, through the eyes of the young narrator, a traitor for negotiating independence, having implied his intention to fight for *l'Algérie française* with his famous "Je vous ai compris" [I have understood you] speech in Algiers in 1958:

> J'entends de plus en plus parler d'un certain général venu de Gaule, qui a levé un jour ses grands bras et de sa voix chevrotante (même lorsqu'il ne parle pas à la TSF) a déclaré qu'il avait tout compris. Il y a aussi les fellaghas et au début j'ai cru qu'il s'agissait de fées là-bas, cachées dans les collines. Mais ces fées-là ne nous veulent pas de bien. Et le général il s'appelle de Gaulle. [. . .] D'abord on pensait que c'était un ami mais il a retourné sa veste et une veste de général en plus, avec beaucoup de galons. C'est si compliqué à comprendre et il ne faut pas poser de questions! (61)

[I hear more and more talk about a certain general from Gaule, who lifted up his big arms one day and in his quavering voice (even when he is not speaking on the wireless) declared that he had understood everything. There are also *fellaghas* and at the start I thought they were "fées" [fairies], "là-bas" [over there], hidden in the hills. But these fairies do not wish us well. And the general is called de Gaulle. [. . .] At first people thought he was a friend but he was a turncoat and what's more, it was a general's coat with lots of stripes. It is so difficult to understand and you must not ask questions!]

This quotation, which foregrounds the narrator's naiveté, stands as a metaphor for her community, which consequently appears as an innocent *peuple jeune*.

Furthermore, Jacqueline's emphasis on the significance of distinctive gender roles from a young age reiterates literary markers of what now form part of a recognizable, communal *pied-noir* identity. Thus, at the age of seven, she claims that she and her nine-year-old sister Lisa have already begun their "apprentissage de bonnes mères de famille" (12) [apprenticeship as blessed mothers of a family]. She is equally aware that the baby her mother is expecting at the beginning of the story must be a boy for the sake of the family's honor (9). A close relationship with indigenous Algerian women also frames descriptions of her childhood. Her best friend at school is called Malika and, in an echo of Cixous's description of Aïcha (as discussed in chapter 2), she imagines that the family's maid, Keltoum, is her mother. A characteristic accent is a further marker of the narrator's identity, which is a source of mockery when she enrolls in school in France (90). The distinctive nature of this identity is also evident through the narrator's reference to typical *pied-noir* expressions, such as the following, which points to both an inherent optimism and modest expectations: "tant qu'on a un croûton de pain et de l'oignon, la vie vaut la peine d'être vécue!" (93) [as long as we have a crust of bread and some onion, life is worth living!]. Moreover, in an echo of *Le Coup de Sirocco*, the narrator credits the *pieds-noirs* with introducing couscous, as well as merguez sausage, to France (94).

While Joé's family in Berreby's *L'Enfant pied-noir* includes both Catholics and Jews, this story privileges Catholicism. Thus, Jacqueline's parents met as children thanks to the Church, as the same babysitter looked after her father and mother while their parents attended mass. The family's reenactment of a live crib, with Lisa using their great-grandfather's cane to act as Joseph and the new baby, Marc, playing the role of the baby Jesus, echoes the nativity scene in *Le Premier Homme* and constructs the settlers' identity in terms of well-intentioned pilgrims. Furthermore, their religion differentiates them from the metropolitan French as Jacqueline notes that her parents, ever loyal to their beliefs, do not send them to a secular school near their new home in

France, instead choosing a convent school at some distance from where they live (89). Her statement on life in Algeria: "Dimanche = religion + famille" (37) [Sunday = religion + family] also reiterates the family as a key feature of *pied-noir* identity. Religious occasions, such as Easter and First Holy Communions, as well as holidays, involve a large clan. Indeed, there are numerous references to her extended family in the book; the narrator claims that a "vraie famille pied-noir" [true *pied-noir* family] consists of countless cousins of all ages (24), and notes, on her arrival in France, that the *pieds-noirs* have family everywhere (80).

It is the presence of her extended family along with another crucial identity marker, a pioneering spirit, which enables Jacqueline and her immediate family to look forward to their future in France. They decide to "«prospecter», chercher un nouveau chez-nous, une terre d'accueil, pionniers à leur tour comme avant eux leurs grands-parents" (85) [prospect, seek a new home, a land of refuge, pioneers in turn just like their grandparents before them]. Thus, unlike many of the other works studied, this one ends on a distinctly hopeful note, as the narrator is ready to adapt to life in France. At the close of the novel, Jacqueline wakes up full of youthful energy and, on visiting her parents' new vineyard with "toute la famille" [the whole family], proclaims: "Les vers de Lamartine [. . .] me reviennent en mémoire: *Et la famille, enracinée sur le coteau qu'elle a planté, refleurit d'année en année.* Voilà c'est là notre nouvelle terre et je sens que je vais l'aimer elle aussi" (95, Gadal's emphasis) [The verses of [Alphonse de] Lamartine [...] come back to me: *And the family, rooted on the hillside where it sowed, flowers again year after year*. There it is, our new land, and I get the feeling I am going to like her too]. In this way, Jacqueline and her family display a French identity constructed through literature and a love for the land and vines, but they also perform a uniquely *pied-noir* identity that is marked by entrepreneurial spirit, Christianity as opposed to secularism, and an emphasis on the family as a key site of affective and ideological investment. Furthermore, her performance as a child enables her to construct a positive memory of the *pieds-noirs* without addressing the still contested political and historical situations of the colonial past. This leads to an exploration of narratives that are more productive in terms of addressing the legacy of colonialism.

4.3 PRODUCTIVE POSSIBILITIES IN PERFORMANCE

Virginie Buisson's *L'Algérie ou la mort des autres* (1978) [Algeria or the Death of Others] provides a potential counterpoint to the above texts. Benjamin Stora describes Buisson as a *pied-noir*.[55] However, a biographical note at the beginning of the novel explains that she was born in 1944 in

France and lived there until the age of ten, which again draws attention to *pied-noir* identity as a site of contestation and performance.[56] This narrative, written in the voice of a young girl who moves to Algeria from France at the age of eleven, is perhaps, like most of the works studied, best considered as semiautobiographical.[57] The front matter implies that writing the narrative was personally cathartic for the author:

> Toute la guerre elle a vue, elle n'a rien demandé, elle disait comme ça pour elle, un jour j'écrirai un livre, il s'appellera *La mort des autres*. Elle a dit cela pendant quinze ans. Aujourd'hui il est là comme on le dit d'un enfant nouveau-né. Il est là et elle est au monde.

> [She saw the whole war; she asked for nothing; she used to say, just for herself, one day I will write a book; it will be called *The Death of Others*. She said that for fifteen years. Today, as you say about a newborn child, it is here. It is here and she has come into the world.]

However, the book is also significant in disseminating information about the conflict, as suggested by its continued publication in collections aimed at women, children, and adolescents.[58] Moreover, its title recalls Jean Guéhenno's critical reflections on World War I, in his *La Mort des autres* (1968) [The Death of Others], thereby suggesting a politically engaged approach.[59]

Buisson's laconic style, using phrases she describes as "taillées jusqu'à l'os" [cut to the bone], is unusual.[60] As discussed in chapter 2, *pied-noir* women have displayed a particular tendency to focus on personal events in an emotional manner. Andrea L. Smith states that men's contrasting tendency to recount events from the war as if reciting from a book, and without connecting them to their personal lives, suggests an active avoidance of memory that she contends, drawing on Stora's work in *La Gangrène et l'oubli* (1992) [Gangrene and Forgetting], inhibits healing.[61] Indeed, according to clinical psychologist and trauma specialist Kathleen Young, recounting traumatic experiences in an emotionally disconnected manner does not promote healing.[62] However, while drawing on emotion is beneficial in allowing people to move on from traumatic events, such narratives work to "distort our recollection" of the relevant events.[63] Perhaps by not engaging emotionally with the subject, Buisson's narrative is a more reliable portrait of the war presented from a young girl's point of view. The liminal space between words and *les non-dits* [what is not said], which, like the responses of Smith's male interviewees, appears indicative of repressed trauma, also reflects the narrator's by now familiar position between childhood and adulthood. Her status as a "patos" (12) [French Frog], who belongs to neither the Arabo-Berber nor *pied-noir* communities, further cements her position as an outsider with the potential to confront the realities of a difficult past.

The story diverges from traditional representations of youth by destabilizing stereotypes of childhood. The narrator does this when she draws attention to conventions to which she chooses to conform in order to avoid punishment, noting:

> Il y a tout un code que je découvre petit à petit, d'abord il faut manger, obéir, ne pas traîner en faisant les courses, ne pas répondre à ma mère, donner mes jouets à mes frères, aimer être à la maison. (25)

> [There is a whole code that I discover little by little. First, I have to eat, obey, not dawdle when doing the shopping, not answer back to my mother, give my toys to my brothers, enjoy being at home.]

Moreover, she is adept at performing childhood and adult femininity as the occasion requires. Thus, she escapes from the role to which she is consigned "en jouant les sacristains" [by playing the sacristan] at the local church (30), where she quickly finishes her chores in order to spend time with the soldiers who are camped next to the presbytery. She also performs as a dutiful child in advance of a date with a soldier, noting that on the day in question, she is generous with her brother, helps her mother, avoids answering back, clears her plate, and dresses in the clothes her mother picks for her (54–55). The narrator then changes her clothes in the church bell tower and puts on nail polish for her date (55). Furthermore, she pretends to a boyfriend, Daniel, that she is seventeen when she is barely fourteen (47). Her ability to act a certain age therefore reveals that "age, like gender, is shaped by a society's expectations and the performance of a populace to achieve what can be approximated as normative behavior."[64]

The narrator's position as a young outsider who can perform both childhood and adulthood, and who is not, therefore, merely a symbol of youthful innocence, is a helpful means of engaging with all sides in the war. Thus, through her detached descriptions of what she sees and hears, she highlights the impact of the war on indigenous families, including the elderly women and children at the gates of the military base where their loved ones are imprisoned (57). The treatment some women receive at the hands of soldiers equally underscores gendered violence in the colonial context: "Ils ont arraché en hurlant le voile des femmes, renversé les couffins de ceux qui avançait mal, éventré les charges des bourricots, répandu la semoule" (69) [They shouted as they tore women's veils from them, knocked over the baskets of those who did not move quickly, ripped open donkeys' loads and scattered semolina].

More crucially still, the narrator's dispassionate descriptions convey the horrific torture perpetrated against the Arabo-Berber population, to which her younger brothers are oblivious and which the army wives support. As with John Boyne's *The Boy in the Striped Pajamas* (2006), the realization that such cruelty is possible becomes even more shocking for the reader when viewed through the eyes of a young narrator:[65]

> Sur le moment j'ai cru que quelqu'un s'était fait mal. Mais les femmes se sont mises à rire. Les enfants ont arrêté leurs jeux. Quelqu'un a deploré que les caves ne soient pas mieux isolées et que les interrogatoires se fassent l'après-midi. Les cris sont devenus prières. Les femmes ont rangé leur tricot, déplacé leur chaise et se sont installées plus loin. Les enfants ont suivi. Mes frères ont continué à jouer avec des fourmis. C'était juste après la sieste. Le sirocco s'était calmé; il restait la chaleur de la terre et la poussière rouge sur les murs. A l'heure du goûter, ma mère nous a rentrés. Elle a fermé les fenêtres sur les cris. (56)

> [At the time, I thought that someone had hurt themselves. But the women began to laugh. The children stopped playing their games. Someone bemoaned the fact that the cellars were not better soundproofed and that the interrogations we carried out in the afternoon. The cries became prayers. The women gathered up their knitting, moved their chairs and sat down further away. The children followed. My brothers continued playing with ants. It was just after the siesta. The Sirocco wind had subsided; the earth's heat and red dust on the walls remained. At teatime, my mother brought us in. She closed the windows on the cries.]

While *Le coup de Sirocco*'s allusion to the wind evokes the turmoil of adolescence and of the Algerian War for *pied-noir* families, a reference to the calm Sirocco above is suggestive of the effects of deliberate violence against the indigenous population. Furthermore, like young Bruno's juxtaposition of normal family life in Boyne's *The Boy in the Striped Pajamas* with the lives of the concentration camp prisoners on the other side of the fence, the narrator's description of being sent to fetch wine from a basement that is filled with prisoners begging for water dramatically highlights their mistreatment:

> Ma mère m'a envoyée à la cave chercher du vin. J'ai descendu les marches, je n'ai pas supporté les corps entravés et je me suis sauvée, des hurlements plein le corps. Les caves étaient pleines de prisonniers, ils passaient leurs mains à travers les barreaux et réclamaient de l'eau. (66–68)

> [My mother sent me to the cellar to fetch wine. I went down the steps; I could not bear the shackled bodies and I ran away, screams bursting from my body.

The cellars were full of prisoners; they were putting their hands through the bars and begging for water.]

Having heard someone crying out while being tortured, the narrator, the next day, asks a shepherd what "Bouyoukh" ("Papa") means (56). The implication that this girl has heard another young person being tortured further emphasizes the horror of the situation. Indeed, this episode recalls the torture of thirteen-year-old Algerian Saïd Ferdi by French soldiers, as described in his autobiography, *Un enfant dans la guerre* (1981) [A Child in War].[66] Significantly, despite excuses by the adults, who justify torture by citing brutal attacks against Europeans, the young narrator in Buisson's text links violence to colonial injustice, through which children die of hunger:

«Parmi eux [les prisonniers], il y a peut-être ceux qui ont coupé le sexe des soldats.» [. . .] Qui les a éventrés, pour quelle colère? Et les quinze cercueils alignés dans le jardin de l'église et le mépris des Européens et des enfants morts de faim dans un gourbi adossé à la ferme d'un colon.[67] La vérité éclatait. (68)

["Among them [the prisoners], there may be those who cut off soldiers' genitals." [. . .] Who disemboweled them, for what angry reason? And what about the fifteen coffins lined up in the churchyard and the Europeans' contempt and the starving children in a lean-to hut beside a colonist's farmhouse? The truth was dawning.]

Thus, the young narrator draws attention to the difficult situation of the colonized population and to the "racisme ordinaire, quotidien" (15) [ordinary, daily racism] that she learns as a child in Algeria. Moreover, the colonial administration appears complicit in confining Muslim women to the domestic sphere; the narrator's parents withdraw her from a girls' primary school (where she is the only French pupil) due to the teacher's sole emphasis on keeping house and on knitting and sewing (17, 24).[68] The narrator's relationship with Nance, a teacher in the boys' primary school next door, is a further indictment of France's *mission civilisatrice* [civilizing mission], despite the young narrator's romanticized vision of their trysts in his classroom after school. Her fairy-tale romance, during which she feels "riche et généreuse, prête à tous les partages" (35) [rich and generous, prepared to share everything], jars with the image of the school teacher's abuse of his position to take advantage of a young primary school girl: "Il disait: «Je veux que tu sois à moi.» Je ne comprenais pas bien, mais sa violence m'effrayait un peu lorsqu'il m'embrassait" (35) [He would say, "I want you to be mine." I did not really understand, but his violence scared me a bit when he kissed me]. Furthermore, having abused his position, Nance suddenly announces that he is leaving for France and his sudden abandonment of her and Algeria prefigures the end of colonialism. Consequently, in the apocalyptic scenes at the end of the novel, it seems as though the spell of French Algeria has been broken as the narrator claims that her love story with the sea, which she previously considered her most certain relationship (76), is over: "La mer a perdu ses sortilèges" (88) [The sea has lost her magic spell].

The war also provokes the sudden end of the narrator's childhood biologically and psychologically. When a soldier asks if he can kiss her, she does not dare to say yes although she wants to, and in the next paragraph, she notes in typically laconic style that he died following an ambush (58). In an echo of Marie Cardinal's bleeding, her trauma manifests itself physically as she begins to menstruate (59). This recalls the young narrator of *pied-noir* author Marie-Jeanne Perez's *Gouttes-de-sang* (1991) [Blooddrops], for whom the onset of puberty and menstruation collides with the bloodshed of the Algerian War.[69] As Philip Dine notes, privileging the child's view and the intimately feminine in this way can potentially destabilize "the apparent certainties of the colonial situation [. . .] particularly its foundation on a set of binary oppositions: inside/outside, male/female, Self/Other, colonizer/colonized, civilized/savage."[70] Buisson's novel, in which the narrator, like the narrator of *Gouttes de sang*, demonstrates a disturbing and defamiliarizing precocious sexuality, thus subverts conventional depictions of what Rose calls the "fantasy of childhood" as it appears in literature.[71] Although the narrator's childhood definitively ends when she witnesses the death of Jacques (a young *pied-noir* conscript with whom she falls in love) at the hands of *Algérie française* activists (92–93), she does not look back to idealized childhood innocence. In consequence, the text does not perpetuate nostalgia and does not appear as an attempt to "recolonize" Algeria through literature.

The narrator's continuing development also facilitates an exploration of psychological disorders.[72] On seeing soldiers carrying a tarpaulin that covers the tortured body of an indigenous Algerian, the narrator takes her first "cachets de l'oubli" (89) [pills to forget]. She ends up "absente" [absent] and perhaps spends some time in hospital, stating that she remembers a brown corridor and crawling on tiles, before leaving for France in September 1962 (93). Her mental instability recalls that of Cardinal, as well as Frantz Fanon's and Bernard Sigg's work on the trauma caused to perpetrators and victims of colonial violence. It is useful to point out here that the narrator reveals her complicity in this violence by failing to intervene when she witnesses a soldier forcing a bottle of beer into the mouth of a young indigenous girl.[73] Her complicity is also evident when she fails to engage with the prisoners in her basement who cry out for water (66–69). Moreover, she actively partakes in colonial violence when she joins a soldier in trampling on some yellow melons (the word "melon" is significant as a racist evocation of the indigenous population) and in then eating one in front of an old Arab man the soldier has been harassing (50–52). However, the narrator confirms her unease at the repudiation of the colonized population when she destroys a can of paint that soldiers are using to mark a cross on every *gourbi* [hut] in the village during a census (50). In consequence, this text differs from the narratives studied above, as it overtly associates the narrator's mental instability with colonial injustice.

Another representation of childhood that engages with the trauma of both sides in a similarly restrained style is Algerian-born author Jean-Noël Pancrazi's semiautobiographical *Madame Arnoul* (1995).[74] This later novel's appeal to a wide audience is evident from the awards it received.[75] Like Buisson's *L'Algérie ou la mort des autres*, the text does not dwell on emotions and is not polemical. The young narrator is another outsider who is largely alone except for the company of a neighbor who becomes his second mother. This is the eponymous Madame Arnoul, herself an outsider who left Alsace as an adolescent and settled in the small town of Batna, in the mountainous Aurès region.

The narrator's performance of masculinity is of particular interest as it varies from the normative heterosexuality emphasized in the majority of works studied so far. It is useful to point out here that sociologist Michael A. Messner, drawing on contemporary scholarship, suggests that the performance of gender by children varies according to the social context.[76] By the same token, the narrator's performance of childhood in *Madame Arnoul* gives him more freedom to perform masculinity as he chooses, particularly as he is frequently on the fringes of social interaction with a wider group. Thus, he describes tender sexual interactions with another boy, Jean-Pierre Vizzavona, although he admits that in public he feigns nonchalance when returning from Jean-Pierre's house (40–41). Moreover, the narrator witnesses Jean-Pierre's later romantic relationship with a girl when both are involved in group activities with their contemporaries—at a Holy Communion party and on another occasion when a group of young friends enjoy increased freedom from their parents, who are preoccupied by the worsening situation of the war (50, 56). It seems, therefore, that society affords youths like Jean-Pierre the freedom of not performing normative heterosexual masculinity, depending on the social setting. The *pied-noir* character Henri in French director André Téchiné's *Les Roseaux sauvages* (1994) [Wild Reeds] makes a similar suggestion in a film that uses the adolescent gaze to approach France's painful colonial legacy with regard to *pied-noir* and metropolitan French youths, although not the Algerian population.[77] In the privacy of their boarding school washroom in South-West France, Henri tells François, who is younger and whom he suspects of engaging in homosexual activities: "À ton âge, je faisais pareil, j'en ai bien profité. C'est normal, c'est la vie" [At your age, I did the same thing; I made the most of it. It's natural, it's part of life].[78] For the narrator of *Madame Arnoul*, his parents are "trop tolérants, ou insuffisamment pieux, pour le croire vraiment" [too tolerant or not pious enough to really believe him] when a priest to whom he confesses his "plaisirs clandestins" [clandestine pleasures] informs them that he is a pervert (42). It appears that his youth is a factor in his parents' decision to ignore his failure to perform normative masculinity.

Once again, the narrator's youth enables him to draw attention to the shocking violence of war and to reject dominant discourses. His child's eye implicitly criticizes violence committed by the authorities in the following disorienting description that gives an insight into his confusion:

> il m'avait semblé distinguer des dizaines de corps enflammés qui dévalaient les pentes de la montagne d'Aïn Timor avant de basculer et de disparaître dans le noir [. . .], le vent de soufre, de bois et de chairs brûlés qui atteignait la terrasse me glaçait d'une colère impuissante et triste. (55)

> [I thought I saw dozens of burning bodies rushing down the slopes of the Aïn Timor mountain before toppling over and disappearing into the darkness. [. . .] The wafting scent of sulfur, wood and burnt flesh that reached the terrace filled me with a sad, powerless anger.]

The below description reveals his horror at the systematic debasement of the indigenous population, thereby pointing to resultant trauma on all sides:

> J'étais envahi par une honte désemparée lorsque, sur le chemin du lycée, je voyais la masse silencieuse des musulmans derrière les rouleaux de fils de fer barbelés. Les soldats les fouillaient un à un, soulevaient leurs gandouras[79] avec le bout des fusils, juste pour exhiber la nudité de leurs corps grelottant de peur et de misère, avant de les obliger à monter sur les plate-formes des camions qui les conduisaient vers les "centres d'hébergement." Les bâches retombaient derrrière eux comme des rideaux de mort. (58)

> [I was overwhelmed with a crippling sense of shame when, on the way to high school, I would see the silent mass of Muslims behind rolls of barbed wire. The soldiers would search them one by one, lifting up their tunics with the tips of their rifles, just to expose the nakedness of their bodies that shivered from fear and destitution, before forcing them to climb up onto the platforms of the trucks that were taking them to "residential centers" [internment camps]. The tarpaulins would fall down behind them like curtains of death.]

The sight, during a school trip, of female detainees working in paddy fields equally haunts him and he fears his beloved Madame Arnoul may be among the women, following her arrest due to suspected activities on behalf of the independence movement (100). It is worth noting here that during this same trip to a Roman amphitheater, the narrator rejects the teacher's premise that Latin Africa is evidence of the "«grandeur» dont [. . .] nous étions les héritiers" [grandeur to which [. . .] we were heirs] (99). His youthful viewpoint also serves to criticize the OAS, as he describes understanding the significance of the mysterious acronym on witnessing attackers shooting an old indigenous woman in an ambush assault (104–5).

Moreover, the narrator underlines the performative aspects of adults' behavior. Indeed, he alludes to a perceived need to perform an exaggerated masculinity due to France's loss of Indochina, following a bloody war from 1945 to 1954. For this reason, his uncle Noël is "de retour d'Indochine [. . .] avide, sans doute, de se retrouver sur la terre d'une autre colonie où il pourrait encore régner" (34) [back from Indochina, [. . .] no doubt eager to get back to the land of another colony where he could still reign]. The concept of powerful masculinity is undermined when the narrator's father and Madame Arnoul's husband join the reservist "unités territoriales" [territorial units] and set off to guard a road. Their ill-fitting uniforms and embarrassed air imply that their behavior is not natural, as the narrator notes: "ils avaient plutôt l'allure de soldats de comédie montant vers un décor de fortins et un ciel de guerre imaginaire" (81–82) [They actually looked like soldiers from a play going toward a set of forts and an imaginary war-torn sky]. The performance of the army is equally theatrical and even meaningless as, when the soldiers suddenly depart without warning, he states that their rubbish "semblait l'élément de décor d'une représentation finie" (101) [seemed like part of the set from a finished performance]. Similarly, the settler women's exaggerated makeup indicates a performance that is revealed as such in the horror of war, as Madame Arnoul, newly released from prison, mocks them for their

> fards outranciers de femmes qui s'efforçaient de masquer leur peur et, s'éloignant [. . .], devenaient les sosies hagards et désarticulés des mannequins qu'elles avaient joué à être lorsqu'en cette saison elles défilaient devant la villa du juge de paix en arborant leurs nouvelles tenues d'été. (117–18)

> [extreme makeup of women who were struggling to mask their fear and [who], from a distance [. . .], became the haunted and shattered doppelgangers of the models they had played at being when parading past the magistrate's villa this season, sporting their new summer clothes.]

Both Buisson's *L'Algérie ou la mort des autres* and Pancrazi's *Madame Arnoul* therefore stand as genuine attempts to engage with the undeniable trauma of the war on both sides. A youthful view is particularly helpful in tackling the issue of torture and subverting stereotypes of childhood and gender, which are revealed as performative, as well as destabilizing normative heterosexuality. This said, the narrator of *L'Algérie ou la mort des autres* evokes Orientalist imagery with her romanticized descriptions of indigenous women (17, 33, 42). Her fear that those close to her—her love interest Jacques and her family—will die, hence her fear of "la mort des autres" [the death of others], referred to in the title of the book, also suggests an overarching sympathy with the settlers and metropolitan French (86). Historic events, when occasionally referenced, further indicate a prevailing sympathy with the settler population.[80] The young narrator of *Madame Arnoul*, meanwhile, appears Camusian in his desire not to choose sides, expressing his unease when some classmates attempt to transform him, "à mon insu en porte-parole d'une cause à laquelle je n'étais pas prêt à adhérer" (59) [unbeknown to me, into a spokesperson for a cause I was not ready to join]. Through his friendship with a classmate, Mohammed Khaïr-Eddine, he also points to a potential fraternity between the colonizing and colonized populations in an imagined, very French model of the Republic:[81]

> une petite république à deux, une enclave de paix, un pays rêvé où il n'y aurait que des classes à l'infini, où la seule rumeur serait celle du crissement des craies sur les ardoises et les seuls drapeaux ceux destinés à fêter les élèves qui, montant sur une tribune, tiendraient leur diplôme de bourse blotti contre le cœur. (97)

> [a little Republic for two, an enclave of peace, a dream country where there would be nothing but endless classes, where the only sound would be chalk grating on slates and the only flags would be those destined to celebrate the students who, standing on a rostrum, would hold their scholarship certificate nestled to their hearts.]

Significantly, the narrator's friendship with this character underscores the difficult future awaiting Algerians as Mohammed despairingly asks: "Pourquoi vous partez?" (131) [Why are you leaving?]. Here, he looks at the narrator with "un regard de clairvoyance attristée—devinant peut-être, déjà, les dérives, les intolérances et les amnésies d'une société nouvelle à l'écart de laquelle il se plaçait d'avance" (131) [a saddened, perceptive expression, perhaps already sensing the downward spiral, the intolerance and the amnesia of a new society from which he was setting himself apart in advance]. Furthermore, the narrator's premature loss of innocence, symbolized by his actions as a go-between for soldiers and indigenous Algerian maids (in an echo of the famous L. P. Hartley novel cited above) and his self-professed identity as an eternal "enfant perdu" (138) [lost child] upon leaving Algeria still suggest that this tragic outsider represents a broader *pied-noir* community.

4.4 A LASTING LEGACY FOR THE NEXT GENERATION

Writers continue to publish works focusing on French Algerian childhoods. One offering that appeared in the context of the fiftieth anniversary of Algerian independence is journalist Brigitte Benkemoun's *La Petite fille sur la photo: La guerre d'Algérie à hauteur d'enfant* (2012) [The Little Girl in the Photo: A Child's View of the Algerian War], which received considerable attention in the French media and is worth considering briefly here.[82] Benkemoun, a *pied-noir* of Jewish extraction, focuses on children such as herself who left Algeria in 1962. Through this prism, she investigates her own family history and interviews others, including well-known figures such as Benjamin Stora, who left Algeria aged eleven, Jean-Jacques Jordi, who left aged seven, and twins Jacques (economist, writer, former special advisor to President François Mitterrand) and Bernard (business executive, former CEO of Air France) Attali, who left aged twelve. One reviewer situates this book as part of a timely decision to "donner la parole aux enfants" [give children a chance to speak].[83] Others underline a younger generation's will and ability to break taboos on the Algerian War.[84] Yet fictionalized works by Buisson and Pancrazi, both of whom left Algeria at a young age, suggest that authors were producing taboo-breaking texts as far back as the late 1970s. By using fiction, these authors had scope to tackle thorny subjects without courting controversy before French authorities officially recognized the war. In contrast, Benkemoun's text is composed of her and her family's real-life experiences and those of her interviewees. Nevertheless, she indicates that her own family rewrote its history on settling in France and suggests that her research will stand in for what she might have remembered had she not left Algeria definitively aged four.[85] Her personal inquiry into her birthplace becomes a published "journal d'un passé recomposé" (15) [diary of a reconstructed past]. Once again, therefore, personal stories take on significance with regard to a collective memory shaped by narratives.

La Petite fille sur la photo diverges from typical nostalgic evocations of Algeria. Benkemoun's family members sometimes talk about their birthplace, particularly her Jewish father's expulsion from school under the Vichy regime and his fearful expedition to Algeria, described in militaristic terms as a "raid," to recover the family's belongings some weeks after independence (12). In general, however, her parents did not dwell on the past, erased traces of their accent and encouraged her to believe that leaving Algeria as a family when she was a child was an "aubaine" [godsend] (29). This book is not an overt attempt to rehabilitate colonialism and the author's engagement with interviewees from outside her community is particularly noteworthy. However, many of the reflections incorporated hark back to familiar territory. A chapter on Algerian-born writer and filmmaker Mehdi Charef focuses largely on Ali, the protagonist of Charef's semiautobiographical film *Cartouches gauloises* who befriends Muslims, Jews, and Christians—providing Benkemoun with the image of the Arab friend she says she would have liked her *pied-noir* interviewees to describe (74). Charef's suggestion that a wealthy colonial family in his region, who did not pay their staff adequately, loved the country too much (76), recalls similar statements about excessive devotion to their country by former settlers, as discussed in chapter 2 of the current book. Furthermore, an Algerian woman called Zohra, whom Benkemoun interviews in France, expresses nostalgia for French primary schoolteachers and emphasizes a colonial society in which all communities coexisted in harmony, although without really mixing (85–86). Zohra's sister, whom the author interviews in Algeria, suggests as the title for Benkemoun's book: "C'était mieux avant!" (190) [It was better before!]—thereby pointing to the deterioration of her country postindependence. An interview with the daughter of a *harki*, meanwhile, allows a non-*pied-noir* to air grievances about the abandonment of her community by politicians and intellectuals (128–34). However, it also reflects the concept put forward by *pied-noir* activists that *harkis* are members of a broader "repatriate" community in what Claire Eldridge suggests is part of "a larger project to reclaim the colonial past from those who would denigrate its value and importance."[86]

Some of the more conventional themes also surface. For example, references to Benkemoun's hardworking grandfather recall pioneering imagery (206–7). Descriptions of her uncle, who was involved in the OAS, point to normative constructions of *pied-noir* gender: "Ancien arbitre de football, sanguin, macho, bel home, il roulait en DS, toujours très élégant, sa femme en manteau d'astrakan" (60) [a former soccer referee, hotheaded, macho, a handsome man; he drove a Citroen DS car and always looked stylish, with his wife in her Astrakhan fur coat]. Moreover, OAS violence, in an echo of Francine Dessaigne's text fifty years earlier, appears as the result of temporary madness sparked by nationalist violence (61). Allusions to herself and other interviewees as part of a "bâtard" [bastard] race made up of multiple identities are equally familiar concepts that minimize the colonial conquest. The author's designation of Oran, following her visit there, as "une vieille femme négligée dont on devine encore qu'elle fut splendide" (178) [a neglected old woman whose former splendor can still be detected] is also familiar. Moreover, the book encourages sympathy for the *pieds-noirs* as the author uncovers details that were previously unknown to her, such as the deaths of many settlers at Oran on July 5, 1962. By the same token, an emphasis on the particular trauma caused to children—such as Nicole Guiraud, a ten-year-old victim of the 1956 Milk Bar bomb in Algiers (interviewed by the author), and the tearful *pied-noir* girl in the newspaper photo that prompted Benkemoun's initial decision to research the subject—contrasts with the famous image of young OAS victim Delphine Renard. Benkemoun's initial disappointment on her arrival in Algeria fifty years after her own departure, when she does not encounter the Camusian community which she had imagined, is of particular interest as it serves as a significant example of Camus's legacy with regard to a younger generation of *pieds-noirs* (178).[87] It is also worth noting here that in addition to stories told during dinners with relations, the story of the fictional Hernandez family, discussed in the introduction to the current book, informs the author's initial impressions of colonial Algeria. She imagines it as a place where "Espagnols, Juifs, Bourguignons, Arabes, Gitanes et Alsaciens vivaient ensemble dans une sorte de sitcom à mi-chemin entre *Plus belle la vie* et *La Famille Hernandez*" (11) [Spaniards, Jews, natives from Burgundy, Arabs, gypsies and those from the Alsace region lived together in a sort of situation comedy half-way between *Plus belle la vie* [A better Life] and *La Famille Hernandez*].[88]

This leads to a consideration of American writer Claire Messud's novel, *The Last Life* (1999).[89] Its plot centers on fallout from the violent actions of the narrator's *pied-noir* grandfather who moved to France following the Algerian War many years previously. The former settler shoots and injures one of the narrator's friends who is among a group of youths taking an illicit nighttime swim in his hotel. For this crime, he goes on trial. The violent lengths to which this elderly *pied-noir* man goes in order to protect his property hints at a dark, repressed, and disturbing past with regard to colonial history. His act of casual violence also echoes that of Meursault. This later novel therefore reveals the enduring legacy of Camus's construction of masculinity. It is equally worth noting that the author has written elsewhere about her *pied-noir* father and grandfather and her chosen plot thus reveals a continued concern with identity and memory politics among later generations.[90] Scholars have also pointed to the autobiographical impression left by the novel, which suggests its resemblance to the other accounts of young adulthood studied.[91] However, the novel, which is set in America as well as France, offers a radical cultural and linguistic break from these other works. The original publication of this text in English before its translation into French as *La Vie après* [After Life] (2001) attests to its appeal beyond a *pied-noir* audience. Moreover, as the daughter of a French Algerian father and an American mother, the narrator occupies a liminal space between cultures and she acknowledges, when she decides to go to boarding school in America as her sixteenth birthday approaches, that she "won't belong" in America any more than she belongs in France, despite having lived there all her life (333). She therefore stands apart from the previously examined young narrative voices, who poignantly evoke personal experiences of their homeland. The narrator's linguistic and cultural hybridity thereby points to the novel's potential for coming to new understandings of a traumatic past.

The narrator's name—Sagesse [wisdom]—evokes the concept of youth as a site of perceptiveness.[92] She also occupies a familiar space between childhood and adulthood. Although she reveals that she is a "history of ideas" graduate student at Columbia University (375), she claims that she has been living a largely interior life up until now. Her admission, at the end of the book, that she feels ready to open up and reveal her true self to a man for the first time—a newly arrived Algerian immigrant called Hamed—symbolizes her imminent entry into adulthood. Moreover, her younger point of view dominates as she recounts, through flashbacks, a year in her life from when she is almost fifteen years old to the aftermath of her father's suicide shortly before her sixteenth birthday. Through her, the author can therefore harness the aforementioned productive "open psychic structure" of the adolescent state theorized by Kristeva. Indeed, Sagesses's viewpoint appears replete with productive possibilities, although she is self-consciously aware that young people frequently miss such opportunities due to their lack of maturity:

> Adolescence [. . .] is a curious station on the route from ignorant communion to our ultimate isolation, the place where words and silences reveal themselves to be meaningful and yet where, too young to acknowledge that we cannot gauge their meaning, we imagine it for ourselves and behave as if we understood. (32)

The novel is particularly significant for drawing attention to the performative nature of collective memory and to apocryphal stories about the colonial past, as Sagesse deconstructs myths about her own family. From the beginning, she underlines the unreliability of her personal history, noting: "The beginning, as I take it, was the summer night of my fifteenth year when my grandfather shot at me" (2). While her initial uncertainty about the timeline of events echoes Meursault's inability to pinpoint the date of his mother's death in *L'Étranger*, Sagesse consciously underscores her construction of a narrative by continuing:

> In this way every story is made up, its shape imposed: the beginning was not really then, any more than was the day of my brother's birth, or, indeed, of mine. Nor is it strictly true that my grandfather shot *at me*: I was not, by chance, in the line of fire; he did not know that I was there. But it was an event, the first in my memory, after which nothing was the same again. (2)

Her (re)construction of events is complicated by her desire to distill the mythical versions of tales about her paternal *pied-noir* grandfather, Jacques LaBasse, that her grandmother tells "with reverent indulgence," and those "repeated with a sneer" and with a different slant by her American mother, in order to "cull the essence of the man, who was so resolutely divorced from them [the stories] in his own person" (55). Moreover, while her grandmother "wove a narrative out of the lives of the LaBasses" and her mother "unraveled these stories [. . .] and put them together again another way, with a different, darker meaning," she observes both women joining forces as her grandfather goes on trial (192–93). During this episode, both women weave the family stories "even tighter" so as "to keep the family whole" (193). Sagesse also admits that events are "filtered, by faulty memory, into a shape that is now useful to us" and reminds the reader that "stories are made up, after all, as much of what is left out" (290, 8). In consequence, her personal story points to what Wood calls collective *lieux d'oubli* [sites of forgetting] or the deliberate avoidance of some memories.[93] Similarly, certain people do not fit into her family's pioneering narrative, but rather fragments of relatives are "pressed into the mosaic of my grandparents' path [. . .] a way simultaneously to remember and to forget those who fell by the wayside, who were lost on the road to the Bellevue [Hotel] and success" (289). This text is therefore unusual in consciously drawing attention to the manner in which settlers construct narratives of memory to unify a *pied-noir* community in exile.

The text is also of significant value as the narrator purposely points to the performative nature of identity. In this way, identity appears as what Judith Butler calls a "regulatory fiction,"—which Sagesse consciously performs according to the social context.[94] As a "shape-shifting" (136) adolescent, she notes that conversation with her boyfriend Thibaud seems to involve a rehearsal of memorized lines (87). She also performs differently depending on which American relatives she interacts with when on a summer trip, and when in the company of pot-smoking teenagers she befriends during the trial, who are also playing a role. Furthermore, when she moves to America to attend boarding school after her father's death, she resolves to master her "guise" as effectively as she can (358).

Of particular interest, however, is the way in which Sagesse's mother performs her identity. As an American who knows little about France's colonial history, she projects a certain concept of French identity onto her *pied-noir* husband when they first meet, deciding he is a "male Marianne" (216), while she will henceforth perform as a Frenchwoman. The narrator's reference to drag with regard to her mother is especially noteworthy as she reveals that "something in her face, in the shape of her head or the way that she held it, gave away her foreignness, the way a transvestite is betrayed by her wrists or the line of her back" (7). This remark suggests a self-conscious allusion to Butler's theorizing on the imitative nature of gender identity, which is bolstered by the narrator's contention that scientists built their analysis of "Woman" on an image of "Her" that "didn't really exist" (114). Her allusion to drag also evokes the compulsion for mimicry of the colonizer, which, as theorized by Homi Bhabha, results in imitations that can subversively highlight the constructed nature of identities by "disclosing the ambivalence of colonial discourse," thereby undermining it.[95] *The Last Life* is consequently a self-consciously postcolonial text in so far as Sagesse draws attention to her mother's mimicry of what she believes to be French culture. Her mother was strongly encouraged in this regard by her mother-in-law. However, the identity she mimics is revealed as an imitation of a *pied-noir* identity, which itself appears as an outdated construct from the colonial era: "Not till too late did she realize that the recipes and expressions she had so studiously mimicked, until they inseparably constituted her French self, were the antiquated trivia of an Algerian life no longer extant, or rather, existing only in such households as her own, and as a result of virtuosic mimicry all round" (224).

Sagesse's searing gaze therefore enables her to point out the artificial nature of identities, in this case those relating to colonial processes and systems. An anecdote about her grandmother's comments on a traditional cake, *la mouna*, specifically alludes to the constructed nature of *pied-noir* identity. Although her grandmother perceives this cake as a distinguishing marker of her identity, she admits that she does not like it, but rather "the idea of it." Yet she is taken aback when Sagesse suggests that Zohra, her grandmother's housekeeper in France, might like to take it home. The older lady's statement, "I think they like stickier cakes, as a rule" (279), implies that persistent efforts to mimic an identity informed by the colonial context have led to the maintenance of related power structures in postcolonial France. One friend of Sagesse's grandparents, Madame Darty, similarly reiterates the binary oppositions of colonial discourse when she states that Arab teenagers "get their fun from terrorizing us" (275). By the same token, Sagesse's grandfather, Jacques, expresses xenophobic views that exclude his American daughter-in-law, his grandchildren, and even himself, as a *pied-noir* of Italian and Maltese extraction, from a "pure" French identity, which he nevertheless believes he represents. His exaggerated nationalism exemplifies what Clarisse Buono calls "surassimilation" [over-assimilation], as some *pieds*-noirs, having represented France abroad, felt themselves to be patriotic representatives of a "pure" nation, which paradoxically affirmed their own cultural difference.[96] Thus, when commenting on the deaths of three young people who accidentally kill themselves when the bomb they had planned to use in a French nightclub frequented by Arabs blows up, Jacques exclaims:

> The FN's [National Front's] not the problem. [. . .] It's just a symptom of the problem. Of the problems. Plural. The problems that this nation faces, overrun with immigrants—Arabs, Africans, the English-speakers, all of them—our culture assailed on all sides. Our children, for God's sake, building bombs for no reason! And our government—this decrepit, farcical liar who fancies himself

emperor [Mitterrand]—our government has nothing to say about it, nothing at all! (24)

Sagesse's narrative is therefore particularly productive in revealing the constructed nature of *pied-noir* memory and identity and its potential, in its exaggerated form, for facilitating xenophobia. Furthermore, the unfavorable situation of characters of Algerian ancestry in the novel, for example Sami who is expelled from school, his girlfriend Lahou who aborts their baby, and the aforementioned Zohra, who lives in social housing on the far side of town, indicates the "rebound" effects of colonialism, as discussed in the introduction to the current study.

That said, the narrator ultimately comes down on the side of the former settlers. When, bereft of friends, she begins reading up on Algeria, she concludes that the *pieds-noirs* continue to pay the price for believing an illusion maintained by the French administration:

> France's error made flesh, the *pieds-noirs*, and with them, the *harkis*, were guilty simply for existing. In the national narrative, my father's family was a distasteful emblem. [. . .] St. Augustine and Camus might have been Algeria's most celebrated offspring, but the former colonials' most vocal champion, at that late date, was no Algerian at all, was Jean-Marie Le Pen. [. . .] This was the political voice of my grandfather's people—and inevitably, of my father's too—the bitter grizzling of those who fought for Catholicism and a nostalgic ideal of France, a pure France that would, and did, label me "foreign" for my American mother (my *pied-noir* father, on the other hand, was foreign only to the great majority). My family believed in a country that could want no part of them, would rather they had been gloriously martyred in Algeria, memorialized in a curly arch or two at metropolitan intersections, and conveniently forgotten. (240–41)

This positioning of *pied-noir* families as scapegoats for colonial history is familiar, as is their associated link with the exceptionally difficult situation of the *harkis*. In the above quotation, far-right politician Jean-Marie Le Pen's non-*pied-noir* identity contrasts with the humanism of Algeria's "offspring"—St. Augustine and Camus. Moreover, the *pieds-noirs* who follow leaders such as Le Pen are mimicking (or, to borrow Buono's term, "overassimilating") an exclusionary concept of French identity that the nation's current practices underscore. This includes its treatment of immigrants from the former colonies as well as its distaste for the former settlers and its desire to erase them from the national narrative through processes of memorialization that constitute Wood's *lieux d'oubli* [sites of forgetting] rather than Pierre Nora's famous *lieux de mémoire* [sites of memory].

In this way, Sagesse draws attention to an urgent need for the French nation as a whole to face up to its colonial past, while the book's publication appropriately, if coincidentally, coincides with France's belated official recognition of the war. However, she ultimately appears to excuse the *pied-noir* population from their role in the colonial past. Indeed, her side has been chosen since the beginning, when, during her elderly grandfather's trial, she realizes that she cannot choose her friends over family and compares her situation, "where every choice was wrong," to that of Camus (182). Apart from the plot's echoes of *L'Étranger* through the trial of a *pied-noir* for a rash act of violence, the author peppers the novel with references to Camus, as well as to St. Augustine. Of particular significance is Sagesse's reiteration of the myth of lost opportunities by imagining a Camusian scenario for her father's secret half brother born to the family's maid in Algeria, about whom the family has no information but whom she christens Hamed. In the narrator's vision, Hamed's only chance of happiness would have been to grow up with her father, Alexandre. During the Algerian War, the half brothers would then have seen the conflict through each other's eyes and, if this had happened on a large scale, the outcome would have been different: "Camus' dream—the city of white stone flashing in the sunshine while its life, a fully lived, multichromatic life providing common succour to every shade and faith and diverse history of the Mediterranean basin—might then have been possible" (324). References here to Algeria's *décennie noire*—a period that Sagesse feels would have made a chosen life in Algeria impossible for Hamed—and to racism in France, which she feels would have made life in France difficult had he emigrated after the Algerian War, serve to condemn both nations for missed opportunities for harmony (322, 320). Sagesse, in her vision of a potentially fraternal relationship between the colonizer and colonized, goes as far as to allude to the possibilities for *métissage* [the mixing of races]. Thus, she notes that Saint Augustine was of Berber and Roman origin. Furthermore, she highlights a "myth, or perhaps fact" involving a group of nuns who landed at Ténès, west of Algiers, in the nineteenth century and wed local men when they found few women left in the town, which had been swept by an illness (324).

Sagesse also emphasizes her family's "burden of Original Sin" (1), which is symbolized for her by her severely mentally and physically disabled brother, whose name, Etienne Parfait [Etienne Perfect], positions him as a permanent site of lost perfection. Moreover, this burden applies to the *pied-noir* community more generally as she notes that it was St. Augustine of Hippo (later Bône, now Annaba) who theorized the concept of Original Sin and hence made it a communal possession: "Ours, as a personal heritage, a gift indeed, most particularly for us, the Europeans of North Africa, was the doctrine of Original Sin" (174). The *pieds-noirs*, therefore, and particularly young Sagesse who is at a remove from Algeria, appear to shoulder the burden of colonial wrongs despite not having personally sinned in this regard.

References to another relative, Serge LaBasse, whose farm was razed to the ground in 1955 (286), similarly portray the settlers in a sympathetic light. His surname, which is also Sagesse's, evokes the French word "bas" meaning low, pointing to a humble background while also recalling the typical *pied-noir* reference to Algeria, from their position in exile, as "là-bas" [over there]. Moreover, despite her recognition of colonial Algeria's violent beginning or "blood-soaked soil" (324), her reiteration of the pioneering myth emphasizes the courage of early settlers, such as Tata [Auntie] Christine, a "solo traveller" who spent the final days of her life acting as a *sage-femme* [midwife] to remote tribes in the Algerian wilderness (93–97). Her grandfather Jacques's rapid rise to success with his hotel business in France following the Algerian War, where "On new soil" he aimed to "accomplish in five years what others took ten to achieve" (54), also suggests the perpetuation of pioneering qualities through the generations, as does her own ability to adapt successfully to life in America.

An apparently ironic allusion to *pied-noir* devotion to the mother figure, which goes back as far as St. Augustine and is therefore "a cultural characteristic of the *pieds-noirs*, if you believe our historians, right up there with the *soubressade* [sausage] and siestas" (175), nevertheless reiterates the Camusian model of *pied-noir* masculinity. The narrative also links masculinity to violence and a death wish that relates to the loss of the motherland. Thus, Sagesse describes her grandfather's life in Algeria immediately after evoking his violent outburst when he shoots at her friends. She also reveals her father's attempted suicide following the traumatic circumstances of his repatriation to France and his eventual suicide years later beside the sea, facing his "invisible [Algerian] home on the far side of the ocean" (238). Indeed, Sagesse portrays suicide as being a particular fate of the *Français d'Algérie*, noting that both St. Augustine, who banned suicide, and Camus asked "whether life was worth living; and both answered 'yes' with a desperation and a defiance that can have been born only of 'no'" (213). While Sagesse comments that St. Augustine and Camus faced their temptation and that "It plays" on her own mind, she states: "It played louder still in the ears of my father, born with Africa in his blood from both sides, and left to live, without revolt, in [*sic*] a dispassionate and alien border" (214).

In this way, the adolescent narrator of this novel highlights the trauma associated with the violence of the Algerian War and with leaving Algeria, which filters down to the next generation. Indeed, Sagesse's decision to go to school in America is informed by her belief, due to her "family's stories," that "departure, once mooted, must be seen as inevitable" (330). Furthermore, as with some of the narrators discussed above and in chapter 2, the atmosphere in Sagesse's home causes a physical manifestation of trauma on the female body—this time in boils that break out all over her back and in panic attacks.

Thus, her adolescent viewpoint proves very effective in drawing attention to France's need to confront its enduring colonial legacy and to the constructed nature of identities born of colonial discourse. Sagesse's struggle with her identity evokes France's problems at a national level, including racism, and her questioning of family narratives draws attention to communal narratives as factitious. However, Sagesse's own story ultimately portrays the *pieds-noirs* in a sympathetic light. While this young girl feels in some way responsible for the ills of colonial history and wishes, as a fifteen-year-old, she could enter a family painting of Algiers, where she "would have altered the course of history" and "willed Camus' dream of a paradise on earth" (291), she has clearly done nothing wrong. References to lost opportunities, Original Sin, and tragic *pied-noir* masculinity, as personified by the suicide of her father and the trial of her elderly grandfather, evoke what are by now familiar themes with regard to memory and identity. However, history appears to repeat itself when, for example, Sagesse mentions Iraq's invasion of Kuwait and the "cordoning of Europe [. . .] as a means of closing out definitively the other worlds, the second and third" (291–92). In consequence, the author highlights the Western world's responsibility for neocolonial actions that repeat colonial mistakes. Indeed, she insists that her family's stories "aren't our stories alone. They seep outwards. Hairline seepages, perhaps, but perceptible, if you look closely" (375). Thus, in "the suicide of Mitterrand's loyal lieutenant Pierre Bérégevoy," Sagesse sees that of her father, while in "the War Crimes trial, much later, of Maurice Papon," she sees a *pied-noir* like her grandfather (375).[97] In trying to address her history, Sagesse therefore prompts readers to pose questions about their own. This novel is perhaps the most effective of those examined in this chapter, in engaging with the continued impact of colonialism as a whole. Moreover, practices by Sagesse's mother and grandmother in which they weave stories to unite a family in exile reveal the ways in which postindependence narratives continue to constitute *pied-noir* memory and identity.

NOTES

1. Marcel Proust, *A la recherche du temps perdu 1: Du côté de chez Swann—A l'ombre des jeunes filles en fleurs* (Paris: Gallimard, 1954). See particularly Section 1, "Combray," 3–187.

2. For more on the significance of these genres, see Louise Hardwick, "The Rise of the récit d'enfance in the Francophone Caribbean," in *Postcolonial Poetics: Genre and Form*, ed. Patrick Crowley and Jane Hiddleston, *Francophone Postcolonial Studies* (Liverpool: Liverpool University Press, 2011), 166–82; and Justin O'Brien, *The Novel of Adolescence in France: The Study of a Literary Theme* (New York: Columbia University Press, 1937). The publication of Orientalist painter and travel

writer Eugène Fromentin's semiautobiographical novel *Dominique* in 1862 is worth noting as a particularly early example of a narrative of adolescence.

3. Rita Bouckaert-Ghesquiere, "Looking Back. The Rise of the Autobiographical Novel in Children's Literature," in *Genres as Repositories of Cultural Memory: Vol. 5 of the proceedings of the 15th congress of the International Comparative Literature Association*, ed. Hendrik Van Gorp and Ulla Musarra-Schroeder (Amsterdam: Rodopi, 2000), 441.

4. Ibid. Bouckaert-Ghesquiere contends that this surge in popularity is due to war children becoming adults and a changing, more open, and realistic society that treats children in a more adult way.

5. Ibid., 443.

6. Ibid., 444, 450.

7. Patricia Pace, "All Our Lost Children: Trauma and Testimony in the Performance of Childhood," *Text and Performance Quarterly* 18, no. 3 (July 1998): 234.

8. Jeffrey Jensen Arnett, *Adolescence and Emerging Adulthood: A Cultural Approach* (Boston: Prentice Hall, 2010), xii. Arnett argues that adolescence is not only starting earlier but also ending later as adult roles "such as marriage, parenthood, and stable full-time work" are delayed. This results in a distinct phase of development called "emerging adulthood."

9. Julia Kristeva, "The Adolescent Novel," in *Abjection, Melancholia and Love: The Work of Julia Kristeva*, ed. John Fletcher and Andrew Benjamin (London: Routledge, 1991), 8, 14.

10. Mary Hilton and Maria Nikolajeva, "Introduction: Time of Turmoil," in Hilton and Nikolajeva, *Contemporary Adolescent Literature and Culture: The Emergent Adult*, ed. Mary Hilton and Maria Nikolajeva (Farnham, Surrey: Ashgate, 2012), 8.

11. Kimberley Reynolds, *Radical Children's Literature: Future Visions and Aesthetic Transformations in Juvenile Fiction* (Basingstoke: Palgrave, 2007), 1. Cited in Georgie Horrell, "Transgression and Transition," in Hilton and Nikolajeva, *Contemporary Adolescent Literature and Culture*, 49.

12. Anne Roche, "La Perte et la parole: témoignages oraux de pieds-noirs," in *La Guerre d'Algérie et les Français*, ed. Jean-Pierre Rioux (Paris: Fayard, 1990), 536.

13. Ibid., 528–29.

14. L. P. Hartley, *The Go-Between* (London: Penguin, 1997), 5. It is worth noting that the narrator of this story becomes aware that childhood is performative on his thirteenth birthday, as he realizes that he has been "playing a part, which seemed to have taken in everybody, and most of all myself. [. . .] They like to think of a little boy as a little boy, corresponding to what their idea of what a little boy should be—as a representative of little boyhood. [. . .] They even had a special language designed for little boys" (228).

15. Nancy E. Virtue, "Memory, Trauma, and the French-Algerian War: Michael Haneke's *Caché* (2005)," *Modern & Contemporary France* 19, no. 3 (August 2011): 282–83. Virtue draws on Dominick LaCapra, *History and Memory after Auschwitz* (Ithaca, NY: Cornell University Press, 1998), 45.

16. Jane Hiddleston, "Introduction," in Crowley and Hiddleston, *Postcolonial Poetics*, 7.

17. Svetlana Boym, "Nostalgia and Its Discontents," *The Hedgehog Review* 9, no. 2 (Summer 2007): 7–8.

18. Bertrand described the youthful adventures of a nascent French Algerian race, most notably through the character of Rafael in *Le Sang des races* (1899) [Blood of Races]. See Louis Bertrand, *Le Sang des races* (Paris: Paul Ollendorff, 1899).

19. Albert Camus, *Essais* (Paris: Gallimard, 2000), 72.

20. Jacqueline Rose, *The Case of Peter Pan or The Impossibility of Children's Fiction* (London: Macmillan, 1984), 141.

21. Ibid., 43.

22. Ibid., 138–39.

23. One educational graphic novel aimed at children, for example, attempts to shape readers' understanding of the war and perhaps to regulate the performance of childhood, as it notes that all populations in Algeria got on well before the conflict and divides descriptions of boys' and girls' games from the period along distinct gender lines. See Gilles Bonotaux and Hélène Lasserre, *Quand ils avaient mon âge . . . Alger 1954-1962* (Paris: Autrement, 2002).

24. For the film version, see Alexandre Arcady, *Le Coup de Sirocco* (France: Films de l'Alma, 1979).

25. William B. Cohen, "The Algerian War and French Memory," *Contemporary European History* 9, no. 3 (November 2000): 490.

26. Raphaëlle Branche, *La Guerre d'Algérie: une histoire apaisée?* (Paris: Seuil, 2005), 24–25.

27. Ibid., 25.

28. Sophie Watt, "Alexandre Arcady and the Rewriting of French Colonial History in Algeria," in *France's Lost Empires: Fragmentation, Nostalgia, and la fracture coloniale*, ed. Kate Marsh and Nicola Frith (Lanham, MD: Lexington, 2011), 69.

29. Ibid.

30. Articles discussing Arcady describe the film as autobiographical. See, for example, Souad Ben Slimane, "Ce que le jour doit à la nuit en chantier—Et pourtant ça tourne!," *La Presse (Tunis)*, June 16, 2011 and Anonymous, "Points forts. Carrière," *Midi Libre: Les journaux du Midi*, September 15, 2012. The film's close resemblance to the novel and the fact that Saint-Hamont cowrote the screenplay would suggest that at least part of these autobiographical elements are from Saint-Hamont's text.

31. Jean-Jacques Jordi, *Les Pieds-Noirs* (Paris: Le Cavalier Bleu, 2009), 80. Jordi cites the narrator's description of his family being overcharged by a taxi, followed by a railway employee's refusal to give them a "repatriate's discount."

32. While the novel begins with the narrator's departure from Algeria, a notable difference in the film, apart from a change of name for some characters, is the addition of thirty minutes of opening footage revealing key events in the narrator's life from his birth in 1945. This adds to the nostalgic feel of the movie by encouraging the viewer to identify with the narrator's homeland.

33. Daniel Saint-Hamont, *Le Coup de Sirocco* (Paris: Fayard, 1978), 185. Although the narrator of the film version begins by telling us he is now thirty, the rest of the film similarly privileges his adolescent gaze through flashback.

34. Ethnologist Victoria M. Phaneuf, having studied cuisine habits of North African and *pied-noir* associations, notes that the former tend to serve "traditional" dishes at public events and worldwide dishes at private events, while the reverse is the case for *pied-noir* associations. One possible explanation for this is that members of the public could easily question the provenance of some of the dishes claimed as *pied-noir*, particularly the traditional North African dish of couscous. See Victoria M. Phaneuf, "Negotiating Culture, Performing Identities: North African and Pied-Noir Associations in France," *The Journal of North African Studies* 17, no. 4 (2012): 682.

35. Lesa Rae Vartanian "Revisiting the Imaginary Audience and Personal Fable Constructs of Adolescent Egocentrism: A Conceptual Review," *Adolescence* 35, no. 140 (Winter 2000): 639.

36. Ibid.

37. Ibid., 640.

38. The "general with the moustache" most likely refers to General Massu who presided over the French army in Algeria during the Battle of Algiers (1956–1957). The French army's use of torture allowed them to win this particular battle of guerrilla warfare, although politically it provoked the loss of international support.

39. Claire Eldridge, "'We've Never Had a Voice': Memory Construction and the Children of the *Harkis* (1962-1991)," *French History* 23, no. 1 (2009): 88–89.

40. Jo McCormack, *Collective Memory: France and the Algerian War (1954-1962)* (Lanham, MD: Lexington, 2007), 169.

41. A *douar* is a North African settlement in which dwellings usually consist of tents.

42. Élie-Georges Berreby, *L'Enfant pied-noir* (Arles: Actes sud, 2007), 22. The Marquise de Sévigné was a seventeenth-century aristocratic writer.

43. Lucienne Martini, *Racines de papier: Essai sur l'expression littéraire de l'identité Pieds-Noirs* (Paris: Publisud, 1997), 45.

44. Anonymous, "Raymond Plante (Quebec) prime à la Foire du Livre de Brive," AFP, November 7, 1994, LexisNexis.

45. Ibid. Quote from the author.

46. Peter Carey uses this term in his historical novel *True History of the Kelly Gang: A Novel* (New York: Alfred A. Knopf, 2000).

47. Anonymous, "Élie-Georges Berreby, un homme pluriel," Berreby, http://www.berreby.net/accueil/ index.html. Date accessed: August 21, 2013.

48. The title of Berreby's play, *Jonas*, referenced on his website as the work through which he became known in France after the Algerian War, also echoes Camus's work, specifically his short story "Jonas" in *L'Exil et le royaume* (1957).

49. Albert Camus, *Actuelles, III: Chroniques algériennes, 1939-1958* (Paris: Gallimard, 1958), 125.

50. Camus, *Essais*, 824. In his consciously Mediterraneanist description of boxing in Oran, Camus proclaims: "à Corinthe, deux temples voisinaient, celui de la Violence et celui de la Nécessité" [In Corinthe, there were two temples next to each other: one of violence and one of necessity].

51. Emmanuel Roblès, *Saison violente* (Paris: Seuil, 1974), 149–51.

52. Joëlle Hureau, *La Mémoire des pieds-noirs: de 1830 à nos jours* (Paris: Perrin, 2010), 298–300.

53. Nono's father funds nationalist revolutionary leader Messali Hadj and Nono informs Joé that his family have already moved a large bulk of their assets out of Algeria. This emphasizes the idea that a minority of *gros colons* [wealthy colonists] bought their way out of trouble while the *petits blancs* [poor white settlers] suffered. The television version of *Les Chevaux du soleil* (episode 11—"Le Tonnere et les Anges") noticeably makes this point when the camera pans over an impressively vast expanse of land and a villa that has been untouched by the war. When the villa's owner refuses to help his neighbors, they conclude that he is funding the FLN.

54. Hélene Gadal, *Petite pied-noir deviendra grande* (Paris: Théles, 2002).

55. Benjamin Stora, "Mémoires comparées: femmes françaises, femmes algériennes: Les écrits de femmes, la guerre d'Algérie et l'exil," in *L'Ère des décolonisations: Sélection de textes du colloque «Décolonisations comparées," Aix-en-Provence, 30 septembre–3 octobre 1993*, ed. Charles-Robert Ageron and Marc Michel (Paris: Karthala, 1995), 175.

56. Virginie Buisson, *L'Algérie ou la mort des autres* (Paris: Gallimard, 1981).

57. Bouckaert-Ghesquiere lists the book as an autobiographical children's novel in Bouckaert-Ghesquiere, "Looking Back," 449.

58. La Pensée sauvage originally published the novel as part of its "Espaces féminins" [feminine spaces] series; "Folio junior" republished it with illustrations in 1981 and it reappeared in Gallimard's "Scripto" collection for adolescents in 2012.

59. Jean Guéhenno, *La Mort des autres* (Paris: Grasset, 1968).

60. Cited by Geneviève Briot and André Cohen Aknin, "Des écrivains et la guerre d'Algérie," http://briot-cohenaknin.hautetfort.com/tag/virginie+buisson. Date accessed: November 8, 2011.

61. Andrea L. Smith, *Colonial Memory and Postcolonial Europe: Maltese Settlers in Algeria and France* (Bloomington, IN: Indiana University Press, 2006), 153–59.

62. Kathleen Young, "Talking vs. Processing in Trauma Therapy," http://drkathleenyoung.wordpress.com/2011/06/09/talking-vs-processing-in-trauma-therapy/. Date accessed: July 31, 2013.

63. James W. Pennebaker and Janel D. Seagal, "Forming a Story: The Health Benefits of Narrative," *Journal of Clinical Psychology* 55, no. 10 (1999): 1251.

64. Nicole Brugger-Dethmers, "Cross-Dressing and Performativity," in Hilton and Nikolajeva, *Contemporary Adolescent Literature and Culture*, 84.

65. John Boyne, *The Boy in the Striped Pajamas* (Oxford: David Fickling Books, 2006).

66. Saïd Ferdi, *Un Enfant dans la guerre: témoignage* (Paris: Seuil, 1981), 42–43. Jules Roy praises this autobiography for bringing to light the horror of war from a child's perspective. See the back cover.

67. A *gourbi* is a hut or simple dwelling.

68. Gouda and Clancy-Smith suggest that efforts to educate indigenous women were born of a fear of the intermarriage of Westernized indigenous men with settler women, a threat that the administration could reduce if indigenous women were suitably educated for future marriages with indigenous men. See Julia Clancy-Smith

and Frances Gouda, "Introduction," in *Domesticating the Empire: Race, Gender, and Family Life in French and Dutch Colonialism*, ed. Julia Clancy-Smith and Frances Gouda (Charlottesville, VA: University of Virginia Press, 1998), 17.

69. Marie-Jeanne Perez, *Gouttes-de-sang: roman* (La Tour d'aigues: Éditions de l'Aube, 1991).

70. Philip Dine, "(Still) À la recherche de l'Algérie perdue: French Fiction and Film, 1992-2001," *Historical Reflections* 28, no. 2 (Summer 2002), 260.

71. Rose, *The Case of Peter Pan*, 138.

72. Hilton and Nikolajeva underline the distinctive possibilities opened up for exploring mental instability in narratives featuring young narrators: "Given its high degree of instability, the intuitive imaginative possibilities open to writers who seek to get inside the adolescent mind can extend its framework beyond the range of normality." See Hilton and Nikolajeva, "Introduction: Time of Turmoil," 14.

73. This description recalls the brutal torture of Muslim women such as Louisette Ighilahriz, who described how French soldiers raped her with objects during the war. See Louisette Ighilahriz, *Algérienne: récit recueilli par Anne Nivat* (Paris: Fayard, 2001), 113.

74. Jean-Noël Pancrazi, *Madame Arnoul* (Paris: Gallimard, 1995). William Cloonan and Jean-Philippe Postel point to the novel's autobiographical elements in "From maison d'édition to librairie: The Novel in 1995," *The French Review* 69, no. 6 (May 1996): 908.

75. The novel won the Prix Maurice Genevoix, Prix Albert Camus, and Prix du Livre Inter. See Anonymous, "Biographie de Jean-Noël Pancrazi," Société des gens de lettres, http://www.sgdl.org/culturel/les-prix-litteraires/les-prix-de-la-session-de-printemps/575. Date accessed: October 4, 2011.

76. Messner notes that while "children are active agents in the creation of their own worlds—often in direct or partial opposition to values or 'roles' to which adult teachers or parents are attempting to socialize them [. . .], varying moments of gender salience [. . .] occur in social contexts such as schools and in which gender is formally and informally built into the division of labor, power structure, rules and values." See Michael A. Messner, "Barbie Girls Versus Sea Monsters: Children Constructing Gender," *Gender & Society* 14, no. 6 (2000): 765–66.

77. Adolescents again appear as a site of truth here as this award-winning and popular film suggests that adults can learn tolerance and flexibility from a younger generation. Nevertheless, close-ups of their bodies and of the French landscape as they play sport and swim invite pleasurable viewing rather than a reflection on the grim realities of war.

78. André Téchiné, *Les Roseaux sauvages* (France: Studio Canal, 1994).

79. A *gandoura* is a long tunic.

80. There are oblique allusions to rejoicing on May 13, 1958, the effective military coup that led to de Gaulle's return to power, to the failed putsch by rebel generals in April 1961 in a bid to stop Algerian independence, and to the Rue d'Isly shootings (35–36, 83, 85).

81. This name is suggestive of the Moroccan poet and novelist Mohammed Khaïr-Eddine, who wrote in French due to his education but in so doing revolted

using "guerrilla linguistics." Lynne Rogers has documented this writer's sense of disenchantment with the political situation following Moroccan independence. See Lynne Rogers, "The Guerilla Linguistics of Mohammed Khaïr-Eddine," in *Writing the Nation: Self and Country in Post-Colonial Imagination*, ed. John C. Hawley (Amsterdam: Rodopi, 1996), 108. The narrator's friend's name also recalls Khaïr Eddin, one of the Barbarossa brothers who reigned in Algiers during the sixteenth century.

82. See, for example, Gilles Chenaille, "Dossier: La sélection littéraire du mois d'avril: La petite fille sur la photo, de Brigitte Benkemoun," *MarieClaire*, July 19, 2013 and Anonymous, "Plus de cent livres pour le 50e anniversaire de la fin de la guerre d'Algérie," AFP, February 4, 2012, LexisNexis.

83. Edith Serero, "Brigitte Benkemoun Pleure Ô Pays Bien-Aimé," *Paris Match*, May 24–30, 2012.

84. See, for example, François-Guillaume Lorrain, "Les enfants brisent le silence; Algérie," *Le Point*, March 15, 2012 and Lydie Steurel, "Les derniers tabous de la guerre sans nom," *Marianne*, March 24, 2012.

85. Brigitte Benkemoun, *La Petite fille sur la photo: La guerre d'Algérie à hauteur d'enfant* (Paris: Fayard, 2012), 29, 15.

86. Claire Eldridge, *From Empire to Exile: History and Memory within the Pied-Noir and Harki Communities* (Manchester: Manchester University Press, 2016), 149.

87. Of her encounter with her friend Zohra's sister, Sadia, Benkemoun notes: "j'espérais trouver un double ou une lointaine cousine qui m'aurait prouvé, comme l'écrivait Camus, qu'un «même ciel, une nature impérieuse, la communauté de nos destins [auraient] été plus forts [. . .] que les barrières naturelles ou les fossés artificiels entretenus par la colonisation»" [I was hoping to find a double or a distant cousin who would have proven to me, as Camus wrote, that a "same sky, an imperious nature, our shared destinies [would] have been stronger [. . .] than the natural barriers or the artificial rifts fostered by colonization"]. She is disappointed, however, by the fact that Zohra wears the hijab. Benkemoun's quotation is from *Cahiers Albert Camus* (Paris: Gallimard, 1987), 39.

88. *Plus belle la vie* is a French soap set in a fictional neighborhood in Marseille featuring families of diverse backgrounds.

89. Claire Messud, *The Last Life* (London: Picador, 1999).

90. Claire Messud "Camus & Algeria: The Moral Question," *The New York Review of Books*, November 7, 2013.

91. Carolyn A. Durham notes the author's insistence that the book is a work of fiction but contends that the "autobiographical nature of the novel is clearly in part a question of interpretation," while William H. Pritchard draws attention to the "autobiographical feel" of the novel. See Carolyn A. Durham, "Mosaics of the Might-Have-Been: Metaphor, Migration and Multiculturalism in Claire Messud's The Last Life," *Journal of Narrative Theory* 32, no. 2 (Summer 2002): 181, 200 and William H. Pritchard, "Fiction Chronicle," *The Hudson Review* 53, no. 1 (Spring 2000): 141.

92. Sagesse notes the likelihood that when naming their baby, her parents "wrongly" assumed she was "the child of their wisdom" (227)—an insight that suggests she is more perceptive than they are.

93. Nancy Wood, *Vectors of Memory: Legacies of Trauma in Postwar Europe* (Oxford: Berg, 1999), 10.

94. Judith Butler, *Gender Trouble: Feminism and the Subversion of Identity* (London: Routledge, 1999), 175.

95. Homi K. Bhabha, *The Location of Culture* (London: Routledge, 1994), 88.

96. Clarisse Buono, *Pieds-noirs de père en fils* (Paris: Balland, 2004), 41, 61.

97. Bérégevoy had been prime minister from 1992 to 1993, when his socialist party was defeated in elections. He died by suicide on May 1, 1993. In 1998, Papon was convicted of complicity in "crimes contre l'humanité" [crimes against humanity] for his role in deporting Jews from France during World War II. The massacre of Algerian protestors in Paris on October 17, 1961, occurred under Papon's leadership as chief of police at the time.

Conclusion

Competing memories of France's colonial past, particularly with regard to the troubling legacy of the Algerian War, highlight an enduring "complex posterity," which is further complicated at national level by the initial suppression of the conflict and contemporary depictions of a modern, postcolonial France.[1] Perhaps unsurprisingly, therefore, its former settlers, as living reminders of *Algérie française*, have remained to some extent underexplored by academics. Against the backdrop of enduring stereotypes and analyses that they or their descendants tend to have conducted in order to win a place in the national narrative, this book takes its place alongside recent efforts by French and non-French academics to reexamine this population from a nuanced viewpoint. A broader trend in recent scholarship, for example by Alec Hargreaves, Jane Hiddleston, and Helen Vassallo, has stressed the importance of studying fictional and autobiographical works by immigrants of Algerian origin in France and their children.[2] As France continues to strive to come to terms with the legacy of its colonial past, a study of semi-fictional works by the former settlers is an equally important part of processes of post-conflict recovery.

This book reveals ways in which colonial and anti-colonial discourses influenced and continue to influence performances of *pied-noir* identity. It also highlights ways in which fictionalized narratives can subvert hegemonic discourses. In the context of ever-contentious debates on the subject of global migration, the focus on storytelling in this study reveals some of the processes through which migrants can construct, in the face of animosity, a communal identity and memory that has the potential to disrupt prevalent discourses or state-sanctioned silence. In fact, many politicians view the former settlers as a cohesive political force despite academic research that reveals that "the *pied-noir* vote" is "multiforme" [multiform].[3] However, literary and cinematic productions are traditional bastions of French identity that are highly valued in its education system. That the *pieds-noirs* strive to construct a unified memory and identity through their production of such works perhaps points to the ultimate Frenchification of the settlers, which was the original aim of French educators in the colonies.

Examining the significant corpus of narratives by *pied-noir* authors through the prism of the family draws attention to the politics of inclusion and exclusion which characterized colonial encounters and which continue to shape policies within nations, even the most hospitable of which, as Jacques Derrida points out, enforce controlling frontiers.[4] Indeed, Ashis Nandy directly links contemporary hostility toward migrants and an attendant fear that a foreign presence will diminish the prosperity of those within Europe or the United States, to a sense of superiority that is a hangover from the experience of colonialism.[5] The current study reveals a renewed investment in the inclusion-exclusion model by many of the settlers following Algerian independence. Drawing on Butler's theories of performativity also points to some of the ways in which the domestic and deeply gendered politics of colonialism crossed over into postindependence constructions of a communal *pied-noir* identity. A focus on the family facilitates an investigation of models of masculinity and femininity for the former settler population as well as their representations of childhood and adolescence. Furthermore, this analysis demonstrates that the *pied-noir* family took on increased significance following 1962 as a means of unifying a community in exile. Moving beyond the *pieds-noirs*, the focus of the current book complements Tina-Karen Pusse's and Katharina Walter's contemporary volume on international literature and film, which suggests that families more generally are performed and underlines "the importance of analyzing and renovating the discourses of 'family,' which, because of their ubiquity, are too often taken for granted."[6]

An examination of a broad range of works by the *pieds-noirs* shows that this frequently essentialized "community" is made up of individuals who were continuously renegotiating their identities in response to personal and political concerns, over which the Algerian conflict and its aftermath did not necessarily take precedence. Indeed, while some commentators cast the *pieds-noirs* as macho males and anti-intellectual figures, this study reveals varying literary and filmic constructions of gender, childhood, and adolescence, as well as pointing to a wealth of significant French Algerian figures who engaged with universal issues. Albert Camus, who is renowned for his philosophy of the absurd and concern with social justice; Marie Cardinal and Hélène Cixous, both known for their feminism; or the homosexual anti-colonialist Jean Sénac, for example, were clearly influenced by thinking from outside this community while at the same time illustrating tensions within it. Indeed, the contested identity of Camus, deemed "un écrivain brûlant" [an incendiary author] in France as well as in Algeria,[7] is suggestive of the complex processes of identity renegotiation that began for the settlers once the colony's demise became increasingly likely. This process continues today. That said, this book's examination of a variety of individual engagements reveals striking similarities as regards some of the themes privileged, with an emphasis on the conflict as a family affair recurring in works by eminent as well as lesser-known authors. In fact, many later and even contemporary works are reminiscent of early narratives that include Camus's variety of masculinity and his positive depiction of pioneering settlers in *Le Premier Homme*. The following message in a 2006 documentary on the *pieds-noirs* reveals Camus's continuing contribution to a collective memory and his position as a *père spirituel* [spiritual father] to many: "'Les Pieds Noirs, histoires d'une blessure' doit énormément à la lecture du 'Premier homme' d'Albert Camus, à la rencontre avec celle qui l'a publié et qui a été un fidèle soutien dans notre travail: Catherine Camus" ["*Pieds-Noirs*: History of a Trauma" owes a great deal to reading "The First Man" by Albert Camus, to meeting the woman who published it and who was a loyal supporter of our work: Catherine Camus].[8]

This study also reveals broader trends over time in the type of works produced since Algerian independence. Following Camus's death in 1960, women's early postindependence texts were particularly significant given the official silence on the war in France at the time. Ostensibly personal narratives published from 1962 serve as metaphors for the *pied-noir* community, as their authors see themselves as custodians of memory. They consciously differentiate the *pieds-noirs* from Arabo-Berber Algerians and the metropolitan French, and foreground certain themes that continue to shape collective memory today. Some works by feminists such as Cardinal, Brigitte Roüan, and Cixous disrupt the narratives woven, although not as much as could be expected since colonial history still appears as a tragic family drama between a mother and her daughter, between sisters and their lovers, or between a Jewish family and an unattainable motherland. Men's voices from the 1970s reveal a reaffirmed attachment to the family and the mother(land) following their settlement in France, most notably by writers who had previously been known for their progressive stance with regard to the indigenous population. Sénac, who continued to live in Algeria, provides a significant divergence from conventional depictions of normative French Algerian masculinity, although his murder in 1973 and disillusionment with the postindependence government position him to some extent as a *pied-noir* outsider. Finally, this study highlights the preponderance of texts focusing on childhood from the late 1970s, which are part of a French tradition and an international trend. The surge of young narrative voices is, however, especially striking from the 1990s—some thirty years after the end of the conflict—and is significant in light of the ability of child and adolescent voices to draw attention to societal issues, including a troubling colonial past. Thus, some of these novels use the benefit of hindsight, facilitated by candid young protagonists, to engage with the trauma caused to the colonizing and colonized populations by an unjust system. However, depictions of happy childhoods under colonialism can overtly or obliquely criticize an independent Algeria in the context of increased violence. Furthermore, some of these works seek to influence a younger generation's perceptions of colonial history and of the *pieds-noirs*, whom they cast in a positive light.

Thus, despite Lucienne Martini's suggestion that an initial angry phase gave way to works of *nostalgérie* and a final, more objective phase that includes the *roman familial* [family saga],[9] this study suggests that an objective phase has not necessarily been reached. Moreover, while Rosemarie Jones suggested in 1995 that *pied-noir* literature was dying,[10] this is not the case as works continue to emerge, including by younger generations. Fifty years after independence, the decision by the daughter of a *pied-noir*, Laurence Fontaine Kerbellec, to publish stories told to her by her mother about her life in Algeria, where she lived until the age of nineteen, underlines the fact that firsthand memories are not necessary to perpetuate the type of narratives studied.[11] The fact that this writer dedicates her publication to her own children and to the duty of memory points to infinite possibilities for the perpetuation of similar stories.

This book also unravels some of the processes by which apparently private stories seek to influence public perceptions of the former settlers and contribute to constructions of a united identity as Algerian independence became increasingly likely. In consequence, the current analysis suggests that many narratives by the former settlers do not reflect a communal identity but rather seek to create one. For many of the authors studied, forming a narrative of familial memory and identity is undoubtedly therapeutic. Indeed, as suggested in the introduction to this study, those with nonvisible stigmatized identities benefit more from writing about being a member of the stigmatized group, rather than of the wider community.[12] This would imply that once the *pieds-noirs* or their descendants no longer feel stigmatized, an affective and ideological emphasis on a French Algerian family narrative will become less important and may even disappear. For the moment, however, the trope continues on-screen and in print, suggesting a continuing desire to preserve a distinctive communal affiliation.

On the subject of France's history in relation to Algeria, Patrick Apel-Muller suggests that "Des traumatismes individuels perdurent, mais aussi collectifs. Dans les blancs de la mémoire, se nichent les ferments du racisme" [Individual trauma persists, but also collective trauma. The catalysts for racism nest in the spaces in memory].[13] One way in which scholars could deconstruct stereotypes regarding the former settlers and the indigenous population might be through comparative studies of works by *pied-noir* and Algerian writers, particularly on the theme of memory and identity. This would promote an inclusive national narrative amid residual resentment and continued "memory wars" that, as Stora points out, can tend to pit opponents according to their "appartenance familiale" [familial affiliation].[14] The reclaiming of Camus and Sénac by some Algerian writers from the 1990s offers further scope for such comparative work and suggests the potential opening up of a Franco-Algerian identity that includes the former settlers as well as the indigenous population. Moreover, Franco-Algerian author Leïla Sebbar as well as writers of the "beur" community, itself a relatively recent construct, convey in their literature "forms of collectivity [that] are created not according to rigid concepts of community and difference but through fluctuating combinations of singularity, specificity and relationality."[15] This flexible approach to a collective identity, which is in reality fragmented, could prove particularly productive for *pied-noir* writers, were they to adopt it in their creative writing.

A text published on the occasion of the fiftieth anniversary of Algerian independence and jointly penned by an Algerian author and a French journalist, who spent five years of her childhood in Algeria, is suggestive of such a fluid form of communal belonging. Karima Berger's and Christine Bey's *Toi, ma soeur étrangère* (2012) [You, My Outsider Sister] is particularly striking as it includes both sides of the colonial divide. In this text, the two women, born the same year but kept apart by the colonial system, discuss and engage with each other's singular points of view, particularly memories of their childhoods and concepts of identity. Camus's shadow once again hangs over this text as Christine defends him and Karima criticizes him.[16] Significantly, the narrative woven here goes beyond the one-way hospitality featured in Camus's "L'Hôte" [The Guest], as each makes a sincere effort to open up to the other. In the words of Karima: "Je suis ton hôte et tu es la mienne" [I am your guest and you are mine].[17] Both writers approach familial identification from a stance of mutual respect that facilitates commonalities and difference. Karima's optimistic vision for a narrative of Algeria's colonial history that includes not just multiple voices but also multiple languages is a fitting way to end the current study as it points to potentially fruitful dialogue and reconciliation:

> je rêverais d'un livre sur l'Algérie écrit à la façon de ces livres de calligraphie chinoise qui se déplient de page en page: une page écrite en arabe, l'autre en face en français, l'autre encore en berbère . . . une littérature à explorer et recueillir les fruits qu'elle féconderait en chacune de nous, dans sa langue, dans sa culture.[18]

> [I would dream of a book on Algeria written in the same manner as those books of Chinese calligraphy which unfold from page to page: one page written in

Arabic, the opposite page in French, the next again in Berber . . . a literature to explore and to gather the fruits that it would fertilize in each one of us, in one's language and culture.]

NOTES

1. Henry Rousso uses this term to describe memories of Vichy France in his *The Vichy Syndrome: History and Memory in France since 1944*, trans. Arthur Goldhammer (Cambridge, MA: Harvard University Press, 1991), 79.

2. See Helen Vassallo, "Re-mapping Algeria(s) in France: Leïla Sebbar's *Mes Algéries en France* and *Journal de mes Algéries en France*," *Modern and Contemporary France* 19, no. 2 (2011): 129–45; Alec G. Hargreaves, ed. *Memory, Empire, and Postcolonialism* (Lanham, MD: Lexington Books, 2005); Jane Hiddleston "Cultural memory and Amnesia: the Algerian war and 'second-generation' immigrant literature in France," *Journal of Romance Studies* 3, no. 1 (2003): 59–71.

3. Emmanuelle Comtat, *Les Pieds-Noirs et la politique: quarante ans après le retour* (Paris: Sciences Po, 2009), 292.

4. Safaa Fathy, *D'Ailleurs, Derrida* (France: Gloria Films, 1999). See also Dominique Dhombres, "Il n'y a pas de culture ni de lien social sans un principe d'hospitalité; ce penseur estime que c'est au nom de ce principe, pris absolument, qu'il faut inventer les meilleures mesures en matière d'immigration," *Le Monde*, December 2, 1997.

5. Ananya Vajpeyi, "Ashis Nandy: Why Nationalism and Secularism Failed Together." Reset DOC: Dialogues on Civilizations, https://www.resetdoc.org/story/ashis-nandy-why-nationalism-and-secularism-failed-together/. Date accessed: July 12, 2018.

6. Tina-Karen Pusse and Katharina Walter, "Introduction," in *Precarious Parenthood: Doing Family in Literature and Film*, ed. Tina-Karen Pusse and Katharina Walter (Berlin: Lit Verlag, 2013), 7.

7. Benjamin Stora and Jean-Baptiste Péretié, *Camus Brûlant* (Paris: Stock, 2013), 10.

8. Gilles Perez, *Les Pieds-Noirs, histoires d'une blessure* (France: France 3, 2006). This text features on a DVD extra, "Albert Camus et l'Algérie: Interview de Catherine Camus" [Albert Camus and Algeria: Catherine Camus Interview]. Here, Catherine Camus discusses a way of life in Algeria that is similar to that evoked by the author. She notes that "On était de plain-pied avec la vie" [We were perfectly in sync with life], that there was a "forte imprégnation du présent" [strong emphasis on the present], and that "Il n'y a pas de la séparation de l'âme et du corps chez nous" [there is no separation between the body and the soul with us].

9. Lucienne Martini, *Racines de papier: Essai sur l'expression littéraire de l'identité Pieds-Noirs* (Paris: Publisud, 1997), 6–8, 44.

10. Rosemarie Jones, "*Pied-Noir* Literature: The Writing of a Migratory Elite," in *Writing Across Worlds: Literature and Migration*, ed. Russell King, John Connell, and Paul White (London: Routledge, 1995), 138.

11. Laurence Fontaine Kerbellec, *Un trait de khôl au bord des yeux* (Paris: Publibook, 2012). This book contains many of the themes already discussed, including the importance of family, elegant clothes, Oriental culture and superstitions, harmonious cohabitation, hospitality, and speedy funerals. It does, however, mention the massacre of Algerians in France on October 17, 1961, in addition to dates such as July 5, 1962.

12. James W. Pennebaker and Janel D. Seagal, "Forming a Story: The Health Benefits of Narrative," *Journal of Clinical Psychology* 55, no. 10 (1999): 1247.

13. Patrick Apel-Muller, "Le long cheminement d'une affaire d'État; un geste magistral reste à accomplir pour que l'affaire Maurice Audin soit un révélateur et, aussi douloureuse soit-elle, le terrain de nouvelles rencontres," *L'Humanité*, January 9, 2014.

14. Benjamin Stora, "Algérie-France, mémoires sous tension," *Le Monde*, March 18, 2012.

15. Jane Hiddleston, *Reinventing Community: Identity and Difference in Late Twentieth-Century Philosophy and Literature in French* (London: Legenda, 2005), 213.

16. Karima Berger and Christine Ray, *Toi, ma soeur étrangère: Algérie-France, sans guerre et sans tabou* (Paris: Rocher, 2012), 82.

17. Ibid., 45.

18. Ibid., 140.

Bibliography

Achille, Etienne, Charles Forsdick, and Lydie Moudileno, eds. *Postcolonial Realms of Memory: Sites and Symbols in Modern France.* Liverpool: Liverpool University Press, 2020.
Ahmed, Catherine and Raphael Eulry, "Aventures et passion en Algérie française," *Le Monde,* August 25, 1996.
Aldrich, Robert. *Colonialism and Homosexuality.* London: Routledge, 2003.
Alleg, Henri. *La Question.* Paris: Minuit, 1961.
Alloula, Malek. *Le Harem Colonial (Images d'un sous-érotisme).* Geneva: Slatkine, 1981.
Al-Mansour, Haiffa. *Wadjda.* Saudi Arabia: Soda Pictures, 2014.
Amrouche, Jean, and Jules Roy. *D'une amitié: Correspondance Jean Amrouche, Jules Roy (1937-1962).* Aix-en-Provence: Édisud, 1985.
Anderson, Benedict. *Imagined Communities: Reflections on the Origin and Spread of Nationalism.* London: Verso, 1991.
Anderson, Kirsteen H. R. "La Première Femme: The Mother's Resurrection in the Work of Camus and Irigaray." *Society for French Studies* 56, no. 1 (2002): 29–43.
Anonymous. "Aix-en-Provence: hommage à Camus, un an après la polémique." *Libération,* October 6, 2013.
———. "Avertissement." LIMAG, http://www.limag.refer.org/Documents/AvertissementNedjma1956.pdf. Date accessed: February 5, 2014.
———. "'Bambi,' quand un petit garçon d'Algérie devient femme d'exception." AFP, June 14, 2013, LexisNexis.
———. "Biographie de Jean-Noël Pancrazi." Société des gens de lettres, http://www.sgdl.org/culturel/les-prix-litteraires/les-prix-de-la-session-de-printemps/575. Date accessed: October 4, 2011.
———. "Élie-Georges Berreby, un homme pluriel." Berreby, http://www.berreby.net/accueil/index.html. Date accessed: August 21, 2013.
———. "France Remembers the Algerian War, 50 Years On." France 24, http://www.france24.com/en/20120316-commemorations-mark-end-algerian-war-independence-france-evian-accords. Date accessed: February 24, 2014.

———. "Il y a 50 ans mourait Albert Camus." L'Association nationale des Pieds Noirs progressistes et leurs amis, http://www.anpnpa.org/?p=166. Date accessed: October 6, 2013.

———. "Michel Onfray ne sera pas le commissaire de l'exposition Camus à Aix." AFP, September 15, 2012, LexisNexis.

———. "Plus de cent livres pour le 50e anniversaire de la fin de la guerre d'Algérie." AFP, February 4, 2012, LexisNexis.

———. "Points forts. Carrière." *Midi Libre: Les journaux du Midi*, September 15, 2012.

———. "1er Novembre 1954 : La Tousssaint algérienne. Les déchirures d'un juste," *Le Monde*, November 4, 1994.

———. "Raymond Plante (Quebec) prime à la Foire du Livre de Brive." AFP, November 7, 1994, LexisNexis.

———. "Suicide d'un écrivain d'extrême droite à Notre-Dame, hommage de Le Pen." AFP, May 21, 2013, LexisNexis.

Apel-Muller, Patrick. "Le long cheminement d'une affaire d'État; un geste magistral reste à accomplir pour que l'affaire Maurice Audin soit un révélateur et, aussi douloureuse soit-elle, le terrain de nouvelles rencontres." *L'Humanité*, January 9, 2014.

Apter, Emily. "Out of Character: Camus's French Algerian Subjects." *MLN French Issue* 112, no. 4 (September 1997): 499–516.

Arcady, Alexandre. *Là-bas mon pays*. France: Alexandre Films, 2000.

———. *Le Coup de Sirocco*. France: Films de l'Alma, 1979.

Arnett, Jeffrey Jensen. *Adolescence and Emerging Adulthood: A Cultural Approach*. Boston: Prentice Hall, 2010.

Bachi, Salim. *Le dernier été d'un jeune homme*. Paris: Flammarion, 2013.

Baïlac, Geneviève. *La Famille Hernandez*. France: Films Etienne Baïlac, 1964.

———. *La Famille Hernandez*. Théâtre du Gymnase Marie Bell, Paris: Antenne 2, 1987.

Barclay, Fiona. "Postcolonial France? The problematisation of Frenchness through North African immigration: A literary study of metropolitan novels, 1980-2000." Unpublished PhD dissertation, University of Glasgow, 2006.

———. "Reporting on 1962: The Evolution of *pied-noir* Identity across Fifty Years of Print Media." *Modern & Contemporary* France 23, no. 2 (2015): 197–211.

Baring, Edward. "Liberalism and the Algerian War: The Case of Jacques Derrida." *Critical Inquiry* 36, no. 2 (Winter 2010): 239–61.

Barthes, Roland. *S/Z*. Paris: Seuil, 1970.

Bartlett, Elizabeth Ann. *Rebellious Feminism: Camus's Ethic of Rebellion and Feminist Thought*. New York: Palgrave Macmillan, 2004.

Basham, Richard. "Machismo." *Frontiers: A Journal of Women Studies* 1, no. 2 (Spring 1976): 126–43.

Béar, Liza, "Brigitte Rouan," *Bomb Magazine*, January 1, 1992, https://bombmagazine.org/articles/brigitte-rouan/. Date accessed: July 9, 2019.

Beaugé, Florence. "Torturée par l'armée française en Algérie, Lila recherche l'homme qui l'a sauvée." *Le Monde*, June 20, 2000.

Beaumont, Peter. "Albert Camus, the outsider, is still dividing opinion in Algeria 50 years after his death." *The Observer*, February 28, 2010.
Begag, Azouz. *Le Gone du Châaba : Roman*. Paris : Éditions du Seuil, 1986.
Bell, Vikki. "Mimesis as Cultural Survival: Judith Butler and Anti-Semitism." In *Performativity and Belonging*, edited by Vikki Bell, 133–61. London: Sage, 1999.
———. "On Speech, Race and Melancholia: An Interview with Judith Butler." In *Performativity & Belonging*, edited by Vikki Bell, 163–74. London: Sage, 1999.
———. "Performativity and Belonging: An Introduction." In *Performativity & Belonging*, edited by Vikki Bell, 1–10. London: Sage, 1999.
Ben Slimane, Souad. "Ce que le jour doit à la nuit en chantier—Et pourtant ça tourne!" *La Presse (Tunis)*, June 16, 2011.
Benassayag, Maurice. "Familles, je vous aime." In *Les Pieds-Noirs*, edited by Emmanuel Roblès, 161–76. Paris: Philippe Lebaud, 1982.
Benkemoun, Brigitte. *La Petite fille sur la photo: La guerre d'Algérie à hauteur d'enfant*. Paris: Fayard, 2012.
Bensalah, Mohamed. "11 Décembre 1960: Du devoir de mémoire au devoir d'histoire." Vinyculture, http://www.vinyculture.com/11-decembre-1960-du-dev oir-de- memoire-au-devoir-dhistoire-par-mohamed-bensalah/. Date accessed: March 26, 2013.
Berger, Karima, and Christine Ray. *Toi, ma soeur étrangère: Algérie-France, sans guerre et sans tabou*. Paris: Rocher, 2012.
Berque, Jacques. *Le Maghreb entre deux guerres*. Paris: Seuil, 1962.
Berreby, Élie-Georges. *L'Enfant pied-noir*. Arles: Actes sud, 2007.
Bertrand, Louis. *Le Sang des races*. Paris: Paul Ollendorff, 1899.
Bey, Maissa. *L'ombre d'un homme qui marche au soleil: Réflexions sur Albert Camus*. Montpellier: Chèvre-feuille étoilée, 2004.
Bhabha, Homi K. *The Location of Culture*. London: Routledge, 1994.
Blanchard, Pascal, and Sandrine Lemaire. *Culture impériale: Les colonies au coeur de la République, 1931-1961*. Paris: Autrement, 2004.
Bonotaux, Gilles, and Hélène Lasserre. *Quand ils avaient mon âge . . . Alger 1954-1962*. Paris: Autrement, 2002.
Bouckaert-Ghesquiere, Rita. "Looking Back. The Rise of the Autobiographical Novel in Children's Literature." In *Genres as Repositories of Cultural Memory: Vol. 5 of the proceedings of the 15th congress of the International Comparative Literature Association*, edited by Hendrik Van Gorp and Ulla Musarra-Schroeder, 441–63. Amsterdam: Rodopi, 2000.
Bourdieu, Pierre. "The Sentiment of Honour in Kabyle Society." In *Honour and Shame: The Values of Mediterranean Society*, edited by J. G. Peristiany, 191–242. Chicago: University of Chicago Press, 1974.
Boyer, Corinne. "Aix-en-Provence tient absolument à une exposition Camus; Les organisateurs de Marseille-Provence 2013 ont renoncé à une exposition consacré au prix Nobel de littérature. La ville d'Aix-en-Provence reprend le projet dans un contexte chaotique." *La Croix*, October 18, 2012.
Boym, Svetlana. "Nostalgia and Its Discontents." *The Hedgehog Review* 9, no. 2 (Summer 2007): 7–18.

Boyne, John. *The Boy in the Striped Pajamas*. Oxford: David Fickling Books, 2006.
Branche, Raphaëlle. *La Guerre d'Algérie: une histoire apaisée?* Paris: Seuil, 2005.
Bree, Germaine. "Camus." *The French Review* 33, no. 6 (May 1960): 541–44.
Briot, Geneviève, and Aknin Cohen. "Des écrivains et la guerre d'Algérie." Briot and Cohen, http://briot-cohenaknin.hautetfort.com/tag/virginie+buisson. Date accessed: November 8, 2011.
Brosman, Catharine Savage. "Les Frères ennemis: Jules Roy et l'Algérie." *American Association of Teachers of French* 56, no. 4 (March 1983): 579–87.
Brown, Stephanie. "On Kitsch, Nostalgia, and Nineties Femininity." *Popular Culture Association in the South* 22, no. 3 (April 2000): 39–54.
Brugger-Dethmers, Nicole. "Cross-Dressing and Performativity." In *Contemporary Adolescent Literature and Culture: The Emergent Adult*, edited by Mary Hilton and Maria Nikolajeva, 77–91. Farnham, Surrey: Ashgate, 2012.
Buisson, Virginie. *L'Algérie ou la mort des autres*. Paris: Gallimard, 1981.
Buono, Clarisse. *Pieds-noirs de père en fils*. Paris: Balland, 2004.
Butler, Judith. *Bodies That Matter: On the Discursive Limits of 'Sex.'* New York: Routledge, 1993.
———. *Gender Trouble: Feminism and the Subversion of Identity*. London: Routledge, 1999.
———. *Trouble dans le genre (Gender Trouble): Le féminisme et la subversion de l'identité*. Translated by Cynthia Kraus. Paris: La Découverte, 2005.
Camus, Albert. *Actuelles, III: Chroniques algériennes, 1939-1958*. Paris: Gallimard, 1958.
———. *Essais*. Paris: Gallimard, 2000.
———. *La Peste*. Paris: Gallimard, 1947.
———. *Le Premier Homme*. Paris: Gallimard, 1994.
———. *L'Étranger*. Paris: Gallimard, 1942.
———. *L'Exil et le Royaume*. Paris: Gallimard, 2003.
———. *The First Man*. Translated by David Hapgood. London: Hamish Hamilton, 1995.
———. *The Outsider*. Translated by Joseph Laredo. London: Penguin, 1982.
Camus, Albert, and Jean Grenier. *Correspondance: 1932-1960*. Paris: Gallimard, 1981.
Cardinal, Marie. *Au Pays de mes racines*. Paris: Grasset, 1980.
———. *Les Mots pour le dire*. London: Bristol Classical Press, 1993.
———. *Les Pieds-Noirs*. Paris: Belfond, 1988.
———. *The Words to Say It*. Translated by Pat Goodheart. London: Picador, 1984.
Carey, Peter. *True History of the Kelly Gang: A Novel*. New York: Alfred A. Knopf, 2000.
Carroll, David. *Albert Camus the Algerian: Colonialism, Terrorism, Justice*. New York: Columbia University Press, 2007.
Chenaille, Gilles. "Dossier: La sélection littéraire du mois d'avril: La petite fille sur la photo, de Brigitte Benkemoun." *MarieClaire*, July 19, 2013.
Choi, Sung-Eun. *Decolonization and the French of Algeria: Bringing the Settler Colony Home*. Basingstoke, UK: Palgrave Macmillan, 2016.

Cixous, Hélène. *Les Rêveries de la femme sauvage: Scènes primitives*. Paris: Galilée, 2000.
Clancy-Smith, Julia. "Islam, Gender, and Identities in the Making of French Algeria, 1830-1962." In *Domesticating the Empire: Race, Gender, and Family Life in French and Dutch Colonialism*, edited by Julia Clancy-Smith and Frances Gouda, 154–74. Charlottesville, VA: University of Virginia Press, 1998.
Clancy-Smith, Julia, and Frances Gouda, eds. *Domesticating the Empire: Race, Gender, and Family Life in French and Dutch Colonialism*. Charlottesville, VA: University of Virginia Press, 1998.
———. "Introduction." In *Domesticating the Empire: Race, Gender, and Family Life in French and Dutch Colonialism*, edited by Julia Clancy-Smith and Frances Gouda, 1–20. Charlottesville, VA: University of Virginia Press, 1998.
Cloonan, William, and Jean-Philippe Postel. "From maison d'édition to librairie: The Novel in 1995." *The French Review* 69, no. 6 (May 1996): 903–11.
Cohen, William B. "The Algerian War and French Memory." *Contemporary European History* 9, no. 3 (November 2000): 489–500.
Comtat, Emmanuelle. *Les Pieds-Noirs et la politique: quarante ans après le retour*. Paris: Sciences Po, 2009.
Condotta, Françoise. "Cimetières d'Oranie: Une décennie de silence." *Midi Libre*, December 18, 2013.
Conesa, Gabriel. *Bab-el-Oued: Notre paradis perdu*. Paris: Robert Laffont, 1970.
Cooper, Frederick, and Ann L. Stoler. "Between Metropole and Colony: Rethinking a Research Agenda." In *Tensions of Empire: Colonial Cultures in a Bourgeois World*, edited by Frederick Cooper and Ann L. Stoler, 1–56. Berkeley, CA: University of California Press, 1997.
Creed, Barbara. "Horror and the Monstrous Feminine: An Imaginary Abjection." *Screen* 27, no. 1 (1986): 44–70.
Daoud, Kamel. *Meursault, Contre-enquête : Roman*. Arles: Actes Sud, 2014.
de Beauvoir, Simone. *Le Deuxième Sexe I: Les faits et les mythes*. Paris: Gallimard, 1976.
de la Hogue, Janine. "Les Livres comme patrie." In *Les Pieds-Noirs*, edited by Emmanuel Roblès, 112–23. Paris: Philippe Lebaud, 1982.
de Montvalon, Jean-Baptiste, and Sylvia Zappi. "Ce que Sarkozy propose, c'est la haine de l'autre." *Le Monde*, December 27, 2009.
Derderian, Richard L. "Algeria as a *lieu de mémoire:* Ethnic Minority Memory and National Identity in Contemporary France." *Radical History Review* no. 83 (Spring 2002): 28–43.
Derrida, Jacques. *Le Monolinguisme de l'autre ou la prothèse d'origine*. Paris: Galilée, 1996.
Dessaigne, Francine. *Journal d'une mère de famille pied-noir*. Paris: France-Empire, 1972.
Dhombres, Dominique. "Il n'y a pas de culture ni de lien social sans un principe d'hospitalité; ce penseur estime que c'est au nom de ce principe, pris absolument, qu'il faut inventer les meilleures mesures en matière d'immigration." *Le Monde*, December 2, 1997.

Dine, Philip. "Big-Game Hunting in Algeria from Jules Gérard to *Tartarin de Tarascon*." *Moving Worlds: A Journal of Transcultural Writings* 12, no. 1 (2012): 47–58.

———. "Fighting and Writing the War Without a Name: Polemics and the French-Algerian conflict." *Aurifex*, no. 2 (2002), http://www.goldsmiths.ac.uk/aurifex/issue2/dine.html. Date accessed: February 17, 2014.

———. *Images of the Algerian War: French Fiction and Film, 1954-1992*. Oxford: Oxford University Press, 1994.

———. "Reading and remembering *la guerre des mythes*: French literary representations of the Algerian war." *Modern & Contemporary France* 2, no. 2 (1994): 141–50.

———. "(Still) À la recherche de l'Algérie perdue: French Fiction and Film, 1992-2001." *Historical Reflections* 28, no. 2 (Summer 2002): 255–75.

———. "The French Colonial Myth of a Pan-Mediterranean Civilization." In *Transnational Spaces and Identities in the Francophone World*, edited by Hafid Gafaiti, Patricia M.E. Lorcin, and David G. Troyansky, 3–23. Lincoln, NE: University of Nebraska Press, 2009.

Djebar, Assia. *Femmes d'Alger dans leur appartement*. Paris: Albin Michel, 2002.

———. *Le Blanc de l'Algérie: récit*. Paris: Albin Michel, 1995.

Dugas, Guy. "Les auteurs." In *Algérie: Un rêve de fraternité*, edited by Guy Dugas, 969–93. Paris: Omnibus, 1997.

Dugdale, John. "Albert Camus centenary goes without much honour at home. Neither France nor Algeria pay much attention to 100th anniversary, leaving job to Google." *The Guardian*, November 7, 2013.

Dunwoodie, Peter. *Writing French Algeria*. Oxford: Oxford University Press, 1998.

Dupuis, Jérôme. "Acte III : «Houellebecq a tout programmé depuis le premier jour»." *L'Express*, September 1, 2005.

Durham, Carolyn A. "Mosaics of the Might-Have-Been: Metaphor, Migration and Multiculturalism in Claire Messud's The Last Life." *Journal of Narrative Theory* 32, no. 2 (Summer 2002): 179–206.

———. "Strategies of Subversion in Colonial Nostalgia Film: Militarism and Marriage in Brigitte Roüan's *Outremer*." *Studies in French Cinema* 1, no. 2 (2001): 89–97.

Elbe, Marie. *À l'heure de notre mort*. Paris: Albin Michel, 1992.

Eldridge, Claire. *From Empire to Exile: History and Memory within the Pied-Noir and Harki Communities*. Manchester: Manchester University Press, 2016.

———. "'We've Never Had a Voice': Memory Construction and the Children of the Harkis (1962-1991)." *French History* 23, no. 1 (2009): 88–107.

Fanon, Frantz. *L'An V de la révolution algérienne*. Paris: La Découverte, 2001.

———. *Les Damnés de la terre*. Paris: Gallimard, 1991.

———. *Peau noire, masques blancs*. Paris: Seuil, 1952.

Fathy, Safaa. *D'Ailleurs, Derrida*. France: Gloria Films, 1999.

Ferdi, Saïd. *Un Enfant dans la guerre: témoignage*. Paris: Seuil, 1981.

Ferrandez, Jacques. *L'Hôte: d'après l'œuvre d'Albert Camus, tirée de L'Exil et le royaume*. Paris: Gallimard, 2009.

Fletcher, John. "Interpreting *L'Etranger.*" *The French Review* 1 (Winter 1970): 158–67.
Foley, John. *Albert Camus: From the Absurd to Revolt*. Montreal: McGill-Queen's University Press, 2008.
Fontaine Kerbellec, Laurence. *Un trait de khôl au bord des yeux*. Paris: Publibook, 2012.
Fortier, Anne-Marie. "Re-Membering Places and the Performance of Belonging(s)." In *Performativity & Belonging*, edited by Vikki Bell, 41–64. London: Sage, 1999.
Foucault, Michel. *«Il faut défendre la société»:Cours au collège de France (1975-1976)*. Paris: Gallimard, 1997.
Foucault, Michel. *L'Archéologie du savoir*. Paris: Gallimard, 1969.
Fouchet, Antoine. "Le souvenir de la guerre d'Algérie divise encore les parlementaires; La proposition de loi PS faisant du 19 mars le jour du souvenir de la guerre d'Algérie n'a pas fait l'unanimité, hier, au Sénat. Les associations de pieds-noirs et de harkis dénoncent le choix de cette date." *La Croix*, November 9, 2012.
Frohock, W.M. "The Failing Center: Recent Fiction and the Picaresque Tradition." *Novel: A Forum on Fiction* 3, no. 1 (Autumn 1969): 62–69.
Fromentin, Eugène. *Dominique*. Paris: Flammarion, 1987.
Gabbard, Krin. "Men in Film." In *Debating Masculinity*, edited by Josep M. Armengol and Àngels Carabí, 42–56. Harriman, TN: Men's Studies Press, 2009.
Gadal, Hélene. *Petite pied-noir deviendra grande*. Paris: Théles, 2002.
Gil, Marie. *De l'autre côté de la mer . . . Oran et l'Oranie*. Empury: Association Réalités du Morvan, 2001).
Gilmore, David. "Cultures of Masculinity." In *Debating Masculinity*, edited by Josep M. Armengol and Àngels Carabí, 31–41. Harriman, TN: Men's Studies Press, 2009.
Gosnell, Jonathan K. *The Politics of Frenchness in Colonial Algeria, 1930-1954*. New York: University of Rochester Press, 2002.
Graebner, Seth. *History's Place: Nostalgia and the City in French Algerian Literature*. Lanham, MD: Lexington, 2007.
Granara, William. "Picaresque Narratives and Cultural Dissimulation in Colonial North African Literature." *The Arab Studies Journal* 11, no. 2 (Autumn 2003/ Spring 2004): 41–56.
Greene, Naomi. *Landscapes of Loss: The National Past in Postwar French Cinema*. Princeton, NJ: Princeton University Press, 1999.
Grine, Hamid. *Camus dans le narguilé* (Paris: Éditions Après la lune, 2011).
Guéhenno, Jean. *La Mort des autres*. Paris: Grasset, 1968.
Haddour, Azzedine. *Colonial Myths: History and Narrative*. Manchester: Manchester University.
Hardwick, Louise. "The Rise of the récit d'enfance in the Francophone Caribbean." In *Postcolonial Poetics: Genre and Form*, edited by Patrick Crowley and Jane Hiddleston, 166–82. Liverpool: Liverpool University Press, 2011.
Hargreaves, Alec G., ed. *Memory, Empire, and Postcolonialism*. Lanham, MD: Lexington Books, 2005.
Hartley, L. P. *The Go-Between*. London: Penguin, 1997.
Hecht, Emmanuel. "Petites phrases de la Ve." *L'Express*, July 6, 2011.

Hiddleston, Jane. "Cultural Memory and Amnesia: The Algerian War and 'Second-Generation' Immigrant Literature in France." *Journal of Romance Studies* 3, no. 1 (2003): 59–71.

———. "Introduction." In *Postcolonial Poetics: Genre and Form*, edited by Patrick Crowley and Jane Hiddleston, 1–12. Liverpool: Liverpool University Press, 2011.

———. *Reinventing Community: Identity and Difference in Late Twentieth-Century Philosophy and Literature in French*. London: Legenda, 2005.

Hilton, Mary, and Maria Nikolajeva. "Introduction: Time of Turmoil." In *Contemporary Adolescent Literature and Culture: The Emergent Adult*, edited by Mary Hilton and Maria Nikolajeva, 1–16. Farnham, Surrey: Ashgate, 2012.

Hobsbawm, Eric. "Introduction: Inventing Traditions." In *The Invention of Tradition*, edited by Eric Hobsbawm and Terence Ranger, 1–14. Cambridge: Cambridge University Press, 1996.

Horne, Alistair. *A Savage War of Peace: Algeria 1954-1962*. New York: New York Review Books, 2006.

Horne, Janet R. "In Pursuit of Greater France: Visons of Empire among Musée Social Reformers 1894-1931." In *Domesticating the Empire: Race, Gender, and Family Life in French and Dutch Colonialism*, edited by Julia Clancy-Smith and Frances Gouda, 21–42. Charlottesville, VA: University of Virginia Press, 1998.

Horrell, Georgie. "Transgression and Transition." In *Contemporary Adolescent Literature and Culture: The Emergent Adult*, edited by Mary Hilton and Maria Nikolajeva, 47–59. Surrey: Ashgate, 2012.

Hubbell, Amy L. *Remembering French Algeria: Pieds-Noirs, Identity and Exile*. (Nebraska: University of Nebraska Press, 2015).

Hughes, Edward J. "Building the Colonial Archive: The Case of Camus's *Le premier homme*." *Research in African Literatures* 30, no. 3 (1999): 176–93.

Hureau, Joëlle. *La Mémoire des pieds-noirs: de 1830 à nos jours*. Paris: Perrin, 2010.

Hussey, Andrew. "The French Intifada: How the Arab banlieues are fighting the French State." *The Observer*, February 23, 2014.

Ighilahriz, Louisette. *Algérienne: récit recueilli par Anne Nivat*. Paris: Fayard, 2001.

Jones, Ann Rosalind. "Writing the Body: Toward an Understanding of 'L'Écriture Feminine.'" *Feminist Studies* 7, no. 2 (Summer 1981): 247–63.

Jones, Linda. "Islamic Masculinities." In *Debating Masculinity*, edited by Josep M. Armengol and Àngels Carabí, 93–112. Harriman, TN: Men's Studies Press, 2009.

Jones, Rosemarie. "*Pied-Noir* Literature: The Writing of a Migratory Elite." In *Writing across Worlds: Literature and Migration*, edited by Russell King, John Connell, and Paul White, 125–40. London: Routledge, 1995.

Jordi, Jean-Jacques. *Les Pieds-Noirs*. Paris: Le Cavalier Bleu, 2009.

Karsenty, Irène. "C'était quoi, déjà, les oubliés?" In *Les Pieds-Noirs*, edited by Emmanuel Roblès, 140–50. Paris: Philippe Lebaud, 1982.

Kassoul, Aicha, and Mohamed-Lakhdar Maougal. *The Algerian Destiny of Albert Camus*. Translated by Philip Beitchman. Bethesda, MD: Academica Press, 2006.

Kateb, Yacine. *Nedjma*. Paris: Seuil, 1996

———. *Nedjma*. Translated by Richard Howard. Charlottesville, VA: University of Virginia Press, 1991.

Keller, Richard C. *Colonial Madness: Psychiatry in French North Africa*. Chicago: University of Chicago Press, 2007.
Kilcline, Cathal. "Constructions of Identity in Mediterranean France: A Study of Sport and other Popular Cultural Forms." Unpublished PhD dissertation, National University of Ireland, Galway, 2009.
Koubi, Richard M. *Pieds-Noirs belle pointure: Onze portraits de famille*. Paris: L'Atlanthrope, 1979.
Kristeva, Julia. "The Adolescent Novel." In *Abjection, Melancholia and Love: The Work of Julia Kristeva*, edited by John Fletcher and Andrew Benjamin, 8–23. London: Routledge, 1991.
Kulkarni, Mangesh. "The Ambiguous Fate of a *Pied-Noir*: Albert Camus and Colonialism." *Economic and Political Weekly* 32, no. 26 (June 28–July 4, 1997): 1528–30.
Lachenaud, Pascal. "Colonisation : Une association de Pieds-Noirs porte plainte contre Macron," *LeParisien.fr*, February 27, 2017.
Lazreg, Marnia. *The Eloquence of Silence: Algerian Women in Question*. London: Routledge, 1994.
Leconte, Daniel. *Camus, si tu savais . . . suivi de Les Pieds-Noirs*. Paris: Seuil, 2006.
Legrand, Lucien. *Autobiographie d'un pied noir gay*. Paris: Publibook, 2011.
Letablier, Marie-Thérèse. "Fertility and Family Policies in France." *Journal of Population and Social Security* 1, no. 1 (2003): 242–58.
Lever, Alison. "Honour as a Red Herring." *Critique of Anthropology* 6, no. 3 (December 1986): 83–106.
Lichfield, John. "It's a French woman's duty to wear a bikini, says ex-minister; Islamophobia row as Sarkozy supporter hits out at Muslim on beach in headscarf," *The Independent*, August 19, 2014.
———. "Why Sarkozy won't let Camus rest in peace: France's right-wing leader stands accused of political bodysnatching with a plan to move the author's remains to the Pantheon—burial place of the country's establishment." *The Independent* January 5, 2010.
Licops, Dominique. "Re-scripting History and Fairy Tales in Brigitte Roüan's 'Outremer.'" *Women's Studies Quarterly* 30, no. 1 (Spring/Summer 2002): 103–19.
Ligner, Isabelle. "Pour des Algériens, le recours à une loi de 1955 est une 'provocation.'" AFP, November 8, 2005, LexisNexis.
Lloyd, Moya. "Performativity, Parody, Politics." In *Performativity & Belonging*, edited by Vikki Bell, 195–213. London: Sage, 1999.
Loesch, Anne. *La Valise et le cercueil*. Paris: Plon, 1963.
Lorcin, Patricia M.E. *Historicizing Colonial Nostalgia: European Women's Narratives of Algeria and Kenya 1900-Present*. Basingstoke: Palgrave Macmillan, 2012.
———. "Teaching Women and Gender in France d'Outre-Mer: Problems and Strategies." *French Historical Studies* 27, no. 2 (Spring 2004): 293–310.
Lorrain, François-Guillaume. "Les enfants brisent le silence; Algérie." *Le Point*, March 15, 2012.
Losch, Richard R. *The Many Faces of Faith: A Guide to World Religions and Christian Traditions*. Grand Rapids, MI: Eerdmans, 2002.

Lottman, Herbert R. *Albert Camus*. Paris: Seuil, 1978.
Louar, Nadia. "At the intersection of queer and postcolonial discourses. Rerouting the queer with Jean Sénac and Jean Genet." In *Rerouting the Postcolonial: New Directions for the New Millennium*, edited by Janet Wilson, Cristina Sandru, and Sarah Welsh Lawson, 232–41. London: Routledge, 2010.
Luciani, Noémie. "Bambi à voir; Marie-Pierre, transsexuelle, ex-reine du Paris by night." *Le Monde*, June 19, 2013.
MacDowell, Laurel Sefton. *An Environmental History of Canada*. Vancouver: UBC Press, 2012.
Margerrison, Christine. "The Dark Continent of Camus's *L'Étranger*." *Society for French Studies* 55, no. 1 (2001): 59–73.
Martin, Maj. "The Madness at Deolali." *Royal Army Medical Corps* 152, no. 2 (2006): 94–95.
Martinez, Henri. *Et qu'ils m'accueillent avec des cris de haine: Oran 1962*. Paris: Robert Laffont, 1982.
Martini, Lucienne. *Racines de papier: Essai sur l'expression littéraire de l'identité Pieds-Noirs*. Paris: Publisud, 1997.
Marx-Scouras, Danielle. "The Specter of Jean Sénac." *L'Esprit Créateur* 43, no. 1 (Spring 2003): 45–57.
Mauss-Copeaux, Claire. *Algérie, 20 août 1955: Insurrection, Répression, Massacres*. Paris: Payot, 2011.
Mazzella, Léon. *Le Parler pied-noir: mots et expressions de là-bas*. Paris: Rivages, 1989.
McClintock, Anne. *Imperial Leather: Race, Gender, and Sexuality in the Colonial Conquest*. New York: Routledge, 1995.
McCormack, Jo. *Collective Memory: France and the Algerian War (1954-1962)*. Lanham, MD: Lexington, 2007.
McDougall, James. "Savage Wars? Codes of Violence in Algeria, 1830s-1990s." *Third World Quarterly* 26, no. 1 (2005): 117–31.
Memmi, Albert. *Portrait du colonisé précédé de Portrait du colonisateur*. Paris: Gallimard, 1985.
Messner, Michael A. "Barbie Girls Versus Sea Monsters: Children Constructing Gender." *Gender & Society* 14, no. 6 (2000): 765–84.
Messud, Claire. "Camus & Algeria: The Moral Question." *The New York Review of Books*, November 7, 2013.
———. *The Last Life*. London: Picador, 1999.
Michel-Chich, Danielle. *Déracinés: les pieds-noirs aujourd'hui*. Paris: Plume, 1990.
Mills, Sara. *Michel Foucault*. London: Routledge, 2003.
Montgomery, Geraldine F. "La Mère Sacrée dans *Le Premier Homme*." In *Albert Camus 20: 'Le Premier homme' en perspective*, edited by Raymond Gay-Crosier, 63–86. Paris: Lettres Modernes Minard, 2004.
Mulvey, Laura. *Visual and Other Pleasures*. London: Macmillan, 1993.

Murray, Alison. "Review: Women, Nostalgia, Memory: 'Chocolat,' 'Outremer,' and 'Indochine.'" *Research in African Literatures* 33, no. 2 (Summer 2002): 235–44.
Nacer-Khodja, Hamid. *Albert Camus, Jean Sénac ou Le fils rebelle*. Paris: Éditions Paris-Mediterranée, 2004.
Nora, Pierre. *Les Français d'Algérie*. Paris: Julliard, 1961.
———. *Les Français d'Algérie: Édition revue et augmentée, précédée de «Cinquante ans après» et suivie d'un document inédit de Jacques Derrida, «Mon cher Nora . . . »*. Paris: Christian Bourgois, 2012.
———, ed. *Les Lieux de mémoire* I: *La République*. Paris: Gallimard, 1984.
O'Brien, Conor Cruise. *Camus*. London: Fontana, 1970.
O'Brien, Justin. *The Novel of Adolescence in France: The Study of a Literary Theme*. New York: Columbia University Press, 1937.
O'Connor, Frank. *Guests of the Nation*. London: Macmillan, 1931.
Onfray, Michel. *L'Ordre libertaire: La vie philosophique d'Albert Camus*. Paris: Flammarion, 2012.
Orme, Mark. *The Development of Albert Camus's Concern for Social and Political Justice: "Justice pour un juste."* Madison, NJ: Fairleigh Dickinson University Press, 2007.
Pace, Patricia. "All our lost children: Trauma and testimony in the performance of childhood." *Text and Performance Quarterly* 18, no. 3 (July 1998): 233–47.
Pancrazi, Jean-Noël. *Madame Arnoul*. Paris: Gallimard, 1995.
Pélégri, Jean. *Les Oliviers de la justice*. Paris: Gallimard, 1959.
———. *Ma Mère l'Algérie*. Algiers: Laphomic, 1989.
Pelissier, Jean-Paul. Polémique sur la colonisation: à Toulon, Macron ose un 'Je vous ai compris.'" *LeParisien.fr*, February 18, 2017.
Pennebaker, James W., and Janel D. Seagal. "Forming a Story: The Health Benefits of Narrative." *Journal of Clinical Psychology* 55, no. 10 (1999): 1243–54.
Penrod, Lynn. "Algeriance, Exile, and Hélène Cixous 1." *College Literature* 30, no. 1 (Winter 2003): 135–45.
Perec, Georges. *Quel petit vélo à guidon chromé au fond de la cour?* Paris: Denoël, 1966.
Perez, Gilles. *Les Pieds-Noirs, histoires d'une blessure*. France: France 3, 2006.
Perez, Joseph. "E Macron: Une compassion bien selective," Communiqué CDHA, http://data.over-blog-kiwi.com/1/43/00/01/20180917/ob_26eb39_2018-09-13 -communique-du-cdha1.pdf. Date accessed: September 13, 2018.
———. "Lettre d'Information du CDHA, Novembre 2012, numéro 19: L'édito." Centre de Documentation Historique sur l'Algérie, http://cdha.fr/sites/default/files/ kcfinder/files/Lettre%20n%C2%B019.pdf. Date accessed: March 22, 2013.
Perez. Marie-Jeanne. *Gouttes-de-sang: Roman*. La Tour d'aigues: Éditions de l'Aube, 1991.
Pervillé, Guy. *Oran, 5 juillet 1962. Leçon d'histoire sur un massacre*. Paris: Vendémiaire, 2014.
———. "Réponse à Emmanuel Macron (2017)." Guy Pervillé, http://guy.perville. free.fr/spip/article.php3?id_article=390. Date accessed: July 2, 2017.

Phaneuf, Victoria M. "Negotiating culture, performing identities: North African and Pied-Noir associations in France." *The Journal of North African Studies* 17, no. 4 (2012): 671–86.

Pontecorvo, Gillo. *La Bataille d'Alger*. Algeria: Casbah Films, 1966.

Pritchard, William H. "Fiction Chronicle." *The Hudson Review* 53, no. 1 (Spring 2000): 136–44.

Prochaska, David. *Making Algeria French: Colonialism in Bône, 1870-1920*. Cambridge: Cambridge University Press, 1990.

Proust, Marcel. *À la recherche du temps perdu I: Du côté de chez Swann – A l'ombre des jeunes filles en fleurs*. Paris: Gallimard, 1954.

Pusse, Tina-Karen, and Katharina Walter. "Introduction." In *Precarious Parenthood: Doing Family in Literature and Film*, edited by Tina-Karen Pusse and Katharina Walter, 1–8. Berlin: Lit Verlag, 2013.

Rae Vartanian, Lesa. "Revisiting the Imaginary Audience and Personal Fable Constructs of Adolescent Egocentrism: A Conceptual Review." *Adolescence* 35, no. 140 (Winter 2000): 639–61.

Rearick, Charles. "Madelon and the Men – In War and Memory." *French Historical Studies* 17, no. 4 (Autumn 1992): 1001–34.

Renard, Delphine. *Tu Choisiras la vie*. Paris: Grasset, 2013.

Rice, Alison. *Polygraphies: Francophone Women Writing Algeria*. Charlottesville, VA: University of Virginia Press, 2012.

Rioufol, Ivan, "Macron confronté à la France déchirée," *Le Figaro*, January 11, 2019.

Rizzuto, Anthony. *Camus: Love and Sexuality*. Gainesville, FL: University Press of Florida, 1998.

Roblès, Emmanuel. *Camus, frère de soleil*. Paris: Seuil, 1995.

———. "Pourquoi pieds-noirs?" In *Les Pieds-Noirs*, edited by Emmanuel Roblès, 15–19. Paris: Philippe Lebaud, 1982.

———. "Préface." In *Les Pieds-Noirs*, edited by Emmanuel Roblès, 11–13. Paris: Philippe Lebaud, 1982.

———. *Saison violente*. Paris: Seuil, 1974.

———, ed. *Les Pieds-Noirs*. Paris: Philippe Lebaud, 1982.

Roche, Anne. "La perte et la parole: témoignages oraux de pieds-noirs." In *La Guerre d'Algérie et les Français*, edited by Jean-Pierre Rioux, 526–37. Paris: Fayard, 1990.

Roger, Patrick. "Colonisation: les propos inédits de Macron font polémique." *Le Monde*, February 16, 2017.

Rogers, Lynne. "The Guerilla Linguistics of Mohammed Khaïr-Eddine." In *Writing the Nation: Self and Country in Post-Colonial Imagination*, edited by John C. Hawley, 108–22. Amsterdam: Rodopi, 1996.

Rolin, Gabrielle. "Kateb Yacine à pied d'oeuvre." Jeune Afrique, http://www.jeuneafrique.com/Articleimp_LIN19013katebervueo0_kateb-yacine-a-pie. Date accessed: May 17, 2013.

Rose, Jacqueline. *The Case of Peter Pan or The Impossibility of Children's Fiction*. London: Macmillan, 1984.

Ross, Kristin. *Fast Cars, Clean Bodies: Decolonization and the Reordering of French Culture*. Cambridge, MA: MIT Press, 1999.
Roüan, Brigitte. *Outremer*. France: Paradise Productions, 1990.
———. *Overseas*. France: Aries Film Release, 1992.
Rouquette-Valeins, Hélène, "L'apport des pieds-noirs," *Sud Ouest*, November 21, 2010
Rousso, Henry. *The Vichy Syndrome: History and Memory in France since 1944*. Translated by Arthur Goldhammer. Cambridge, MA: Harvard University Press, 1991.
Roy, Jean-Louis, "Jules Roy contre la torture," *Le Monde*, July 22, 2000.
Roy, Jules. *Adieu ma mère, adieu mon coeur*. Paris: Albin Michel, 1996.
———. *La Guerre d'Algérie*. Paris: Julliard, 1960.
———. *Les Chevaux du soleil: La saga de l'Algérie de 1830 à 1962*. Paris: Omnibus, 1995.
Saadia, Manu, "To understand the Paris 'Yellow Vests' riots, look to French Guiana," *The Washington Post*, December 4, 2018
Said, Edward W. *Culture and Imperialism*. London: Chatto & Windus, 1993.
———. *Orientalism*. London: Penguin, 2003.
Sainson, Katia. "'Entre deux feux': Jean Sénac's Struggle for Self-determination." *Research in African Literatures* 42, no. 1 (Spring 2011): 32–48.
Saint-Hamont, Daniel. *Et le Sirocco emportera nos larmes: roman*. Paris: Grasset, 2012.
———. *La valise à l'eau, ou, Le voyage en Alger: roman*. Paris, Fayard, 1981.
———. *Le Bourricot*. Paris: Fayard, 1974.
———. *Le Coup de Sirocco*. Paris: Fayard, 1978.
———. *Le Macho*. Paris: Fayard, 1979.
Sanson, Hervé, "Jean Sénac, citoyen innommé de l'Ailleurs." *Insaniyat: Revue algérienne d'anthropologie et de sciences sociales*, no. 32–33 (2006): 127–39, http://insaniyat.revues.org/3432#text. Date accessed: February 28, 2014.
Savarèse, Éric. *L'Invention des pieds-noirs*. Paris: Séguier, 2002.
Schmidt, Lynda W. "Review: The Words to Say It by Marie Cardinal." *The San Francisco Jung Institute Library Journal* 4, no. 4 (Summer 1984): 55–63.
Sénac, Jean. *Avant-corps précédé de Poèmes iliaques et suivi de Diwân du Noûn: poèmes*. Paris: Gallimard, 1968.
Sénac, Jean. *Ébauche du père: pour en finir avec l'enfance: roman*. Paris: Gallimard, 1989.
———. "Jean Sénac: Carnets inédits (extraits)." In *Algérie: Un rêve de fraternité*, edited by Guy Dugas, 845–54. Paris: Omnibus, 1997.
———. *Oeuvres poétiques*. Arles: Actes sud, 1999.
Serero, Edith. "Brigitte Benkemoun Pleure Ô Pays Bien-Aimé." *Paris Match*, May 24–30, 2012.
Séry, Macha. "Exposition: Albert Camus à Aix-en-Provence: autopsie d'un gâchis." *Le Monde*, October 8, 2013.
Shepard, Todd. *The Invention of Decolonization: The Algerian War and the Remaking of France*. Ithaca, NY: Cornell University Press, 2008.

———. "Pieds-Noirs, Bêtes Noires: Anti-'European of Algeria' Racism and the Close of the French Empire." In *Algeria & France 1800-2000: Identity, Memory, Nostalgia*, edited by Patricia M. E. Lorcin, 150–63. New York: Syracuse University Press, 2006.

Shohat, Ella, and Robert Stam. *Unthinking Eurocentrism: Multiculturalism and the Media*. London: Routledge, 1994.

Sigg, Bernard. *Le Silence et la honte: Névroses de la guerre d'Algérie*. Paris: Messidor, 1989.

Sivan, Emmanuel. "Colonialism and Popular Culture in Algeria." *Journal of Contemporary History* 14, no. 1 (January 1979): 21–53.

Smith, Andrea L. *Colonial Memory and Postcolonial Europe: Maltese Settlers in Algeria and France*. Bloomington, IN: Indiana University Press, 2006.

Stafford, Andy. "Ambivalence and Ambiguity of the Short Story in Albert Camus's 'L'Hôte' and Mohammed Dib's 'La Fin.'" In *Postcolonial Poetics: Genre and Form*, edited by Patrick Crowley and Jane Hiddleston, 219–39. Liverpool: Liverpool University Press, 2011.

Steurel, Lydie. "Les derniers tabous de la guerre sans nom." *Marianne*. March 24, 2012.

Stoler, Ann L. *Carnal Knowledge and Imperial Power: Race and the Intimate in Colonial Rule*. Berkeley, CA: University of California Press, 2002.

Stora, Benjamin. "Algérie-France, mémoires sous tension." *Le Monde*, March 18, 2012.

———. *La Gangrène et l'oubli: La mémoire de la guerre d'Algérie*. Paris: La Découverte, 1998.

———. *Le Livre, mémoire de l'Histoire: Réflexions sur le livre et la guerre d'Algérie*. Paris: Le Préau des Collines, 2005.

———. "Mémoires comparées: femmes françaises, femmes algériennes: Les écrits de femmes, la guerre d'Algérie et l'exil." In *L'Ère des décolonisations: Sélection de textes du colloque «Décolonisations comparées», Aix-en-Provence, 30 septembre–3 octobre 1993*, edited by Charles-Robert Ageron and Marc Michel, 172–94. Paris: Karthala, 1995.

———. "Women's Writing between Two Algerian Wars." *Research in African Literatures* 30, no. 3 (Autumn 1999): 78–94.

Stora, Benjamin, and Jean-Baptiste Péretié. *Camus Brûlant*. Paris: Stock, 2013.

Strachan, John. "Between History, Memory, and Mythology: The Algerian Education of Albert Camus." In *France's Lost Empires*, edited by Kate Marsh and Nicola Frith, 55–68. Lanham, MD: Lexington, 2011.

———. "From Poverty to Wretchedness: Albert Camus and the psychology of the *pieds-noirs*." *Journal of Colonialism and Colonial History*, no. 2 (Summer 2013), Project Muse.

———. "Reshaping the Mythologies of Frenchness: Culture, History and Identity in European Algeria, 1870-1930." Unpublished PhD dissertation, University of Manchester, 2006.

Susini, Micheline. *De Soleil et de larmes*. Paris: Robert Laffont, 1982.

Téchiné, André. *Les Roseaux sauvages*. France: Studio Canal, 1994.

Thierry, Maël, "Gilets jaunes: Je crains une forme de scission à l'intérieur du pays." *L'OBS*, December 3, 2018.
Todd, Olivier. *Albert Camus: une vie*. Paris: Gallimard, 1996.
Vajpeyi, Ananya, Ashis Nandy: Why Nationalism and Secularism Failed Together." Reset DOC: Dialogues on Civilizations, https://www.resetdoc.org/story/ashis-nandy-why-nationalism-and-secularism-failed-together/. Date accessed: July 12, 2018.
Vassallo, Helen. "Re-mapping Algeria(s) in France: Leïla Sebbar's *Mes Algéries en France* and *Journal de mes Algéries en France*." *Modern and Contemporary France* 19, no. 2 (2011): 129–45.
Verdès-Leroux, Jeannine. *Les Français d'Algérie de 1830 à aujourd'hui*. Paris: Fayard, 2001.
Villiers, François. *Les Chevaux du soleil*. France: Koba Films 1980.
Vircondelet, Alain. *Maman la Blanche*. Paris: Albin Michel, 1981.
Virtue, Nancy E. "Memory, Trauma, and the French-Algerian War: Michael Haneke's *Caché* (2005)." *Modern & Contemporary France* 19, no. 3 (August 2011): 281–96.
Watt, Sophie. "Alexandre Arcady and the Rewriting of French Colonial History in Algeria." In *France's Lost Empires: Fragmentation, Nostalgia, and la fracture coloniale*, edited by Kate Marsh and Nicola Frith, 69–80. Lanham, MD: Lexington, 2011.
Weber, Eugen. *Peasants into Frenchmen: The Modernization of Rural France, 1870-1914*. London: Chatto & Windus, 1977.
Weiner, Susan. "Two Modernities: From Elle to Mademoiselle. Women's Magazines in Postwar France." *Contemporary European History* 8, no. 3 (November 1999): 395–409.
Wilson, Colin. *The Outsider*. London: Indigo, 1997.
Wood, Nancy. *Vectors of Memory: Legacies of Trauma in Postwar Europe*. Oxford: Berg, 1999.
Yacono, Xavier. "Pourquoi pieds-noirs?" In *Les Pieds-Noirs*, edited by Emmanuel Roblès, 15–19. Paris: Philippe Lebaud, 1982.
Yee, Jennifer. "The Colonial Outsider: 'Malgérie' in Hélène Cixous's *Les rêveries de la femme sauvage*." *Tulsa Studies in Women's Literature* 20, no. 2 (Autumn 2001): 189–200.
Young, Kathleen. "Talking vs. Processing in Trauma Therapy." Young, http://drkathleenyoung.wordpress.com/2011/06/09/talking-vs-processing-in-trauma-therapy/. Date accessed: July 31, 2013.
Zouache, Abdallah. "Socialism, Liberalism and Inequality: The Colonial Economics of the Saint-Simonians in 19th Century Algeria." *Review of Social Economy* 67, no. 4 (December 2009): 431–56.

Index

abusive mother (France as), 8. *See also marâtre* (France as)
adult children's literature, 147, 150
Aldrich, Robert, 135
Algerian War, 1–2, 4–6, 8, 10–11, 13, 19–22, 33, 43, 46, 58, 61–62, 64–68, 72, 74, 76, 79, 80–84, 106–7, 114, 119, 129, 131, 137, 139, 147–48, 151–53, 156–59, 164–66, 168–71, 173, 175, 180–81, 191, 193; cease-fire, 5, 76. *See also* Roy, Jules
l'Algérie de papa, 109, 117, 119
Alleg, Henri: *La Question*, 111
Al Mansour, Haiffa: *Wadjda*, 103n127
Amrouche, Jean, 109
Anderson, Benedict: imagined communities, 11, 65
Anderson, Kirsteen, 24
Apel-Muller, Patrick, 194
Apter, Emily, 48
Arcady, Alexandre, 150–51; *Là-bas mon pays*, 142n43; *Le coup de Sirocco*, 150–51
Arnett, Jeffrey Jenson, 148
Attali, Bernard, 173
Attali, Jacques, 173
Audin, Maurice, 6
Audisio, Gabriel, 120

Bab-el-Oued, 10, 63–64, 68, 70, 156, 158; siege, 68, 121. *See also* Conesa, Gabriel
Bachi, Salim, 48
Baïlac, Geneviève: *La Famille Hernandez*, 9–10, 38, 64, 175
Bambi (Jean-Pierre Pruvot), 137–38
banlieues, 1–2
Barbarossa, Khaïr Eddin, 188n81
barbouzes, 69
Barclay, Fiona, 3, 90
Bardot, Brigitte, 107
Barthes, Roland, 90
Bartlett, Elizabeth Ann, 48
Basham, Richard, 37
La Bataille d'Alger, 70, 73
Battle of Algiers, 62, 111. *See also La Bataille d'Alger*
Begag, Azouz: *Le Gone du Chaâba*, 111
Bell, Vikki, 79, 84
Benassayag, Maurice, 8, 78, 106–7
Benkemoun, Brigitte, 13, 150; *La petite fille sur la photo*, 173–75
Ben M'Hidi, Larbi, 63
Ben Sadock, Mohamed, 55n122
Berger, Karima and Christine Bey: *Toi, ma sœur étrangère*, 195–96
Berque, Jacques, 26, 41

215

Berreby, Élie-Georges, 13, 150; *L'Enfant Pied-Noir*, 155–60, 162
Bertrand, Louis, 61, 120, 149; *Le sang des races*, 184n18
Bettelheim, Bruno, 82
beur, 195
Bey, Maissa, 48
Bhabha, Homi: mimicry, 177; Third Space, 89, 148
blood sacrifice, 98n38, 161
Blum-Violette bill, 26
Bonotaux, Gilles and Hélène Lasserre: *Quand ils avaient mon âge . . . Alger 1954–62*, 184n23
Bouckaert-Ghesquiere, Rita, 147
Bouhired, Djamila, 70
Boym, Svetlana, 149
Boyne, John: *The Boy in the Striped Pajamas*, 166
Branche, Raphaëlle, 151
Brosman, Catherine Savage, 109
Brown, Stephanie: kitsch, 69, 71
Bruel, Patrick, 151
Buisson, Virginie, 13, 150, 173; *L'Algérie ou la mort des autres*, 163–69, 171–72
Buono, Clarisse, 8, 108, 178–79
Butler, Judith, 84, 192; drag, 11, 68; gender as performative, 10–11, 14, 19, 22, 44, 177; melancholia, 79, 130

Cain, 46, 48, 87, 159
Camus, Albert, 3, 13–14, 19–49, 65, 81, 86, 92, 106, 109, 112, 114–15, 117, 119–20, 122, 129, 131, 135, 149–50, 154, 158, 175, 179–82, 192–93, 195; *Actuelles III*, 22, 27; *Cahiers*, 188n87; *Essais*, 17n47, 39; *L'Été*, 22, 25, 28, 46, 159; "L'Été à Alger," 21, 28–29, 149; *L'Étranger*, 22–33, 35–36, 39–40, 42–43, 47–48, 109, 120, 125, 130, 154, 175–76, 180; *L'Exil et le Royaume*, 22, 33; "L'Hôte," 22, 33–36, 43, 46–48, 90, 130, 195; "Jonas," 54n105, 185n48; "Lettre à un militant algérien," 158; "Le Minotaure ou la halte d'Oran," 159; "Misère de la Kabylie," 23; "Les Muets," 29, 34, 43; *Le Mythe de Sisyphe*, 14; *Noces*, 21–22, 25, 28, 41, 149; "Noces à Tipasa," 41; "La Nouvelle Culture Méditerranéenne," 17n47; *père spirituel*, 22, 193; *La Peste*, 22, 24–25, 27, 29, 32; "Petit guide pour des villes sans passé," 28, 45–6; *Le Premier Homme*, 22, 36–48, 76, 87–88, 94, 111, 115, 159, 162, 193; "Le vent à Djémila," 28
Camus, Catherine, 36, 193
Camusian, 22, 24, 59, 70, 77, 82–83, 111, 114, 119, 124–25, 135, 153–54, 158, 172, 175, 180–81
Cardinal, Marie, 13, 59, 78, 88, 168, 192–93; *Au pays de mes racines*, 82; *Les mots pour le dire*, 78–83; *Les pieds-noirs*, 71, 78, 83
Carroll, David, 36, 44, 46
Charef, Mehdi: *Cartouches gauloises*, 173–74
Chirac, Jacques, 6
Choi, Sung-Eun, 3
Cixous, Hélène, 13, 59, 78, 88, 162, 192–93; *Les Rêveries de la femme sauvage*, 88–95, 130
Clancy-Smith, Julia and Frances Gouda, 7
Cohen, William B., 13
Comtat, Emmanuel, 3
Conesa, Gabriel, 13, 108, 119, 125, 129, 158; *Bab-el-Oued: notre paradis perdu*, 119–24
Cooper, Frederic and Ann Laura Stoler, 7
Corneille, Pierre, 60
Creed, Barbara, 43
critical witnessing, 149

Daniel, Jean, 135
Daoud, Kamel: *Meursault, contre-enquête: roman*, 23–24, 48
de Beauvoir, Simone, 75, 119
décennie noire, 48, 114, 136, 155, 180

de Gaulle, Charles, 4, 6, 74, 87, 112, 116–17, 154, 161–62, 187n80
Delacroix, Eugène, 72
de la Hogue, Janine, 13, 111
Derderian, Richard, 5
Derrida, Jacques, 23, 33–34, 36, 88, 192; *Le monolinguisme de l'autre ou la prothèse d'origine*, 23, 95n6
Dessaigne, Francine, 13, 59; *Journal d'une mère de famille pied-noir*, 59–65, 71, 76, 174
Dey of Algiers, 106
Dib, Mohammed, 117
Dine, Philip, 6, 12, 34, 61, 65, 109, 168
discourse, 3, 8, 10–11, 19, 57, 81, 89, 93–94, 105, 107, 147–49, 170, 178, 182, 191–92
Djebar, Assia, 48; *Femmes d'Alger dans leur appartement*, 72
drag, 69, 132, 138, 177. *See also* Butler, Judith
Dreyfus, Alfred, 111

Eberhardt, Isabelle, 57
École d'Alger, 19, 26, 38, 108–9
egocentrism, 151–52
Elbe, Marie, 13, 59; *Et à l'heure de notre mort*, 66–71, 76–77, 130–31
Eldridge, Claire, 3, 174
emerging adulthood, 148, 151

Fanon, Frantz, 8, 79, 107, 168
Fassin, Éric, 68
Fathy, Safaa: *D'Ailleurs, Derrida*, 196n4
Feirstein, Bruce, 129
fellagha, 80, 152, 161–62
feminism, 48, 75, 78, 81, 192
Feraoun, Mouloud, 117
Ferdi, Saïd: *Un enfant dans la guerre*, 167
Fontaine Kerbellec, Laurence: *Un trait de khôl au bord des yeux*, 194
Forestier, Denis, 20
Fortier, Anne Marie, 69

Foucault, Michel: discourse, 10; rebound effect of colonialism, 3
Frank, Anne, 60
Fromentin, Eugène: *Dominique*, 182–83n2
Front de libération nationale (FLN), 4, 19, 49n4, 62, 68, 70, 110–12, 130, 132
Front national (National Front), 2, 178

Gadal, Hélène, 13, 150; *Petite pied-noir deviendra grande*, 160–63
gaouri, 133
Garcia Lorca, Frederico, 131
Genet, Jean, 131
Gide, André, 135–36
Gil, Marie: *De l'autre côte de la mer... Oran et l'Oranie*, 72
gilet jaune movement, 1–2
gilet noir movement, 2
Gilmore, David, 108
good-willed colonizer, 117
Graebner, Seth, 26, 114–15, 124
Granara, William, 129
Greene, Naomi, 86
Grenier, Jean, 27
Grine, Hamid, 48
gros colons, 6, 186n53
Guéhenno, Jean: *La Mort des autres*, 164
guerres de mémoires, 6–7, 150, 160, 195
Guiraud, Nicole, 174

Haddour, Azzedine, 29
Hanin, Roger, 151
Hargreaves, Alec, 191
harkis, 5–6, 153, 174, 179
Hartley, L. P.: *The Go-Between*, 149, 172
Henry, Jean-Robert, 21
Hernandez, Philippe, 107
Hiddleston, Jane, 191
Hilton, Mary and Maria Nikolajeva, 148
honor, 21, 30, 35, 38, 70, 106, 118, 124, 162
Horne, Alistair, 33

Horne, Janet R., 57
hospitality, 34, 36, 46, 90, 195, 197n11
Houllebecq, Michel: *Soumission*, 2
Hubbell, Amy, 3, 31
Hughes, Edward, 44
Hureau, Joëlle, 8–9, 129, 159
Hussey, Andrew, 1
hybridity, 13, 31, 112, 118, 120, 134, 136, 175
hyperfemininity, 59, 67
hypermasculinity, 22, 92, 106–8, 125–26, 128, 132, 138

Ighilahriz, Louisette, 111; *Algérienne*, 187n73
imaginary audience, 152
Indochina, 106, 171
invented tradition, 10–11, 61

Jameson, Frederic, 11
Jeanson, Francis, 21
Joissains, Maryse, 20
Jones, Linda, 39
Jones, Rosemarie, 107, 194
Jordi, Jean-Jacques, 5, 8, 132, 151, 173

Kabylia, 61. *See also* Camus, Albert
Kateb, Yacine, 117; *La Femme Sauvage*, 88; *Nedjma*, 23, 47, 129
Khaïr-Eddine, Mohammed, 187–88n81
kitsch, 92, 139. *See also* Brown, Stephanie
Koubi, Richard, 9
Kristeva, Julia, 24, 43, 148, 176

Legrand, Lucien, 13, 108; *Autobiographie d'un pied noir gay*, 136–40
Le Pen, Jean-Marie, 2, 179
Leroy, Michel, 71
Lever, Alison, 106
lieux de mémoire, 5, 43, 160, 179
lieux d'oubli, 177, 179
Lifshitz, Sébastien, 137

Loesch, Anne, 4, 13, 59; *La valise et le cercueil*, 64–66, 71–73, 76–77, 81–82
loi du 23 février, 6
Lorcin, Patricia, 8, 57, 75
Lottman, Herbert, 45

machismo, 13, 30, 37–38, 47, 69, 73, 107–8, 110, 119, 124, 136, 138, 174, 192. *See also* Saint-Hamont, Daniel
Macron, Emmanuel, 6
Mammeri, Mouloud, 117
Manifeste du Peuple Algérien, 26
marâtre (France as), 66, 119
Margerrison, Christine, 25
Martinez, Henri, 32
Martini, Lucienne, 3, 66, 69, 155, 194
Massu, Jacques, 111, 185n38
May 13 1958, 74, 121, 187n80
McCormack, Jo, 153
McDougall, James, 107
Messner, Michael A., 169
Messud, Claire, 13, 150; *The Last Life*, 175–82
métissage, 180
Michel-Chich, Danielle, 78
Mills, Sarah, 10
mimicry, 178–79, *See also* Bhabha, Homi
mission civilisatrice, 57, 61, 167
Mitterrand, François, 173, 179, 182
Montgomery, Geraldine F., 24
mouna, 178
Mulvey, Laura, 84, 86
Murray, Alison, 83, 86–87
Musette, 120; *Cagayous*, 129
myths: eternal Mediterranean, 61, 66, 106, 110; Latin Africa, 61, 106, 171; missed opportunities, 65, 94, 119, 180, 182
memory wars. *See guerres de mémoires*
mental illness, 68, 79, 137, 139, 168–69
melancholia, 84, 91. *See also* Butler, Judith

naming the *pieds-noirs*, 59, 61. See also *pied-noir*
Nandy, Ashis, 192
Napoleonic *Code Civil*, 75
narratives: conduits of collective memory, 11, 43, 58–59, 64, 119, 139, 160; health benefits of, 12, 67, 164, 194
Nora, Pierre, 5, 33–34, 58; *Les Français d'Algérie*, 5, 32–34, 58, 107; *Les Lieux de mémoire*, 5, 179
nostalgérie, 57, 64, 125, 194
nostalgia, 7, 26–27, 57, 83, 86, 90, 94, 111, 115–16, 123, 136, 149, 151, 153, 168, 173–74, 179
novel of adolescence, 147

O'Brien, Conor Cruise, 23
Occupation, 22. See also Vichy
O'Connor, Frank: "Guests of the Nation," 36
Onfray, Michel, 20
Oran, 5, 24, 72, 124, 134, 159, 174; July 5, 1962, 5, 174
Organisation de l'armée secrète (OAS), 4–6, 20, 32, 49n4, 58, 62–64, 68–72, 74, 85, 97n22, 107, 112, 130, 142n57, 146n117, 171, 174–75
Oriental European femininity, 72, 115
Orientalism, 84, 134, 172. See also Said, Edward
Original Sin, 180, 182
Orpheus and Eurydice, 87

Pace, Patricia, 148
Pancrazi, Jean-Noël, 13, 150, 173; *Madame Arnoul*, 155, 169–72
pataouète, 17n47, 129
patos, 139, 164
Pazzi, Roberto, 66
Pélégri, Jean, 13, 108–9, 133; *Ma mère l'Algérie*, 117–19, 136; *Les Oliviers de la justice*, 28, 116–17
Perec, Georges: *Quel petit vélo- à guidon chromé au fond de la cour?*, 103n124

Perez, Joseph, 6
Perez, Marie-Jeanne: *Gouttes-de-sang*, 168
performance of identity, 3, 8–12, 14, 19, 29–30, 32, 35, 41–42, 44, 57, 59, 64, 67–71, 74–75, 79–80, 84–85, 88, 91–92, 105–6, 112–13, 115, 120, 123–26, 128–30, 132, 135–39, 147, 149, 151–53, 163–65, 169–71, 177, 191–92
performativity: of collective memory, 11, 19, 58–59, 64, 84, 176; of identity, 10–11, 19, 59, 68, 89, 126, 130, 148, 171–72, 177, 192
personal fable, 152–53
petits blancs, 6, 20, 186n53
peuple jeune (youthful people), 28, 65, 77, 120–21, 149, 162
picaresque, 129
pied-noir: term (origins of), 12
pied-rouge, 144n86
pied-vert, 131
pioneering tradition, 30, 38, 44, 59, 61–62, 65, 83, 92, 110, 121, 125, 130, 133, 137–38, 158, 161, 163, 174, 177, 181, 193
Plantié, Jeanine, 66. See also Elbe, Marie
politics of seeing, 84
Pontecorvo, Gillo, 73. See also *La Bataille d'Alger*
Prochaska, David, 89
Proust, Marcel: *À la recherche du temps perdu*, 147
Pruvot, Jean-Pierre. See Bambi (Jean-Pierre Pruvot)
Pusse, Tina-Karen and Katharina Walter, 192

quinze glorieuses, 5

Racine, Jean, 60, 124
radicalization, 2
Rae Vartanian, Lesa, 152
Rassemblement national. See Front national (National Front)

ratonnade, 62
razzia, 112
rebound effect of colonialism, 179. See also Foucault, Michel
récit d'enfance, 147
Renard, Delphine, 62, 107, 175
Rhaïs, Elissa, 57
Rice, Alison, 42
Rizzuto, Anthony, 42
Roblès, Emmanuel, 13, 34, 108–9, 114, 117, 119, 125, 129, 133, 158; *Camus, frère de soleil*, 49n5; *Les Hauteurs de la ville*, 115; *Saison violente*, 115–16, 124–25, 130, 156, 159
Roche, Anne, 67, 148
Rose, Jacqueline, 149–50, 168
Ross, Kristin, 70, 75, 107
Roüan, Brigitte, 13, 59, 78, 193; *Outremer*, 83–88
Rousseau, Jean-Jacques, 88
Roy, Jules, 13, 108–9, 117, 119, 134; *Adieu ma mère, adieu mon cœur*, 113–14; *Les Chevaux du soleil*, 111–13, 116; *Étranger pour mes frères*, 109; *La Guerre d'Algérie*, 109–11; *J'accuse le général Massu*, 111
Rue d'Isly, 5, 63, 66, 68, 72, 120, 154, 187n80

Saadia, Manu, 1
Said, Edward, 23, 26–7; *Orientalism*, 93
Sainson, Katia, 132, 138
Saint Augustine, 179–81
Saint-Hamont, Daniel, 13, 108, 150, 160; *Le coup de Sirocco*, 150–55, 162, 166; *Le Macho*, 125–30, 150–51
Saint Simonian movement, 133
Sansal, Boualem, 48
Sanson, Hervé, 132, 135
Sarkozy, Nicolas, 2, 20
Sarradet, Jean, 64–65
Sartre, Jean-Paul, 20–21, 33
Savarèse, Éric, 3, 61, 80, 131
Sebbar, Leïla, 102n118, 195

Sénac, Jean, 13, 108, 117, 131–36, 157, 192–93, 195; *Avant-corps*, 131, 134; *Carnets*, 131; "La course," 134–35; "Des vierges vont se donner," 135; *Ébauche du père*, 132–34; "Lettre à un jeune Français d'Algérie," 132–33; *Le mythe du sperme-Méditerranée*, 134–35; "Paix en Algérie," 141n33
Sétif, 63–4; May 1945, 26, 63, 117
Shepard, Todd, 58, 105, 107
Shohat, Ella and Robert Stam, 11
Sigg, Bernard, 79, 168
Sivan, Emmanuel, 122
Smith, Andrea L., 12, 30–31, 67, 106, 164
Stafford, Andy, 34, 36
Stora, Benjamin, 7, 13, 20, 57–58, 67, 72, 163–64, 173, 195
Strachan, John, 7, 38, 43
stranger groups. See Prochaska, David
Susini, Jean-Jacques, 64, 71, 74–75
Susini, Micheline, 13, 59; *De soleil et de larmes*, 64, 71–77

Taubira law, 139
Téchiné, André: *Les Roseaux sauvages*, 169
Thomas, Nicholas, 11
time (accelerated), 27–29, 47, 114, 129, 134
time (lessness), 47–48, 87, 94, 118, 128
Todd, Olivier, 21
tombs (abandonment of), 113–14
torture, 2, 4, 6, 62, 110–12, 152–53, 166–68, 172
Tournoux, J. R., 65
Trente Glorieuses, 5

la valise ou le cercueil, 4. See also Loesch, Anne
Vassallo, Helen, 191
veil, 2, 41, 74, 76, 93, 127, 165
Verdès-Leroux, Jeannine, 111, 119

Vichy, 34, 88, 173
Vircondelet, Alain: *Maman la Blanche*, 97n22
Virtue, Nancy E., 149

Watt, Sophie, 151
Weber, Eugen: *Peasants into Frenchmen*, 14n3
Weiner, Susan, 75
Whitman, Walt, 131
Wilde, Oscar, 135

Wood, Nancy, 11, 47, 177, 179
World War I, 40, 42, 75, 106, 161, 164
World War II, 5, 13, 23, 26, 70, 76, 106, 115, 147, 156, 189n97; Allied landings, 23, 68

Yacef, Saadi, 70
Yee, Jennifer, 89, 94
Young, Kathleen, 164

Zola, Émile, 111

About the Author

Dr. **Aoife Connolly** lectures in French studies at Technological University Dublin. She previously worked as a French lecturer at Queen's University Belfast and at National University of Ireland, Galway. Her research focuses on French decolonization, particularly on memory communities of the Algerian War.

www.ingramcontent.com/pod-product-compliance
Lightning Source LLC
Chambersburg PA
CBHW050904300426
44111CB00010B/1368